SOUTH AFRICA
THE STRUGGLE FOR
A BIRTHRIGHT

MARY BENSON

SOUTH AFRICA
THE STRUGGLE FOR A BIRTHRIGHT

MARY BENSON

International Defence and Aid Fund for Southern Africa
November 1985

First published by Penguin Africa Library 1966
Published by IDAF 1985

The International Defence and Aid Fund for Southern Africa is a humanitarian organisation which has worked consistently for peaceful and constructive solutions to the problems created by racial oppression in Southern Africa.

It sprang from Christian and humanist opposition to the evils and injustices of apartheid in South Africa. It is dedicated to the achievement of free, democratic, non-racial societies throughout Southern Africa.

The objects of the fund are:

(i)   to aid, defend and rehabilitate the victims of unjust legislation and oppressive and arbitrary procedures;

(ii)   to support their families and dependants;

(iii) to keep the conscience of the world alive to the issues at stake.

In accordance with these three objectives, the Fund distributes its humanitarian aid to the victims of racial injustice without any discrimination on grounds of race, colour, religious or political affiliation. The only criterion is that of genuine need.

Under its third objective, the Fund runs a comprehensive information service on affairs in Southern Africa. This includes visual documentation. It produces a regular news bulletin 'FOCUS on Political Repression in Southern Africa', and publishes pamphlets and books on all aspects of life in Southern Africa.

The Fund prides itself on the strict accuracy of all its information.

ISBN No. 0 904759 67 9 (paperback)
ISBN No. 0 904759 68 7 (hardback)

Real generosity to the future lies in giving all to the present.

CAMUS

NKOSI SIKELEL' I-AFRIKA

Composed in 1897 by the Xhosa composer Enoch Sontonga and by a missionary at Lovedale College
Translated by Todd Matshikiza

Nkosi Sikelel' I-Afrika	Lord Bless Africa
Maluphakanyisw' Uphondo Lwayo	Let its Horn (of Hope) be Raised
Yiva Nemithandazo Yethu	Listen also to our Pleas
Nkosi Sikelela	Lord Bless
Nkosi Sikelela	Lord Bless
Yiza Moya	Come Spirit
Yiza Moya	Come Spirit
Oyingcwele	Spirit
Nkosi Sikelela Thina	Lord Bless Us
Lusapho Lwakho	Us, thy Children

Contents

CONTENTS

Preface

In December 1960 friends in London urged me to write a history of the African National Congress. I protested that I had no academic qualifications; besides I thought an African writer should produce such a book, but these friends were insistent: time was running out, they said, and most of the founders of the ANC had already died while the survivors were now very old. So I agreed and, with a publisher's princely advance of £200, returned to South Africa early in 1961.

The excitement and tensions of that time – just a year after the Sharpeville massacre – are described in Chapter 17. The ANC was outlawed; Nelson Mandela was leading the struggle from underground while Oliver Tambo headed the ANC in exile. Under the Suppression of Communism Act merely talking about the Congress could be legally construed as 'furthering the aims of a banned organization' and – quite apart from my own trepidation – it was essential to approach former members discreetly. I envolved a kind of code for my notes: for instance Mandela became Traf (Trafalgar) while communist or communism became Golders or Green due to my belief that Karl Marx was buried in Golders Green cemetery!

However everyone I contacted as I travelled the country seemed eager to reminisce, eager for this opportunity to contribute to the history of the movement. Some were old friends from 1957 when I had been secretary of the Treason Trials Defence Fund: Mandela and Walter Sisulu and several Indian leaders were among those I had met during the early 'fifties, through my association with Michael Scott; and interviewing Ahmed 'Kathy' Kathrada in the flat which Ismail Meer had once occupied *(pages 94-6)* was but one of innumerable experiences when the past sprang to life.

Darting from distant past to present, both figuratively and physically, I went from Mweli Skota's fascinating and moving recollections of the early years of the SA Native National Congress, across the passage to another office in the same building where Sisulu and Duma Nokwe were installed and where they and the ebullient Lilian Ngoyi described their lives and travels and vicissitudes; not only darting but having to dodge Sisulu's shadow, the funereal Sgt. Dirker.

In Pietermaritzburg, Selby Msimang added his reminiscences of the founding of Congress in 1912 but was it he or the old man I met in Port Elizabeth, a butcher, who said, 'To us freedom was only around the corner.' Later, when I visited the location in Bloemfontein where that first conference was held and walked along the road with its drooping, dusty eucalyptus trees, their recollections, and the memories of the Rev. Nimrod Tantsi, who lived in the location, peopled my mind with that great gathering of delegates from all parts of Southern Africa.

Another white-headed clergyman, the Rev. Zaccheus Mahabane, was happy to recall the 'twenties and 'thirties when we met in his home in Kroonstad location; he had been President-General of Congress and was still a leading figure in religious circles.

But if I were to choose one leader who impressed and moved me more than any other, it would be Canon James Calata who during the 'thirties, when the ANC was at its lowest ebb, almost single-handed and despite poverty and serious ill-health, revived the organization. When I set off from a hotel opposite the Dutch Reformed Church to visit him in Cradock location, I was followed by two members of the security police – white and black – but Calata was used to that and waved aside my anxiety on his behalf. Only a few weeks earlier he had been sentenced to six months' imprisonment for having two ancient pictures of ANC delegations on his walls – found guilty of 'furthering the aims' of the ANC, his case was under appeal; he had already spent weeks in prison. That night, in the location hall, he conducted his choir of young men and women performing the freedom songs he had written – yet another illegal act on his part, and on theirs.

Calata, the name still reverberates: the Canon's grandson, Fort, was among the four community leaders from Cradock – members of the United Democratic Front – who were brutally murdered by a 'death squad' on June 29 1985; from far and wide people came to their funeral and sang James Calata's freedom songs in honour of these young martyrs.

As Professor Z.K. Matthews said when we met in Alice, the small town where he had been an eminent figure at Fort Hare University until he resigned in protest against Bantu Education, 'The security police in these dorps have nothing better to do than harass us! Well', he added, leading me from my hotel to his car, and indicating a Volkswagen waiting nearby 'we'll give them a little excitement.' And he proceeded to drive round and round the square, peering into the rearview mirror, chuckling at the sight of the police grimly following our gyrations.

In Cape Town Annie Silinga, a large woman in a small block house, entertained me with stories of how she had adamantly refused to carry a pass and resisted every kind of police retribution; her room – each wall a different pastel shade – reflected her cheerfulness. Oscar Mpetha – now in his seventies and still persecuted despite severe illness – was among the other Cape Town members who described their work for the ANC, as did Frances Baard and Florence Matomela, who met me in a church in New Brighton – vital, strong and humorous women who had been Treason Trial defendants.

Also in Port Elizabeth, Govan Mbeki, who I had first met when he was a speaker at a Multi-Racial Conference at the University of the Witwatersrand in 1957, introduced me to Raymond Mhlaba. And I interviewed Caleb Mayekiso and Vuyisile Mini. When possible, I later sent extracts from the first draft of the history to my informants and I treasure an anonymous note dated September 12, 1962 which says, 'The manuscript has been read and corrected by Mr. Caleb Mayekiso and Mr. Vuyisile Mini': Mayekiso was to die in security police hands during the detentions which preceded Winnie Mandela's trial in 1969; Mini was hanged in November 1964.

In October 1961 came the announcement that Chief Albert Lutuli was to be awarded the Nobel Peace Prize. At the request of Sisulu and Nokwe I flew from Johannesburg to Natal to assist 'Chief' who was inundated with requests for interviews as representatives of the international press descended on Stanger, the nearest town to his home in Groutville where he lived under partial restriction. The magistrate granted a permit to go to Lutuli's house provided I did not 'interfere in the affairs of the Bantu' and did not talk politics. Under his banning orders, Chief was not allowed to join us in the packed meeting which celebrated the award but, beforehand, we had a lunch party at which he joined in the singing and dancing, and Alan Paton and M.B. Yengwa, rehearsed the 'praise' poems they had prepared for the celebration:

> You there Lutuli, they thought that you were chained
> Like a backyard dog
> Now they discover

They are in prison, but you are free
declared one verse in Paton's poem, while Yengwa's 'Nkosi yase Groutville! Nkosi Yase world!" (Chief of Groutville, of the world) set the
crowd laughing and ululating.

Mandela, meanwhile, was 'underground', the security police's most
wanted man. My first of three interviews with him took place in May
1961, just after police and army had massively crushed the stay-at-
home protest strike he had called. Ruth First arranged for correspondents from the *Observer* and *Financial Times* and myself to meet him in
a small flat in Johannesburg. His welcome was typically exuberant, but
when he came to discuss State repression, his demeanour was sombre:
'There are many people who feel it is useless and futile for us to continue talking peace and non-violence against a government whose
reply is only savage attacks against an unarmed and defenceless
people. The time has come for us to consider whether the methods
which we have applied so far are adequate.' His intimation that
Umkhonto we Sizwe was about to be formed.

When the first (illustrated) edition of his history was published as
The African Patriots in 1963, I stated frankly: 'This is a committed book.
During the year spent in historical and personal research in South
Africa I found it impossible not to become engaged by the spirit of the
ANC.' The following year, I used the opportunity to bring the Ameri-
can edition up-to-date with a passage which now, more than twenty
years later, has an appalling topicality: '. . . . at least 5,000 political
prisoners are in gaol. Hundreds are charged with sabotage or member-
ship in "unlawful organisations". Six have been condemned to
death . . . six to life imprisonment and 141 to between 10 to 25 years.
Saboteurs continue to act. Increasingly refugees escape (to Botswana,
Lesotho and Swaziland), risking kidnapping or attack from South
African police and armed civilians.

'International pressures mount . . . The African States . . . lead the
growing insistence for economic sanctions . . . Dr. Verwoerd has
declared "we will never give in." . . . And so South Africa lurches
towards disaster'. 'Will we in the West', I asked, 'enable this non-
violent form of intervention (sanctions) to succeed? Or will we consign
Southern Africa, and perhaps the world, to a bitter race war?'

Returning to South Africa in 1965-6 I was able to bring the history further up to date, concentrating especially on the trials in the Eastern Cape where the security police were intent on purging the entire area of all political activity, *The Struggle for a Birthright*, published in 1966 was the result, and in the preface I made a somewhat premature statement:

'There is . . . the surge in American concern exemplified by the Congressional enquiry into apartheid and into American policy towards South Africa, with Dr. Martin Luther King among those testifying, an inquiry apparently unique in the history of Congress. The concern is also evident in the United Automobile Workers' initiative towards legislation to penalize American firms profiting from South Africa's uncivilized labour conditions; this should particularly affect American companies in that area of notorious police activity and political trials, the Eastern Cape.

'It has become a truism that Britain, with a billion pounds invested in the Republic, waits on American policy, and American policy cannot but be empowered by this new concern and by the growing force of the Negro vote in the States. So far Britain's role in South Africa has amounted to a prolonged and profitable betrayal.'

The preface, written in Johannesburg, continued: 'In the heat and dangers of this day much of what cries out to be told has been made illegal. But it is important it should be told because historical facts are being actively corrupted. In Court records, in press reporting of political trials, on which future historians must rely to give a representative picture of this confused and wretched period, there are recorded allegations blatantly nonsensical to anyone knowing the facts. For instance ANC and PAC may be treated as interchangeable; Sobukwe is alleged to be Poqo or to have initiated the Paarl riots which happened long after he had been imprisoned: ANC stay-at-homes under Lutuli are said to have been violent, while the M plan, conceived by Mandela in 1952 for street to street organizing of non-violent resistance is declared a "sabotage" plan. Many such "facts" go unchallenged.

'One of the propagators of this sort of squalid "evidence" – one of the State's itinerant, I might say ubiquitous, African witnesses – has helped to send men to Robben Island for long terms of imprisonment, and helped to send Vuyisile Mini and five others to the gallows. Of his evidence in a trial where the accused was acquitted, the Judge (sitting with two other judges in the Natal Supreme Court) said: ". . we regard this

13

witness as an unscrupulous and completely unreliable witness and would not act with any feeling of safety upon anything he said . . .'"

I went on to indulge in speculation: what if the ludicrously inaccurate terms 'European' and 'white' had been replaced by E.M. Forster's 'pinko-grey': what if our reserved benches, buses, station entrances, lavatories, immigration, civilization, were labelled: FOR PINKO-GREY ONLY – would the colour bar have become so rampant? And why, in Britain, had we allowed the disease of racialism to take hold and to spread? 'South Africa,' I added, 'is a microcosm of our world: in its races, its religions, in its perilous division into "haves" and "have-nots". If we in South Africa fail, how can our world survive?'

Umkhonto we Sizwe's first guerrilla incursions into Rhodesia (Zimbabwe) and the beginning of SWAPO's armed struggle in South West Africa (Namibia) impelled the International Commission of Jurists to state on 13 December 1967: 'Justice and humanity demand that the principles embodied in the Geneva Conventions for the treatment of prisoners of war should be extended to African freedom fighters captured under arms.'

The preface to the American edition in 1968 gave an opportunity to quote that urgent attempt to save guerrillas from the death penalty. To this day the demand has not been fulfilled and remains a vital objective for international pressure.

I have always wished – perhaps immodestly – that this book could be read in my home country but it was long ago banned – an indeed remains listed as 'objectionable literature'. However, occasionally I get intense pleasure from messages: one from a stranger, who wrote: '*Struggle for a Birthright* was the first book that gave me, as a teenager just becoming politically conscious, a comprehensive view of the history of our struggle. I'm not sure whether the book was actually banned, but we treated it as such, passing it on as soon as someone had finished reading it.'

And one from Nelson Mandela: writing from behind 'forbidding and notorious walls', he expressed the wish that it could be widely read in South Africa, 'because each reader would regard it as telling his or her own story, an account of the striving to realise a fond dream, or as the pursuit of a goal which corresponds with one's own convictions.'

MARY BENSON
London, October 1985

Prologue 1819–1910: The Struggle for a Birthright Begins

Found guilty, 'with others of his countrymen, of no other offence than fighting for their native land against its *civilized* invaders', he was 'condemned to be imprisoned for life on Robben Island – the Botany Bay of the Cape – a spot appropriated for the custody of convicted felons, rebellious slaves, and other malefactors. . . .'

The man? Makana, Xhosa warrior-chief-prophet. The time? August 1819. Yet that account by a contemporary of Makana's could well describe events 145 years later, when African leaders – Nelson Mandela, Robert Sobukwe and Walter Sisulu – were likewise condemned to imprisonment on Robben Island: 145 years of travail for the African people of South Africa as they have struggled for their birthright.

Makana, a commoner whose extraordinary gifts led to his being acknowledged by 'elders and warriors of the nation' as a powerful chief, had at first been hospitable to the Europeans whose devastating encroachment had just begun. But when a Cape commando ravaged his people's lands, killing many women and old people and stealing 20,000 cattle, he led an attack on their outposts, Grahams Town; 'animating' his army of some eight thousand men, with the legendary urge: drive these accursed white men into the sea from which they came. The attack was beaten off. The Colony's militia were called up to burn villages, to massacre old and young, and to threaten extermination of Makana's followers unless they gave him up. Despite their hunger and despair, not one betrayed him.

But on 16 August Makana himself walked unattended into the Commando Camp with an 'air of calm pride and self-possession', according to one of the officers, and with 'magnanimity' offered himself up to restore peace. In expecting generous treatment 'he gave the colonial rulers credit for feelings to which, unfortunately, they were utter strangers', remarked his contemporary Thomas Pringle. For the 'Christian commando' plundered all the cattle they could find from the 'famishing and despairing natives', and Makana was sent to Robben Island.

After about a year, he and others rose, disarmed the guards and escaped in a boat, only to be capsized at sea. Several men who survived related that 'Makana clung for some time to a rock, and that his deep sonorous voice was heard loudly cheering on those who were struggling with the billows, until he was swept off and engulfed by the raging surf'.

Thomas Pringle – poet-journalist-philanthropist – wrote at that time:

The facts, established beyond dispute by so many respectable witnesses, cannot fail to speak to the heart of every candid reader. As regards the Chief Makana, it is melancholy to reflect how valuable an instrument for promoting the civilization of the Caffer tribes was apparently lost by the nefarious treatment and indirect destruction of that extraordinary barbarian, whom a wiser and more generous policy might have rendered a grateful ally to the colony, and a permanent benefactor to his own countrymen.[1]

Makana's leadership of Xhosa people came halfway through a century of frontier wars and skirmishes as blacks defended what they had against whites wanting what they had: land. In the eighth and longest of the 'Kaffir' wars, the Tembu lost much of their land. Twenty years later, in 1877, Pondoland was annexed by the colonials. Meanwhile, wars between Zulus and British flared and then faded with the British annexing Zululand in 1887.

In all these wars, not only were the tribes defeated by the sophisticated weapons of the invaders, but they were weakened by their own divisions – by their very tribalism. But the Basuto, federated from quarrelling tribes and scattered refugees into a

1. For this and the earlier quotations, see Pringle's *Narrative of a Residence in South Africa* (pp. 98–100), and *Afar in the Desert* (p. 238).

nation by Moshoeshoe, were able to withstand the Boers. Moshoeshoe, a man of vigour, thoughtful, a superior man, used to commanding others and above all himself,[1] played off Boer against Briton with superb diplomacy while his people learnt the use of firearms. Yet he too lost rich lands and, though the Basuto retained national cohesion, they were eventually forced to seek British protection and their country became virtually a labour reserve.

For in 1870 diamonds were discovered in Kimberley with immediate drastic effects which were increased twentyfold when in 1886, gold was discovered in the Transvaal. As capital and European immigrants poured into the country – to the dismay of the Boer trekkers who sought rural security – Africans, who were desperately needed for all kinds of labour, were taxed in order to force them into work, while they themselves came to need cash whether for taxes, simply to exist at all, or – some of them hopefully but belatedly – to buy guns. A black proletariat of a landless cheap labour force was thus precipitated.

Military defeat through superior weapons had brought this about. Moreover the use of the 'law' had been as effective as war. Ancestral lands illegally occupied, or occupied under misunderstanding of tribal customs of usage, were marked off by speculators from Britain who acquired legal title, turning thousands of tribesmen into squatters on their own ground. Military and 'legal' defeats, and economic enslavement – for that is what it would amount to – and beguiling ideas, all combined to bring about a profound upheaval in the life of the tribesmen.

Africans, from 1880, began to work within the modern frame and to think in terms of political rather than military action. The first African political association – the *Imbumba Yama Africa* (Union of Africans) – was formed in the Eastern Cape in the early 1880s; at the same time, incidentally, as Afrikaners formed their first political party, the Afrikander Bond. Looking back, two contrary trends emerge – Africans, already influenced by

1. Eugène Casalis on a visit in 1832.

the teachings of Victorian humanitarians and Christian missionaries, began to discover themselves as part of mankind, while Afrikaners, anxious to preserve their small 'nation', and feeling themselves threatened, sought isolation from the rest of mankind.

Of course the nascent political consciousness was apparent in the activities of only a few Africans and in the main the tribesmen and the labourers were ignorant and insular. But those few were significant. Some helped to form African organizations in various parts of the country although political expression was scattered and hesitant. The first African Christian Church was established and the first African newspaper published. By 1880 Africans in the Cape had two generations of missionary education behind them, for the Church of Scotland's College, Lovedale, had been founded before comparable schools were provided for whites.

Furthermore, Africans had been voters on the common roll of the Cape Colony since 1854 and although their proportion of the votes was negligible, in a few constituencies of the Eastern Cape they were beginning to make themselves felt. At this the Government raised the franchise qualifications and an African petition to Queen Victoria appealing against this proved ineffectual, so that at the turn of the century they formed only 4·7 per cent of the voters in the Cape Colony. Yet they were seen as a threat.

All the same Cape policies were broadly liberal, whereas in British Natal, contrary to Queen Victoria's declaration that all races would be equal, the Zulus were being confined to diminishing reserves as European immigrants took their land for sugar estates. From all accounts there was not much to choose between the attitude of Natal farmers and of the Boer Governments of the two Republics of the Transvaal and the Orange Free State, where there was 'no equality in church or state'. The representative of Natal farmers expressed the view to a Native Affairs Commission:

The native is the most tractable man going, as long as he knows you have your foot on his neck. . . . I think the thing that should be used very freely is the lash, for it is bodily pain that the native fears.

When the Boer War broke out many Africans supported the British forces – some for wages but some acting upon principle – and in 1901 the British Government assured them that there would be no peace that did not give them the same privileges as whites. But when the Peace Treaty was signed at Vereeniging Africans found it to be a 'shameless betrayal'.[1] The British Government – a Liberal Government – far from fulfilling the assurance, had become so intent on reconciling the defeated Boers to their new status of becoming British subjects, that ironically the victory became the basis for the ultimate ascendancy of Afrikaner nationalism with its renunciation of the British connexion.

This gave impetus to African political activity though the groups that sprang up all over the country were as yet small. Among them was the Natal Native Congress, of 'Christian and civilized' Africans, led by Martin Lutuli of Tugela. Meanwhile a young Indian lawyer, M. K. Gandhi, since his arrival in South Africa had already formed the Natal Indian Congress in 1894, and the Coloured people in the Cape set up the African People's Organization. Again, a petition was sent to the Imperial Government, this time in 1906 from the Transvaal Natives' Congress who 'respectfully' reminded the House of Commons of their loyalty and claimed, as British subjects, their right to liberty, freedom and equality. They said that the pass laws in the Transvaal – conceived in Southern Africa by the Netherlands East Indies Company 250 years before – were 'repugnant, unnecessary, undesirable and un-British'. Their petition was ignored.

Perhaps it was symbolic that in that same year, 1906, as well as the petition there were two other forms of protest made against the increasing deprivation of land and liberty. In Natal, Zulu anger flared again at renewed seizure of Zulu land by Europeans and the sudden imposition of a tax at a time of extreme poverty. Bambata, a chieftain, led the rebellion. He and some 4,000 Africans and 25 whites were killed in the fighting. And in the Transvaal Gandhi originated the method of passive

1. *Contact* article by Selby Msimang, 2 April 1960.

resistance when he organized Indians against an attempt to force them, like Africans, to carry passes.

By 1909[1] it was clear that Britain was proposing to hand over the non-white population to the rule of the privileged white minority, in a union of Boer and Briton. African political associations rallied to resist. Led by three editors of African newspapers, the Rev. Walter Rubusana, John Tengo Jabavu and the Rev. John Dube, they met and while they approved the principle of Union, they emphatically protested against the colour bar in the proposed constitution. This restricted the vote to whites in all provinces except in the Cape, and even there deprived Africans of the right to elect one of themselves to Parliament. They requested 'full and equal rights' for all persons. The Coloured people also registered their protest.

When the all-white National Convention, representing the four parts to the proposed Union, met in Bloemfontein in 1909 it did not even discuss these protests.

Representative of the many protests from whites, who included the Anglican Archbishop of Cape Town and other leading churchmen, and liberals, was the warning given by Olive Schreiner if white South Africans, 'blinded by the gain of the moment', saw nothing in the 'dark man' but 'a vast engine of labour'. With astonishing foresight she envisaged a South Africa in which the white man dispossessed the African of his land and forced him 'permanently in his millions into the locations and compounds and slums of our cities, obtaining his labour cheaper'. She foresaw that if 'uninstructed in the highest forms of labour, without the rights of citizenship, his own social organization broken up, without our having aided him to participate in our own' – if the whites reduced 'this vast mass to the condition of a seething ignorant proletariat' – then she would rather 'draw a veil over the future of this land'.[2]

1. At this time just over 165,000 whites and 186,000 Africans were at schools, although the quality of education for Africans, apart from the few missionary schools, can be judged from the fact that the education grant for the million whites was sixteen times as great as that for the four million Africans.

2. *Closer Union* by Olive Schreiner.

Warnings went unheeded. The National Convention approved the draft constitution for Union.

However final responsibility rested with Parliament in Britain and an African deputation, led by Rubusana, Jabavu and W. P. Schreiner, a former Prime Minister of the Cape, went there in the hope of persuading the British Government to reject the colour bar in the constitution. They met with the retort from the Colonial Secretary that the question must be settled in South Africa itself. When the House of Commons considered the Bill to establish Union, only the Labour Party and about thirty Liberals stood against the colour bar. The rest, although they unanimously regretted it, sent the Act on its way 'respectfully and earnestly' begging white South Africa, sooner or later, to modify its provisions.

To Africans the Act of Union became an act of ultimate betrayal by the British Government. Not only did it give the whites unlimited power over the non-whites, it also paved the way for the Afrikaners – who already formed the majority of white voters – eventually to win control over the people of British stock who had so passionately worked for Union.

The first South African Cabinet in 1910 included the two pro-British Boer Generals – Louis Botha as Prime Minister and Jan Smuts, his deputy – and there was a third General, J. B. M. Hertzog. One of their first acts prevented employment of Africans in certain jobs and restricted them to low-paid labour, thus protecting the white workers. Soon another Act so regulated African labour that it became a criminal offence for them to break a contract or to strike. Yet another disarmed the African constabulary, who were put into short trousers and a little cap, while the African mounted police were retitled 'police boys'. The Africans, their tribal society and pastoral economy disrupted by the expanding migrant labour system, and naturally drawn to the few towns, were indeed becoming 'a vast engine of labour'. Potential Makanas were thrown into a fantastic new world, of kitchen 'boys', mine 'boys', garden 'boys', cleaners; pass-bearers; vagrants; forced to earn wages in order to pay tax, turned into criminals if they failed to pay tax or to produce a pass; their chiefs turned into servants of the white Government, sons of chiefs, often, into domestic servants. In essence, their humanity was denied.

The Act of Union had sealed their fate.

I 1910–18: The People Unite, but their Land is Lost

The Act of Union was seen by Africans as an act uniting white South Africans against black. The African organizations scattered through the four provinces were shocked by the British Government's abuse of trust in surrendering all power to a white minority government which, as a fundamental principle, opposed the extension of democratic rights to the non-white majority. But their people remained divided into many separate tribes, thinking tribally, and most of them illiterate.

At this critical moment Pixley Ka ('son of ') Izaka Seme returned to South Africa after studying overseas. He had been one of the one hundred and fifty or so young 'Natives' who had gone to the United States through the help of various missionaries. From the hills of Zululand he had been plunged into life in New York City. At Columbia University he did well and distinguished himself as a speaker. He went on to study law at Jesus College, Oxford, and was later called to the bar at the Middle Temple in London.

On his return to South Africa, the young attorney – able, ambitious, impatient, humorous, a bit of a snob – naturally headed for the centre of progress. New York, Edwardian London, and now Johannesburg – a rough mining town with wide dusty streets and a few elaborate Victorian public buildings amongst brick and corrugated-iron shops and offices. He was at once confronted by the humiliation to which Natives were subjected there, and he was appalled. Africans were not allowed to walk on the pavements and had to raise their hats to white men; they had to travel fourth class on trains in a sort of cattle-truck; white politicians openly admitted that taxes were imposed on

Natives to make them work; policemen repeatedly demanded to see their passes and tax receipts, even raiding churches on Sundays to do so, arresting those without the documents; they were hardly heard, seldom believed, in the courts; politically they had no voice; children were not allowed high school education.

At Oxford Seme had dreamed of rebuilding the Zulu nation; now he was provoked into thinking in wider political terms. He called together three other African lawyers who had also just qualified in England. One of them, Richard Msimang, son of the founder of the Independent Methodist Church in South Africa, after becoming a solicitor in Somerset, returned home to be imprisoned straightaway for not having a pass. In this situation, Seme pointed out, the Xhosa-Fingo feud was an aberration; the animosity between the Zulus and the Tongas, between the Basuto and every other Native, must be buried and forgotten. 'We are one people,' he insisted. 'These divisions, these jealousies, are the cause of all our woes and of all our backwardness and ignorance today.' The four young lawyers agreed that the first step was to call a conference of all chiefs and leaders.

In January 1912, from kraals in the highveld and lowveld of the Transvaal, from Zulu villages, from the beautiful bare uplands of the Transkei, from the arid expanses of Bechuanaland and the royal capital of Swaziland, from the Paramount Chief's fastness in the mountains of Basutoland, came chiefs and their followers, some of them from tribes that had long been mutually hostile. From locations in the brash mining areas of Johannesburg and Kimberley, and near the growing ports of Durban, Port Elizabeth and Cape Town, and from the small farming towns of the Eastern Cape and Free State, came the sprinkling of educated men and representatives of political associations – lawyers and clergymen and teachers – as well as clerks and messengers and servants, members of the new African urban proletariat. By train, travelling uncomfortably in their fourth-class carriages, by ox-wagon, on horseback and on bicycles, they came to Bloemfontein as the geographical centre of the Union, a favourite place for national conferences. An unremarkable dorp with colonial iron-roof verandahed buildings, it lay beside a bush-covered kopje. Along its roads the trees – eucalyptus and fir – with their drooping foliage gave an air of dusty dejection to the hot January day. But in the location, well known for its hospitality, there was an enthusiastic and happy atmosphere.

On 8 January the delegates crowded into the location hall. The platform was filled with eminent formally dressed Africans, some in frock-coats with top hats, carrying furled umbrellas. A Sergeant-at-Arms in a tunic with sergeant's stripes, breeches and gaiters, and carrying a hide shield, knobkerrie and axe, kept order.

The Rev. Henry Ngcayiya, a teacher and leader of the Ethiopian Church, opened the dignified proceedings with a prayer. This was followed by an anthem by a Xhosa composer, Enoch Sontonga: *Nkosi Skelel' i-Afrika* – 'Lord Bless Africa' – which was sung for the first time at a great African gathering.

Seme explained his purpose: 'Chiefs of royal blood and gentlemen of our race,' he said, 'we have gathered here to consider and discuss a scheme which my colleagues and I have decided to place before you. We have discovered that in the land of their birth, Africans are treated as hewers of wood and drawers of water. The white people of this country have formed what is known as the Union of South Africa – a union in which we have no voice in the making of laws and no part in the administration. We have called you, therefore, to this conference so that we can together find ways and means of forming *our* national union for the purpose of creating national unity and defending our rights and privileges.'[1]

The delegates were greatly excited at the prospect of unity and, as one of them said, 'even the difficulties of language did not prevent us exchanging pleasantries for we recognized that we were trying to find one another and we felt wonderfully optimistic. To us freedom was only round the corner.' The conference resolved to 'unite together and form a federation of one Pan-African association'.

Thus the South African Native National Congress was formed. It was a score or more years before comparable organ-

1. Quoted by R. V. Selope Thema, *Drum*, July 1953.

izations were set up in Nigeria, the Gold Coast, Kenya, and Northern Rhodesia and Nyasaland.

The conference accepted Seme's recommendation to model it on the American Congress, with British parliamentary structure and procedures added in an Upper House of Chiefs and a Lower House of Commoners, each with a President. The Paramount Chief of the Basuto, Letsie II, was unanimously elected Honorary Governor, leader of the Upper House in which 'Princes of African blood' were to hold their seats for life.

When it came to the election of a President-General, it would have been obvious for a distinguished Xhosa to be chosen as they had been the first to be educated and their outstanding representative, the Rev. Walter Rubusana, teacher and author, and the only African ever to be elected to the Cape Provincial Council, was present. But the Xhosa delegates at the conference decided that the Cape should take a back seat in order to unite people from the other provinces who besides suffered under greater restrictions. A renowned Zulu was elected: the Rev. John Langalibalele ('the bright sun') Dube.

Dube, at forty-one years, though a staid man, proved to be determined and had practical vision. In 1889 he had gone to the United States, worked his way through college, become a teacher, then studied theology. He was influenced by great Negroes, some of whom had founded colleges, such as Booker T. Washington of Tuskegee and Dr John Hope of Atlanta University, and he had been all the more dismayed on his return to Natal to find that the Government was still not providing Natives with high school education. He at once tried to establish an industrial school. The obstacles were immense. For one thing, where could an African possibly raise the necessary capital? People scoffed at his dream and the Boer War made fund-raising doubly difficult so, almost penniless, he returned to America and through forceful lectures raised enough money to go back and establish Ohlange Institute, high on a hill at his birthplace, Inanda. Pupils helped in the building, and when he later decided to open a girls' school as well, he again toured the States, this time with his wife, raising funds by lecturing and singing. His vision for his people went further: in 1904 he founded the first African newspaper in Natal, *Ilanga lase Natal* ('sun of Natal'), and he became President of the Natal Native Congress. But first and foremost he was a Zulu patriot, related to the royal house, adviser to the Paramount Chief, and he had courted arrest by protesting outspokenly against the execution of Zulus during the Bambata rebellion in 1906.

Seme became Treasurer-General and the others elected to office were also earnest men, intent on self-improvement of their people.

Not all the leaders were highly educated. The Secretary-General was Solomon Tshekiso Plaatje, a young man largely self-taught. He had not only passed the Cape Civil Service examinations, coming top in typing, Dutch and Native languages, but spoke English and German. In the Boer War he had reported on the Native situation for the British in Mafeking during the siege, afterwards interpreting for the Duke of Connaught. He contributed to English-language newspapers in the Union besides founding and editing a Tswana newspaper. A lucid orator himself, he hated inarticulate speakers.

Another self-made man was Thomas Mapikela who, after training as a carpenter in the Grahamstown Native College, eventually became a successful builder and a leading citizen in the location of Bloemfontein. His character, his experience as a member of the Free State Native Congress since the beginning of the century, and on the delegation to London in 1909, together with his respect for the traditions of the Imperial Parliament, made him an ideal person for Speaker of the Congress, a role which he filled with tactful strength. He spoke English, Zulu and Sotho, and was known as 'Map of Africa' because of his name, Mapikela, and because he used to say that the whole of Africa and not just the south was the Africans' country.

These Congress leaders aimed to seek redress of grievances by constitutional means and to agitate for the removal of the colour bar in education, in industry, in Parliament and in the administration. They hoped to educate the white Parliament, enlist the sympathy of Europeans, and teach the African people to understand their rights and duties and to be industrious, clean and thrifty. Also they would encourage the establishment of national colleges. These were considerable aims and the Eastern Cape newspaper, *Imvo Zabantsundu* ('African Opinion')[1] commented that the S.A.N.N.C. 'is nothing less than a Native Parliament'. So this alliance of solid middle-class urban men with chiefs and tribesmen from rural areas was formed, the lawyers, clergy and journalists representing a new form of leadership. The significance of the event was completely overlooked by white South Africans.

Later in the year Pixley Seme launched the first national African newspaper, the *Abantu-Batho* ('People') published in English and three Bantu languages. It embraced several other African newspapers which had been confined to particular provinces or towns. The Queen Regent of Swaziland, Natotsibeni, a public-minded woman who sympathized with his aim of uniting the African people, gave Seme financial backing.

'We were dreaming of changes,' said one editor of *Abantu-Batho*, 'of the day when Africans would sit in Parliament and would be able to buy land.' However, in the country at large the people remained divided, unaware, and faced by a new danger.

Two years after Africans had formed their Native National Congress, Afrikaners formed the National Party, led by General Hertzog. Meanwhile in 1912 Hertzog was dropped from Botha's Cabinet because of his fervent anti-British nationalism. Before this crisis Hertzog had been Minister of Native Affairs and Justice, thus appointed to placate the Afrikaner voters. When he had taken over Native Affairs racial extremists hailed him as future Prime Minister and the right man to fix up the Natives. He toured the Orange Free State, lecturing farmers on their folly in letting land to the Natives, for in some cases, where farmers had rushed to the mines leaving their farms in the care of Native servants, on a half-share system, the servants were heading for prosperity and this was seen to menace white supremacy.

Meanwhile in the Eastern Transvaal, Seme had caused con-

1. 26 March 1912.

sternation amongst white farmers by buying four farms and establishing the African Farmers' Association to encourage Africans to buy land and learn modern farming methods. The neighbouring whites complained that in these circumstances South Africa could never be a white man's country. In response to such clamour the Rt Hon. Abraham Fischer, former Prime Minister of the Orange River Colony, as a Member of Parliament, asked his constituents: 'What is it you want? We have passed all the coolie laws and we have passed all the kaffir laws . . . what more can the Government do for you?'

They wanted more labour on their farms and an end to the Natives' right to buy land.

Land: the African's only security. Effective political rights had been denied him by Union; now something far more precious was to be plundered. The Government pushed ahead with the Native Land Bill. The million whites would have access to more than 90 per cent of the country while the four million Africans would be restricted to 7·3 per cent of the country – with rights of freehold ownership or of leasehold, and of transaction in land, only in 'reserves'. Much of these were of poor fertility, indeed certain areas in the Northern Cape and the Northern Transvaal were permanently drought-stricken. The Bill also made it a crime for any but servants to live on white farms and ordered the immediate eviction of Native squatters, of whom there were nearly a million living as families with their small herds on such farms, in return for services to the farmer.

In face of this terrible threat the Native National Congress organized protest meetings and a deputation to the Minister, and appealed to the British Governor-General. Every effort failed. Meanwhile Mission Councils representing, it was said in the House of Assembly, hundreds of thousands of African souls, made their protest. The Government rejected this and innumerable similar African petitions. It accepted thirteen petitions signed by 304 whites. In Parliament, though the Bill met with strong opposition from the best brains in both Houses, the Government, mindful of the backveld farmers who must be retained as loyal voters, steam-rollered it through. Lord Gladstone signed it on behalf of the King and, on a Friday morning, 20 June 1913, 'the African woke', as Sol Plaatje put it, 'to find himself a pariah in the land of his birth'.

Congress resolved that there was nothing left to do but to appeal to His Majesty's Government and to 'apprise the British public of the kind of Government ruling South Africa under the Union Jack'. They had for so long felt close to Britain that it did not seem pointless, but one influential Cape leader mocked their intention: John Tengo Jabavu, editor of *Imvo* – perhaps bemused by his friendship with the new Minister of Native Affairs, J. H. Sauer, who was one of *Imvo*'s shareholders – supported the Land Act as sponsored by a 'sincere friend' of the Natives.

Meanwhile Congress fund-raising went ahead with the Secretary-General, Plaatje, touring the Free State, and other leaders the Transvaal, gathering evidence for the deputation. It was mid-winter and white farmers had begun to evict African squatters and half-share farmers. On many occasions Plaatje found families bivouacked, their beasts dying of starvation, as they rested from going to and fro in the country in search of a place to live. One such man was Kgobadi. He had been earning a hundred pounds a year on an Afrikaner's farm while he and his wife had looked after their own cattle. When the Act went through the farmer demanded the services of Kgobadi, his wife and his cattle, in return for thirty shillings a month. Kgobadi refused. The farmer evicted them. One night in the veld Plaatje found them with their children huddled together on their ox-wagon. A blizzard whipped across the flat land. Kgobadi's goats were to kid and the kids had been dying as they trekked. And Mrs Kgobadi had been nursing a sick baby in the jolting wagon. The baby died that night. Plaatje told how the death of the child added a fresh perplexity to the stricken parents. They had no right or title to the farm lands through which they trekked: they must keep to the public roads – the deceased child had to be buried, but where, when and how?

So the father dug a grave at night, when no one was looking, and in that crude manner their baby was buried.

As Plaatje came across more – hundreds and hundreds – of

people wandering, his writing became the more impassioned. Some farmers told him that they had wanted their squatters to stay on because 'we were living so nicely with your people', but they would have risked a fine of a hundred pounds.

He met an Afrikaner policeman on horseback who said jovially, 'If ever there was a fool's errand, it is that of a kaffir trying to find a new home for his stock and family.'

'And what do you think, baas officer,' asked Plaatje with a deference likely to elicit a reply, 'must eventually be the lot of a people under such unfortunate circumstances?'

'They had no business to hanker after British rule,' was the policeman's reply. 'Why did they not assist the forces of their Republic during the war instead of supplying the English with scouts and intelligence? . . . Serve them right, I say . . .'

Plaatje followed a case of an evicted family who, after a fruit-less search for a place to live, took a travelling pass to Basutoland, the near-by British colony. But before they could reach it they were ambushed by some Afrikaners who shot them and took their stock. One of the whites was arrested. The stolen cattle had been found in his possession; a bullet near the bodies fitted his pistol. In his trial in Bloemfontein General Hertzog defended him. The white jury acquitted him. His friends acclaimed him. Subsequently the police arrested him on a charge of stealing the murdered African's cattle; he was convicted and sentenced to three years' imprisonment with hard labour.

Another factor which Plaatje observed was the irony of South Africa 'which so tyrannically chased her own Natives from the country', receiving 'at this very time with open arms, Polish, Finnish, Russian and German Jews, fled from the tyranny of their governments'.[1]

Meanwhile the Government and even their own white liberal friends were appealing to Congress leaders not to go to England on the grounds that the Land Act was a domestic affair. The deputation was elected: Dube, Sol Plaatje and Rubusana,[2] among others.

1. *Native Life in South Africa* by S. Plaatje.
2. Rubusana, and the African people of the Eastern Cape, had just suffered

The deputation were surprised to be invited by the Governor-General, Lord Gladstone, to Government House, when they arrived in Cape Town. There hope sprang. But all he wanted was to urge them not to go to Britain. They were firm. They told him of the barbarous cruelties inflicted by the Land Act. They believed they saw astonishment and pity on his face, then His Excellency remarked: 'The Natives are not the only sufferers. Even in England people have suffered hardships . . . till they were compelled to emigrate to America and other places.'

One last attempt to dissuade them from appealing to Britain was made by no less a person than General Botha himself who, as Plaatje put it, 'condescended' to meet the deputation. They hoped he would make some offer of a compromise. He simply told them that he and his acquaintances had refrained from evicting their own Natives. When they suggested that he should at least amend the law to legalize the settlement of tenants, he replied: 'Parliament will think I'm mad.'

On reaching London the deputation saw the Colonial Secretary, the Rt Hon. L. Harcourt, who took no notes, asked no questions, told them that the Prime Minister of South Africa had assured him that the Natives had too much land already and, on every point they made, replied that he had the assurance of General Botha to the contrary. He concluded that they should have made their case to their own Parliament. Questions were asked on their behalf in the House of Commons, and it was pointed out that in the Transvaal 300,000 whites had 31 million morgen of land while the 1 million natives were confined to half a million morgen, but the Colonial Secretary brushed all points aside. However the deputation found a sympathetic Press. The *Daily News* said they were obviously men of culture who had given a reasonable account of the set-up in South Africa; it was time Parliament gave attention to its obligation; the South

---

a bad setback when, due to the intervention of Jabavu, who split the vote, Rubusana lost his seat on the Cape Provincial Council to a white candidate. Never again was an African elected and however distinguished Jabavu was in the educational field, he never retrieved his political reputation.

African Native 'has no vote and no friends'. *The Globe* pointed to the anomaly that the Basuto and Gold Coast Africans had just successfully appealed to London but South African Natives, with far more serious grievances, had no constitutional right to do so.

Back at home meanwhile there was continued assault on Africans' freedom of movement. In the Orange Free State African women were degraded and impoverished by the pass laws; forced to buy a fresh pass each month costing one shilling at a time when two pounds a month was an excellent wage. Petitions and deputations having proved ineffectual, the women of the Free State 'threw off their shawls' and took the law into their own hands, as Plaatje put it. In Bloemfontein in July 1913, 600 indignant but calm women marched to the Municipal offices and asked for the Mayor. He was out. When the Deputy Mayor saw them they deposited at his feet a bag of passes and said they would not buy any more.

For the first time South Africa witnessed passive resistance from the African people. This action by African women took place at the time of the suffragettes' protests in England.

The idea caught on. In Jagersfontein, a small dorp, fifty-two women led by 'a jet-black Mozambique lady' went to jail rather than carry passes. There was not enough room in the Jagersfontein jail so they were taken in donkey-carts to another prison. In other dorps the jails were flooded. Plaatje, before leaving for England, had visited thirty-four of the passive resisters who were doing hard labour in Kroonstad. He was shocked to see how emaciated they had become; besides it was exceptionally cold and their socks and shoes had been taken away. He at once telegraphed the Prime Minister pointing out that all these women were in jail not for committing a crime but for resenting a crime which had been committed against them. Botha replied in Afrikaans: 'It shall be my endeavour, as hitherto, to safeguard the just interests of the inhabitants of this land irrespective of colour.' Nothing was done.

Soon after, Dube returned from England and reported back to a special meeting of the Congress in Bloemfontein. Congress expressed disappointment at the cold reception given by the Imperial Government to their deputation, and gratitude to the British public for their warm welcome. While the conference was in session news came that Britain had declared war on Germany. At once the Africans decided 'to hang up Native grievances' and to render the Government every assistance. Dube and other leaders set off for Pretoria to offer the services of Congress. The African women of the Free State halted their passive resistance campaign and joined sewing classes to send clothing to the afflicted Belgians. From African people throughout Southern Africa there were offers of assistance: one Congress leader, for instance, organizing a touring choir to raise money for the Governor-General's fund while the Rev. Walter Rubusana, who had so much influence among the Xhosa, offered to help recruit 5,000 men to assist the South African forces fighting the Germans in South-West Africa.

The reply came: 'The Government does not desire to avail itself of the services, in a combatant capacity . . . of citizens not of European descent. Apart from other considerations, the present war is one which has its origins among the white people of Europe and the Government are anxious to avoid the employment of its native citizens in a warfare against whites.'

But the patriotism of the Africans was irrepressible; they could be heard in country places singing 'Tipperary' in Xhosa, and as soon as they were called for to do menial tasks, they joined up in their tens of thousands. Plaatje commented that Turcos, Algerians, Moroccans, Jamaicans, were doing wonderful deeds for the cause of the Allies; that the Canadian troops included Red Indians; but the non-whites of South Africa were required only as wagon drivers and orderlies. Exposed to all the risks of war, if they were shot they were not even mentioned in casualty lists. Native drivers were classed with transport mules, except that if a mule were killed the owner was compensated.

When in 1914 the Boer Rebellion broke out, among the 10,000 rebels to be detained was Piet Grobler, the Member of Parliament who had originally moved the Native Land Bill in 1913.

After the rest of the Congress deputation had returned to

South Africa, Plaatje remained to tour Britain addressing meetings. When he ran out of money he managed somehow to make a living by journalism. His book *Native Life in South Africa* was published later. He found the audiences so kind that for a time he forgot he was an African. He told about his people: he was not, he said, appealing on behalf of naked hordes of cannibals such as were displayed in fantastic pictures in shop windows in Europe, but on behalf of five million loyal British subjects. He described how recently in Johannesburg, when the Governor-General had congratulated a fashionable crowd on the maintenance at full pitch of the gold industry despite the strain of war, Lord Buxton had had no word for the African miners, the 200,000 'subterranean heroes, who by day and by night, for a mere pittance', Plaatje pointed out, 'sacrificed their lungs to the rock dust which develops miners' phthisis', and who paid taxes that were used towards beautifying white homes and maintaining the Government schools from which Africans were excluded.

More than 84,000 non-whites had joined the South African army, and among their casualties were the 600 African volunteers drowned at sea when the troop ship *Mendi* struck a mine and sank. It was at this time in 1917 that General Smuts, by then a world hero, made a celebrated speech at the Savoy Hotel in London in which he said, 'it has been our ideal to make it [South Africa] a white man's country'. The speech long rankled in the minds of Congress leaders.

Meanwhile Congress had troubles of its own. The executive, separated by great distances with difficulties of communication, met irregularly. The newspaper suffered from lack of funds and war-time paper shortages. Seme turned against Dube, quarrelled with him and drove him to resign. He himself lost interest in Congress and concentrated on his law practice. The personality squabble almost destroyed the organization.

Yet the will to survive won, largely due to Daniel Letanka, a reserved diligent man, for long the editor of *Abantu-Batho*. Samuel Mapoch Makgatho, a Transvaler, was elected President. This was logical when Johannesburg and the surrounding Reef had attracted many of the Africans driven off the land and becoming urbanized. Makgatho, educated partly in England, was a Methodist lay preacher and founder of the Transvaal African Teachers' Association. Since 1906 he had led successive African political organizations in the Transvaal, and although not an outstanding personality, he was a man 'who would not budge' and was practical: for instance, he challenged the railway segregation policy at the risk of assault from an infuriated Afrikaner next to whom he sat on the train. Others followed his example and eventually won the right to have carriages of all classes for Africans, albeit segregated ones.

At the end of the war Makgatho sent a cable to His Majesty the King, expressing Africans' loyalty and pride at their contribution to the war effort. On behalf of Congress he went on to call for a removal of the colour bar in the franchise and, looking further afield, wanted an assurance that the High Commission Territories would not be incorporated in the Union and that South-West Africa would not be disposed of until the inhabitants had been consulted. This concern about South-West Africa showed considerable prescience. His Majesty thanked them for their congratulations on the glorious victory.

2 1918–24: The People Resist, but Opportunities are Missed

The post-war years were a time of general industrial unrest. The cost of living had soared, there was a drought and crop failures. All over South Africa white workers came out on strike, but the Africans endured greater tribulation. Though they had to pay the same prices or more for goods as had the whites, for them even in Johannesburg £4 a month was regarded as a good wage; against this their rent cost 10s. a month, tax £1–£2 a year, and they still had to pay for food, clothing, fu nd the children's education. The crop failures in the over-crowded reserves sent thousands of illiterate peasants searching for work in the few towns. Even from the comparatively contented Cape, hunger was driving people to live under the restrictions of the Transvaal. Around the expanding white towns and suburbs, Native 'locations' proliferated and – denied Municipal services – inevitably became slums.

These conditions set off a chain of protests, despite the Master and Servants Act which made it a criminal offence for an African to break his contract or refuse to obey an order from his employer, and despite the risk of criminal prosecution if Africans dared to strike.

The first African strike, in 1918, was of 'night-soil boys' – sanitary workers – in Johannesburg who downed buckets and demanded sixpence a day more on their wage. 152 of them were arrested. Congress instructed a European lawyer to defend them. The magistrate found them guilty and sentenced them to two months' hard labour.[1] They were told they would be shot or beaten if they tried to escape or disobeyed orders. Congress led

1. *Cape Argus*, 11 June 1918.

the storm of protest by calling for a general strike for a shilling a day increase in wages. The police promptly arrested Letanka and other Congress leaders, as well as S. P. Bunting and two other members of the International Socialist League who had been organizing labour. They were charged with incitement to violence. For the first time Africans and Europeans were arrested together for political activity, but it was largely a coincidence for Congress had no connexion with the socialists nor they with the 'bourgeois' Congress. The case fell away when the main witness repudiated his evidence.

Another attempted strike took place in Bloemfontein when Africans demanded four and six a day instead of two shillings. The authorities declared martial law.

Though their grievances proliferated, Africans remained difficult to organize. Many workers in the towns were herded into easily controlled compounds; many, illiterate and bewildered by the white man's world, were too busy trying to adapt to that world to think much about politics.

The Government's most effective instrument in controlling their movement and maintaining their subjection was the hated pass system which turned any African outside the Native reserves into a vagrant unless he were working for a European. If he were a clergyman, lawyer or the like, he could be exempted from these laws although he would still have to produce on demand a certificate proving this. An African needed passes to get a job, to travel, and to be out after curfew. Anyone not producing a pass on demand was liable to a fine or imprisonment and the resentment against the laws was exacerbated by the way many policemen administered them.

In Johannesburg in March and April 1919, Congress organized the bitter resentment into massive demonstrations. Several thousand Africans gathered to hand in their passes. The leaders emphasized: 'no violence'; the picketers collected and put away any sticks or sjamboks that men might be carrying. The speeches over, they all sang 'Rule Britannia', 'Nkosi Sikelel' i-Afrika' and 'The King'. The crowd cheered enthusiastically for the King and for the Governor-General. For President Wilson of the

United States there were especially loud cheers because he had aroused their imagination with his Fourteen Points of freedom for dependent peoples. The business of collecting passes went on. The Johannesburg *Star* remarked that there were no untoward incidents: 'as a matter of fact there was a sort of humorous atmosphere among the Natives'. Several thousand Africans had already marched to the pass office, to leave sacks full of passes. The evening paper carried the headline: NATIVE MENACE.

White workers who were simultaneously on strike came forward to say that if there were 'native trouble' they would stand by the community. African picketers were arrested. A police officer told them they had gone against the laws of the country and against the King; they would be punished for their 'traitorous behaviour'. Meanwhile a strike of white barbers which had lasted a week was now settled and the men resumed work 'satisfied with the concessions granted'. As soon as white builders, plumbers, butchers and hairdressers had started striking, the Government appointed an Industrial Commission to look into their grievances. A Congress leader told a journalist: 'The white man fights for his rights and when he does not get them he goes on strike . . . and you don't put them in jail. But if we want to fight for our rights the police lock us up. . . .'

The passive resistance spread rapidly through the mining villages. From all over the Witwatersrand, Congress leaders took sacks full of passes and dumped them at the pass office, undeterred by hundreds of arrests.

A huge crowd gathered outside the court for the first trial of two hundred people arrested on a charge of disturbing the public peace. They all pleaded 'Not guilty'. Sentences ranged from one to six months' imprisonment with hard labour, in some cases with lashes. When the magistrate pronounced sentence, from the non-white public gallery came audible 'clicks' of indignation.

Outside the court the crowds waited. Some of them were women with children on their backs, including wives who had brought food to their husbands on trial. A Johannesburg resident, a Mr William Hosken, was to describe what happened. Police, mounted and on foot, arrived, to be greeted by hearty cheers from the Natives, then some booing, followed by 'absolute quiet'. Not a single hostile move was made by the Natives. Then – 'to my astonishment', said Hosken, 'the mounted police suddenly spurred their horses and charged on the crowd'. The police used their staves vigorously, riding over Natives – who included women. Whereupon a civilian began 'slashing with a stick at every Native he came near, and finally struck a Native woman a severe blow'. Hosken remonstrated and demanded the man's name but was ignored. He heard one bystander exclaiming: 'Would I had a machine-gun, and I could then do some execution.' As he went along the street he came across more whites intercepting Natives.[1]

All was quiet at the Magistrates' court the next day. Natives, the Press reported, were in a subdued mood. A police official declared: 'Yesterday's little charge has had the right effect, and I am confident that the back of the trouble has been broken.'

Meanwhile Congress leaders were arrested, at a time when white members of the Government were arriving in Johannesburg to confer with the white strike leaders.

Yet the protests continued for a few more days. On one occasion Africans stoned the police and on another whites shot and killed an African demonstrator.

The Government appointed a one-man commission of inquiry into the allegations of police ill-treatment in Johannesburg, which exonerated the police 'in view of the difficult circumstances'. However, it did bluntly suggest that the Government should modify the pass laws as it was apparent that the Natives were determined to resist them. The Government ignored his suggestion, as it ignored a subsequent recommendation by a Committee from the Department of Justice and Native Affairs 'that the present system of pass laws should be abolished'.

Evidence of the Natives' 'determination to resist the pass laws' came powerfully from another source as, with the ending of the war, African women felt free to renew their protest. They

1. Letter to the *Star*, April 1919.

had acquired a remarkable leader, Mrs Charlotte Maxeke. As a girl she had toured England in an African choir, performing before Queen Victoria. The choir went on to New York where it broke up and Charlotte found herself stranded. Negro friends sent her to Wilberforce University in Ohio, where she graduated as a Bachelor of Science in 1905. She married a missionary of the African Methodist Episcopal Church and together they established a school in the Transvaal where Maxeke also edited a local African newspaper and became a prominent member of the Native Congress.

Mrs Maxeke founded a women's section of Congress. One of her friends said she 'could strike terror into those who crossed swords with her and yet be gentle and kind to those who needed her sympathy'. As President of the Women's Congress she was fearless. Although women had been so active in anti-pass protests years before, it was a revolution in African life for them to be directly involved in politics, and at that time they were hardly seen in the big towns. Now again they invited imprisonment by demonstrating against passes in many parts of the country. In some areas the authorities relaxed the laws.

But no headway had been made in the crucial question of Parliamentary representation. The hopes of Congress leaders again turned towards the first object of their loyalty, the King of England. The recollection of President Wilson's declaration that even small nations were entitled to the right of self-determination encouraged them to send a second deputation not only to Britain, but to the Peace Conference at Versailles.

The deputation that went to Versailles included Sol Plaatje, while the principal spokesman was Selope ('Don't Beg') Thema, Secretary-General of Congress since 1915 and a contributor to *Abantu-Batho*. He came from a poor family in the Northern Transvaal and as a child during the Anglo-Boer War had been commandeered by the Boers to be at one time or another a kitchen-boy, cook, batman, waiter and labourer. After matriculating at Lovedale College he became a clerk, but one day an incident changed his life. As he cycled to work, his hat on his head, he passed a white policeman on horse-back who veered round and demanded to know where Thema's hat was. Thema replied: 'On my head,' whereupon the policeman knocked him off his bicycle and kicked him for not taking his hat off. There and then Thema decided to join the Native National Congress.

Versailles 1919: the deputation found that apart from the official delegation led by Generals Botha and Smuts, there was another unofficial deputation from South Africa, lobbying hard, which consisted of General Hertzog, Dr D. F. Malan, and other Afrikaner Nationalists who wanted sympathy for their aim of a Republic of South Africa. The Afrikaners followed President Wilson to America when the Peace Conference ended, but the Native National Congress deputation could not afford to do so. Nor did they get any hearing in Versailles, and when they went to the Colonial Office in London they were at once advised to return to South Africa and work patiently within the limits of the Union's constitution. Interviews with Lloyd George, the Prime Minister, and with the Archbishop of Canterbury, left the deputation with no alternative but to try once again to arouse British public opinion to compel their Government to influence the South African Government. As before they had a good Press and the British people were friendly; but they were arguing a hopeless case and their funds ran out. All but Plaatje returned to South Africa and reported back to a Congress that at last was disillusioned. As one of its leaders, the Rev. Z. R. Mahabane, said a year or two later, they felt that England 'had finally washed her hands of the innocent blood of the Bantu races, divested herself of all responsibility – although like Pilate in sacred history' she would never be 'absolved from responsibility in the shameful "selling away" of a whole nation'.[1]

Sol Plaatje became the first of South Africa's leaders to make political contact with Africans from other parts of the continent and with American Negroes, when he attended the Pan-African Congress in Paris, organized by Dr W. E. B. Du Bois, with the object of influencing the Peace Conference. From France, Plaatje went on to tell people in Canada and the United States about conditions in South Africa.

1. *Three Presidential Addresses*, Lovedale Press.

Meanwhile in the Union industrial discontent once again drove Africans to action. In February 1920 the Native Congress helped organize more than 40,000 African miners on the Witwatersrand who came out on strike with a demand for higher wages. But after a meeting on one mine had been broken up by white civilians shooting on the crowd, the organizing petered out and the strike was soon crushed by a combination of white miners 'scabbing', of police and civilians violently driving Africans back to work (several Africans being killed), and by sheer lack of trade union know-how.

Besides, Smuts – who since the death of Botha in 1919 had been Prime Minister and Minister of Native Affairs and of Justice – was showing he was not to be trifled with. A threatened strike of Africans in Port Elizabeth in October 1920 was crushed by police and white civilians: more than twenty non-whites were killed. A few months later at Bulhoek in the Eastern Cape a fervid religious sect illegally camping on common ground was eventually removed by the army. The Israelites armed with rough tools charged; the police fired, killing 163 Israelites and wounding nearly as many. The Bulhoek massacre is a story told to African children 'as an incident that has passed into what one might call the political history of the people'.[1]

A few months later Smuts's army, supported by bombing planes, moved into the mandated territory of South-West Africa to attack the Bondelswarts, a Hottentot tribe, who because of poverty refused to pay a heavy dog tax imposed on them. More than a hundred men, women and children were killed and many mutilated.

Again in 1922 on the Rand a white miners' strike turned into a full-scale revolt over a Chamber of Mines proposal to lower the colour bar to enable African miners to do more of the lower skilled work reserved for whites. Smuts personally directed the forces to smash this revolt. Africans were not involved and the tiny minority of Marxists who fought for their rights as fellow-workers were easily isolated and two of them were shot. During the two months of rioting Africans were spontaneously attacked;

1. Z. K. Matthew's Evidence in Treason Trial, 1961.

seven were killed and thirty-six wounded. Thousands were rendered unemployed and returned by the Chambers of Mines to the reserves.

The Native National Congress declared it had no confidence in the Government. And for the first time it passed a motion of no-confidence in the British Government. Speakers even supported the idea of a Republic. Smuts's comment was that the Congress was not representative, 'it consisted of a body of intellectuals', which drew from the Johannesburg *Star*[1] the retort that Smuts himself was an intellectual and there was 'scarcely less wide a gap between his mental outlook and that of some illiterate *bywoner* (white squatter) of the backveld' than between Congress leaders and ordinary Africans. The editorial concluded: 'Of course the Native Congress does not represent all the Natives. How could it in the circumstances prevailing in South Africa?... But upon questions directly affecting the interests of the Natives as a whole, the Congress probably represents Native opinion a good deal more faithfully than an Assembly elected by European voters.'

Smuts's handling of the mine strike had greatly weakened his Government among white workers and at the next election in 1924 white voters put into power a Government which demonstrated the extent to which political expediency could go: the Afrikaner Nationalists joined with the Labour Party – which had been backed in the election by the Communist Party, all intent on representing the interests of white workers and of getting rid of Smuts who had put down the white miners – to form an anti-capitalist coalition. General Hertzog was the new Prime Minister, just as his followers had predicted at the time of the Native Land Act.

1. 2 June 1923.

3 1924–9: Workers are Organized and Philosophies found Wanting

One of Hertzog's first actions was to threaten total segregation, but for the time being he lacked the majority necessary to make good the threat. Things were bad enough: the country was exceptionally prosperous, yet the Johannesburg *Star* could describe the Native 'crowded off the land . . . denied a permanent foothold in urban areas . . . exploited at every point, badgered from pillar to post, and under disabilities of all kinds whether he stays at home or seeks work away from it!' The crux of the matter was that 'unorganized and inarticulate he is powerless'. And in this situation Congress leaders remained more concerned with dignity than poverty and the cost of living.

A dynamic clerk from Nyasaland, Clements Kadalie, swept into the breach. The Industrial and Commercial Workers' Union, which he founded with the aid of a European in Cape Town in 1919, promised to win higher wages and better conditions for the African people. Africans began to pay their fees and join in their thousands. Though the I.C.U. had begun as a trade union of dock workers, with twenty-four members who each contributed one shilling, through the restless energy and organizing ability of Kadalie, by 1925, when I.C.U. headquarters moved to Johannesburg, it had become a country-wide organization representing grievances expressed in innumerable small strikes. It called for a minimum wage for African workers and for the first time gained recognition by white workers, when the S.A. Trade Union Congress supported the call.

The leaders of the two organizations typified their strengths and weaknesses. Kadalie – demagogic, magnetic, with his odd high-pitched voice – rallied the masses as no one had done before: promising reforms, cursing Hertzog. He was soon wielding such power that even European politicians thought it worth their while to woo him. He recruited as chief lieutenant George Champion, a Zulu who had organized the Native clerks on the Rand mines, big, bold-voiced and ruthless, with charm.

On the other hand the new President General of the Native National Congress, the Rev. Zaccheus R. Mahabane, a Methodist, thoughtful, slow-speaking, with a jolly face, felt the work of Congress was to try to educate Africans about their rights, to make representations against the colour bar and for better wages, and to hold frequent meetings.

Kadalie enhanced his prestige by challenging the pass laws. He had been warned he must get permission from the Native Affairs Department to travel about South Africa. When he applied for a permit to visit Natal, and was refused, he nevertheless went to Durban, addressed meetings – including one of 8,000 I.C.U. supporters – and returned to Johannesburg unchallenged. The best way to deal with the pass laws, he announced, was to defy them, and, though belatedly brought to court, he won the case. However, his power and personal boldness were not translated into mass action; nor did the I.C.U. reach the miners or the farm workers. Yet its membership soared; in 1926 it had some 50,000 members.

Meanwhile the Congress decline continued. It was during this period, in 1925, that it was retitled the South African African National Congress; adopted *Nkosi Sikelel' i-Afrika* ('Lord Bless Africa') as its anthem; and chose a flag: black for the people, green for the land, and gold for the riches. The anthem was to be adopted by Congresses in East and Central Africa, while thirty-six years later Tanganyika hoisted such a flag to mark her independence. Incidentally the Congress leader mainly responsible for such moves, T. D. Mweli Skota, though defeated in his desire to call a great All-African Conference, did subsequently, in 1932, edit a unique book that symbolized this dream: *The African Yearly Register* contained biographies of eminent Africans throughout the continent from the Emperor of Abyssinia down, and a copy of it was accepted by the Prince of

Wales. A South African newspaper praised it as 'every bit as engrossing as a novel'.

Skota's interest in the continent of Africa had grown partly through the influence of Marcus Garvey, the Jamaican who had fired African imagination from West Africa to South Africa through his 'Back to Africa' cry to Negroes and the flamboyant soap-box meetings with a uniformed band that he held in New York. Indeed even in remote corners of the Ciskei and Transkei, peasants suddenly became wildly excited over the anticipated advent of Garvey to liberate them; while later, Kwame Nkrumah was to say that Garvey's writings did more than any other to fire his enthusiasm.[1]

Another foreign Negro with great influence in the Union was the West African educationist, Dr J. E. K. Aggrey. But while Garvey fired both the man in the street and nationalist intellectuals, Aggrey's statements about the harmony of white and black piano keys had been given form in Joint Councils of Europeans and Natives established in South African towns after his visit in the early twenties. These made recommendations about Parliamentary matters affecting Natives. Thus some Congress leaders became associated with the small group of white liberals; a natural association for those who had had Christian liberal education in the schools of the Eastern Cape, who had learnt English history, and whose parents had revered the distant Queen Victoria. The Joint Councils, in unconsciously accepting another of Aggrey's tenets, that half a loaf was better than none, neutralized African nationalism.

Africans did not judge whites by their philosophy so much as by their actions. Liberals in the Joint Councils, instead of helping them to win and defend their rights, urged them to abandon militancy, believing that by education, moderation and patience Africans could win white sympathy. So-called socialists in the Labour Party were engrossed in the needs of white workers. This left the communists who after 1924, disillusioned by white labour, concentrated more on providing trades union and political education for non-white workers. The

1. K. Nkrumah's *Autobiography*.

communists best known to Africans were two Englishmen, S. F. Bunting, the lawyer who came from a non-conformist humanitarian family, and Bill Andrews, both of them 'always ready to help us in our battles' explained a Congress leader: 'they had their meetings and we had our meetings and Bunting would come and discuss things with us. In all the cases he defended for Congress I don't think he was paid for three of them. He was a wonderful man.' And the Rev. C. F. Andrews, Gandhi's Anglican friend, after visiting the country in the twenties, said his whole heart went out to the communists there because they were the only Europeans 'ready to admit Indians, Cape Coloured and Bantu on equal terms'.[1]

Kadalie and the I.C.U. were faced by these opposing philosophies in concrete form when sympathetic liberals urged him to expel the four African communists on his Executive, a move which they said could result in the I.C.U. joining the International Federation of Trade Unions. He was anyway angry at the communists' call for strict supervision of the Unions' increasingly dubious finances, and for the reiterated demands for action. The left-wing wanted strikes and pass burnings, the right sought caution – *Hamba Kahle* – go carefully. The quarrel came to a head in December 1926 when he just succeeded in getting a resolution passed that no member of the I.C.U. could be a member of the Communist Party.

Africans could ill afford divisions for Hertzog was enacting his 'Colour Bar' Bill, the Mines and Works Amendment Act of 1926, which debarred Africans from a variety of better paid jobs *whatever* their skills or potential. He strengthened the Masters and Servants Act and dealt with the influx of Africans driven to towns by economic need by even stricter segregation and discriminatory laws. Next, he enacted the Native Administration Act of 1927 which named the Governor-General the Supreme Chief, giving the Government total power in the appointment and deposition of chiefs and intimidating them from supporting the A.N.C., which meant withdrawal by their followers as well. The Act also forbade the holding of meetings

1. *Time Longer than Rope* by E. Roux.

in tribal areas without the white Native Commissioner's permission, thus limiting African political activity increasingly to urban areas. And it embraced a notorious 'hostility clause' under which anyone promoting 'any feeling of hostility between Natives and Europeans' was liable to imprisonment of up to one year or a fine of a hundred pounds or both. Never used against white politicians but only against Africans and their white friends, here was yet another deterrent to political action.

These onslaughts brought together non-white organizations, but only momentarily. In June 1927 the notable Coloured leader Dr A. Abdurahman, with D. D. T. Jabavu, Professor at Fort Hare Native College, called a Non-European Conference with representatives of A.N.C., I.C.U. and Indian Congress, but their hope of a continuing Non-European front was postponed to another day.

Even the I.C.U. at the zenith of its power in 1928 with 200,000 members, and some impressive strikes to its credit, failed to combat these laws. It had gone through a series of paroxysms to deteriorate in a confusion of quarrels over misuse of funds, or between clashing personalities, or over the old problem, inaction: Kadalie's call for a day of prayer in face of Hertzog's 'Colour Bar' Bill drove an ex-communist member of the I.C.U., Thomas Mbeki, to cry out that people could no longer endure the injustice; 'the failure of the A.N.C. was due to too much prayer and no direct action. For God's sake,' he urged Kadalie, 'don't turn chameleon. Are you going back to the masses to ask them to pray, or will you tell them to depend on their numerical powers?' But Kadalie was off to London, Paris, Geneva to win the sympathy of European trade unions. In his absence there were many spontaneous strikes, which petered out. Meanwhile George Champion, who had skilfully organized the Natal I.C.U., used Kadalie's absence to entrench himself, and when Kadalie returned the two men quarrelled bitterly. The outcome was two organizations with Champion controlling the I.C.U. Yase (of) Natal. Later, when British sympathizers sent out William Ballinger to restore order in the I.C.U.'s affairs, there was a further split.

Mahabane of the A.N.C. and its first President, Dr Dube, also went to Europe in the late 1920s to attend the International Missionary Conference in Belgium. Dr Dube warned that the situation in South Africa was very dangerous, 'and the attitude of the present Government alarms us', he said. 'The Colour Bar Bill seems more than we can patiently bear. . . . If the Government persists with its present attitude, we can only think that it desires to exterminate us': strong words from a moderate man. Mahabane, in his address to the Missionary Conference, which included men as prominent in Imperial affairs as Sir Frederick Lugard and J. H. Oldham, spoke of the reaction 'that has taken place in the African's mind through the advance of Western civilization . . . Some of us know,' he said, 'that not every white man is a Christian, but the average African looks upon every white man as a Christian, and if he does not lead the Christian life then the mind of the African revolts against Christianity.'

Not surprisingly, there was a sharp swing to the left in the A.N.C., and the new President-General, when he went to Belgium in 1927, did not attend a missionary conference but a communist-front conference of the League Against Imperialism. There were eminent men present, only this time not administrators but revolutionaries from Asia and Africa – including the coming leader of the Indian National Congress, Pandit Nehru. The new leader of the A.N.C. was James Gumede, a broad-minded Roman Catholic, who, having twice pinned his hopes on Britain helping to free the non-whites of South Africa – once in a deputation from a tribe which had helped the British in the Boer War, and the other time in the 1919 deputation – had begun to look elsewhere. The Brussels conference, concerned with the 'War Danger' and with the 'penetration of Latin America by Yankee Imperialism' could not have been of particular interest to him, but when it came to an end, for the first time in the history of the A.N.C., its President was invited to visit a foreign country – Russia. Gumede, a middle-aged, upright man, had in South Africa been subjected to the usual humiliations. He now found himself fêted 'as though I was the Prime

Minister of the Union' and visited Asiatic parts where he saw that non-Europeans, some as dark as himself, enjoyed the same political and social rights as the whites. Back in Cape Town he told a crowded reception that he had come from the 'new Jerusalem'; Russia was a land of equality and freedom raised from serfdom. 'Your land and yourselves,' he told South Africans, 'are held in bondage. You must redeem your heritage.'[1]

He met with strenuous, even virulent opposition, for although the Communist Party was the only non-racial political party and ran night schools for Africans and helped them form trade unions very few Africans had actually joined it. The majority remained suspicious because, explained one Congress leader, 'it does not believe in God, in Kings or Chiefs. Africans have always believed in a God. They are not materialists.'

And when the A.N.C. for the first time debated a resolution disapproving of the growing fraternization with the Communist Party, one chief pointed out, 'The Tsar was a great man in his country but where is he now?' However, President-General Gumede remarked that the Native Administration Act, the very Act that so undermined the chiefs' power, had been initiated by Hertzog who declared the communists to be the only opposition to his Native policy that he feared; and that the Government, the South African Party, and the English language Press run by the Chamber of Mines, alike hated the Communist Party because it spoke for the masses and was against oppression. Thereupon the chiefs withdrew their motion though rumblings of dissatisfaction continued.

At one conference when the handful of communists in Congress moved that it affiliate with the Communist Party, they were defeated by a large majority, as was their second proposal, that Congress should join with other African organizations in a 'mass revolutionary movement to combat the evil measures' which Hertzog was again threatening in the form of Bills to bring about segregation of the races.

But again Hertzog had to postpone his Bills while the election took place in 1929. During the campaign Smuts, leader of the

1. *Cape Times*, 28 January 1928.

opposition South African Party, spoke of 'British states in Africa' which would 'all become members of a great African Dominion, stretching unbroken throughout Africa'. At once Hertzog accused Smuts of wanting 'a kaffir state' from South Africa to London, with equal rights. Hertzog, Dr D. F. Malan and Tielman Roos issued a manifesto, which became known as the 'Black Manifesto', describing what would become of South Africa if Smuts's policy were accepted. The terms 'kaffir land', 'black kaffir state', 'a kaffir ocean' were liberally sprinkled through it. 'Our national pride, our patriotism, the honour we have to uphold', the three Nationalist leaders said; our 'glorious heritage' all would be 'scrapped' if Smuts had his way.[1] Useless for Smuts's supporters to point out that his plea had simply been one for the unity of whites for mutual protection. The cry of a black bogey, together with the singular prosperity South Africa had enjoyed since 1924, brought the Nationalists into office, for the first time with an overall majority.

The A.N.C. replied to the 'extraordinary and mischievous' manifesto that whereas in the previous century there had been over ten Natives to every white, at the present time there were only three Natives to each white. 'How in the face of that,' they asked, 'could the European be depicted as a drowning man, gasping for breath, catching at every straw, and threatened to be engulfed in a single "kaffir ocean"?'

Congress was still a respectable body, its conference opened by the Mayor, the Bishop, the Chief Magistrate and the Superintendent of Locations. When they met to consider new legislation they discussed the Riotous Assemblies Amendment Bill which gave the Minister of Justice power to banish anyone from any district if he considered the person's presence might stir up hostility; a weapon fit for Oswald Pirow, the Minister, a man who was to visit and admire Hitler. Champion of the A.N.C. and I.C.U. suggested that Hertzog and Pirow should be indicted for creating hostility by calling on whites to unite against blacks. But this was not formally moved, whereas the perennial resolutions were passed calling for abolition of the

1. The *Star*, 29 January 1929.

pass laws and the colour bar and for Parliamentary representation. 'Respectfully' yet 'strongly' Congress urged the Government to appoint a commission to consider wages, cost of living,
and the exclusion of Natives from the Old-Age Pensions Act,
and to study the effect of conditions on the moral integrity of the
African people.

Hertzog was now set on his path. His Minister of Justice,
Pirow, made a personal debut in November 1929 when he flew
dramatically from Pretoria to supervise tax collection in Durban.
The Minister of Finance did not object to this poaching, for the
Minister of Justice was not concerned to see that white voters
paid up, but that voiceless Africans – who if they failed to pay
were automatically criminals – should do so. He literally com-
manded an invasion of 500 white police armed with machine-
guns and bayoneted rifles, together with 200 Native police. At
3 a.m. they 'invested' Native compounds 'silently and swiftly'
(to quote the Johannesburg *Star*) in search of tax defaulters.
While 5,000 Africans were searched, tear-gas was thrown at
spectators. Some 350 men were arrested for failure to produce
tax receipts. Unless they paid at once they were imprisoned for
a month.[1] 'We first advertise in the illustrated periodicals,'
remarked the *Star*,[2] 'the charm of our seaside resorts and then
proceed to give them a unique and world-wide advertisement of
this sort.'

In the recriminations that followed, the feelings of the people
affected were barely considered. The results of an unofficial
inquiry by the Joint Council into the inability of Africans to pay
tax showed that Native wages in Durban had not been raised
since 1914! Many were earning three pounds a month. The
Government's retort, according to the *Rand Daily Mail*, was
that its action had been based on information more sensational
than the Zinoviev letter which had led to the downfall of the
first Labour Government in Britain. It gave no details of this
information but the smear was effective and whites in Durban
remarked that the Zulus were good-humoured people, so it must

1. In 1931–2 convictions under the Native Taxation Act numbered 50,000.
2. 14 November 1929.

be the Communist Party and Soviet money behind the discontent. The A.N.C. and the I.C.U. published a joint denial of communist influence and were supported by William Ballinger, the member of the British Labour Party sent to South Africa to help reorganize the I.C.U., who cabled London: 'Discount press report communist influence in Durban. Causes unrest deep-seated economic wrongs. Critical situation.'[1]

Non-white frustration burst out in protest meetings against Pirow's 'law of oppression' – the Riotous Assemblies Amendment Bill; in Johannesburg all sections of the I.C.U. joined with the Communist Party and with the A.N.C. in burning effigies of 'Pirow the tyrant', and of Hertzog and Smuts; demonstrations which spread to all parts of the country.

One of these protest meetings was held on 16 December 1929, in the location at Potchefstroom, a seat of Afrikaner nationalism. Several thousand Africans turned up as did several hundred Europeans. The principal speakers were Edwin Mofutsanyana and J. B. Marks, who belonged both to the Communist Party and to the A.N.C. Their speeches were broken up by coarse shouts such as '*Hou jou bek kafir!*' ('Shut up kaffir!'). Their appeals to the police to control the hooligans were fruitless and African anger was rapidly rising when one of the rowdies aimed a revolver at the speakers and fired several shots. Marks and Mofutsanyana escaped by diving from the platform but one African was killed and six injured. The crowd turned on the whites who were saved by the arrival of the magistrate who assured the Africans that they would get justice. Subsequently, a white man, brother of the location superintendent, was arrested and charged with murder. The evidence was that he had discharged the contents of his revolver at the Africans and was reloading when he had been caught by the police. The white jury gave its verdict: 'Not guilty.'[2]

The decade of unrest had ended, as it had begun, in violence.

1. *Manchester Guardian*, 20 November 1929.
2. Potchefstroom had been the scene of an earlier disturbance with white civilians precipitating shooting, and there had been similar incidents in other areas, for instance in Bloemfontein in 1925 and in Durban in 1928.

4 1930–5: Divisions at a Time of Depression

The Wall Street crash struck South Africa at a time of severe drought. The poorest people – white and black – were badly hit. Poor whites took kaffir work and hundreds of blacks were thrown out of work. Having nowhere to go, thousands of Africans became displaced persons in their own country, in danger of arrest under the pass laws. In Natal, men were working for six months at 10s. a month and women at 2s. 6d. a month. Rich sugar planters were using umfaans (small boys) taken from Pondoland by white recruiters and on these plantations some Africans, on becoming ill, had been turned out of their jobs and left to wander. Plaatje pointed out that Native labour was in the same market as white, paying the same price for a pound of coffee and a pair of shoes, yet having to work five or six times as long for the same amount.

At this critical time the Africans' national organizations were in a sorry condition. Kadalie had escaped from the disintegration of the I.C.U. to set up the Independent I.C.U. in East London, where he organized a strike demanding an increase in daily wages from 3s. to 6s. 6d. After a week 90 per cent of the labour was out, but feeling the pinch. Kadalie, imprisoned, called for a return to work. He was fined £25. The wages were raised to 3s. 6d. This was the last spurt of what had been a great mass party.

The A.N.C.'s upheaval centred on Gumede's 'communistic tendencies'. He was replaced by Pixley Seme, the founder of Congress, whose status had been enhanced by a doctorate from Columbia University. Alas, he whose dream had been to encourage divided tribes to cooperate was himself incapable of cooperating with colleagues and, once in office, he proved domineering and jealous of newcomers. To Champion, still the

leader of the I.C.U. Yase Natal, Dr Seme wrote: 'All organizations should fall into line with the A.N.C. . . . I must command
all under me.'

Gumede made a last appeal to Congress for Africans to rely
on their own strength and the strength of the colonially oppressed
peoples, to demand equal rights by using organized labour
unions, going in for strikes, demonstrations, the burning of
passes and refusal to pay taxes. The appeal was dismissed by
Seme, who favoured self-help of a different kind – through
Africans getting rights to trade and through social clubs. He
condemned boycotts and strikes because they 'never leave any
pleasant impression in the public mind'.

Gumede had said there were two wings of their movement for
emancipation from the tyranny of European rule, the right and
the left, both 'absolutely necessary for our progress . . . just as
a bird must have two wings for successful flight, so must any
movement have the conservative and radical wings, that is to
say, we may differ in our views but this should not necessarily
mean divisions and bickering'. Not necessarily, but almost
unavoidably there *were* divisions, complicated by disagreement
over the form and timing of action, and frequently aggravated
by conflicts of personality.

This had become particularly true of the Cape Peninsula. In
the mid-twenties such organizers as the A.N.C. had were usually
Coloured men who joined it on the decline of the African
People's Organization, but they soon found more scope in the
Communist Party when it came to organize trade unions and
night schools. It was in any event exceptional for Coloured
people to be involved in politics: the majority were concerned
to maintain their meagre privileges – better wages and opportunities than Africans as well as freedom of movement. Their
great social ambition was to belong to white society rather than
to black.

In the late twenties and early thirties, when the A.N.C. became quite a force in the Peninsula, divisions became sharp,
for the men who put it on the map – James Thaele (pronounced
Ty-ele) and Bransby Ndobe and Elliot Tonjeni – represented

not only a right and left wing but disagreed fiercely about timing and type of action. As personalities they clashed on sight. Ndobe and Tonjeni were 'young militants', Thaele, President of the Cape Western A.N.C., was a political opportunist, son of a Basuto chief and a Coloured mother, who had studied for fifteen years in the United States, before Marcus Garvey inspired him to return to South Africa. In Cape Town he founded a private school for Africans and was called Professor. He encouraged non-whites to start social centres and to apply to use the City Hall for their dances – to them a daring move. It was when he came to organize people in the villages that he clashed with Ndobe and Tonjeni. He accused them of being communists (which they denied) and they told him that he ought to be a bishop, not a Congress leader, while their communist friends suspected him of being a tool of the C.I.D.

Nevertheless between them the three men had succeeded in establishing branches of Congress in the beautiful mountain and fruit-growing areas, where wages for non-whites were pitifully low, but tragic events checked their progress. In Worcester location anger aroused by a police liquor raid led to the death of a white police officer. The police retaliated and five Africans were killed and others wounded. Civilians went about assaulting Africans. One, who was wandering around with a rifle taking pot-shots at Africans, was arrested by the police and fined five shillings by the magistrate for being in possession of a rifle without a licence. He was complimented by the magistrate for his public spirit. He said he was trying to shoot Tonjeni. Humorists among the Africans said he was fined because he missed![1] There was good reason to believe the disturbances had been instigated by an *agent provocateur*; at all events they provided Pirow with a convenient opportunity to ban all A.N.C. meetings in the Western Cape.

As if it was not enough that the Government was thus enfeebling Congress, Thaele tried to divide Tonjeni from Ndobe, but the friends remained mutually loyal and broke away to set up the Independent A.N.C., which achieved the support of *Abantu-*

1. *Time Longer than Rope* by E. Roux.

Batho, the Congress paper in Johannesburg. Their new organization was short-lived. Pirow, having found that the banning of A.N.C. meetings did not subdue its leaders and supporters, proceeded to prohibit and banish a number of them, including Tonjeni and Ndobe.

In Natal too Pirow set about banishing Africans but, ironically, he picked on Champion whose hey-day was past and left the radical African leader of the moment at large. This was Johannes Nkosi, a twenty-five-year-old Zulu, who had worked on Dr Seme's farm in the Transvaal and, at the age of fourteen, taken part in the A.N.C.'s anti-pass campaign of 1919. In 1926 he had attended the Communist Party's night school in Johannesburg and joined the Party. With Champion deported and Dube so moderate as to be no problem, Nkosi found himself with an open field to organize a pass-burning campaign initiated by the communists. The pass laws had become so persistent a persecution that even the prudent newspaper *Imvo* sympathized with the call, referring to the 'damnable pin-pricks and inconveniences suffered by all classes of Natives in their daily lives' and asking: 'Why grumble when violent forms of protest have ultimately to be resorted to, and the aid of communists solicited? We do not love communists as such; but a white man would never hesitate to snatch a nigger's hand that saves him from drowning. Neither would a black man hesitate to call in a communist, or any other hated and despised person for that matter, who helps him to discard the yoke of bondage.'

In December 1930 the A.N.C., represented by Plaatje, Mahabane and Selope Theme, protested to the Native Affairs Department against the demoralization and degradation caused by the pass laws which, they pointed out, had outlived their usefulness and were no protection to Europeans. By this time more than 40,000 Africans were convicted under the laws each year. The Minister for Native Affairs asked for patience.

A few weeks later, on 16 December, Dingaan's Day,[1] the pass-burning campaign took place with only Durban, where

1. The anniversary of the defeat of the Zulu Chief Dingaan at Blood River – for the whites a day of victory, for Africans, of protest.

Nkosi had worked hard, producing a substantial protest. Nearly 4,000 passes were collected at a huge gathering there and a procession was being organized to carry them through the town when a large force of police arrived and advanced on the speakers' platform. Nkosi, trying to control the frantic crowd, was shot down. He and two other men died the next day. No policeman was charged. Twenty-six Africans were sentenced to several months' hard labour for 'incitement to violence'. The campaign was over.

The police ordered 'idle, dissolute or disorderly persons' to be banished from Durban and announced that the resulting deportation of about 200 Africans 'shook the foundation of communism' there. Not for the last time Government exaggeration of the strength and influence of communism enhanced its reputation among the oppressed, while a blessing from the Department of Justice on the Natal Native Congress for 'doing considerable good among the Natives' with its 200 members 'steady and most law-abiding', damned Dube's Congress in many eyes.

Even so, the communists, considering the almost classical situation in which they were functioning, made extraordinarily little progress. However, they had played a constructive and effective role in organizing non-racial, which meant largely non-white, trade unions. A notable example was the achievement of Ray Alexander, who as a girl had come from Lithuania to the Cape where she helped to found a dozen new unions and soon had trained African and Coloured organizers to take over much of the work. But the communists' launching of the anti-pass campaign despite warnings that it was premature, and the suffering caused, was a factor in their failure. Another was Moscow's interventions in a situation that was going nicely for them. In 1929 the Comintern had ordered the dissolution of a League of African Rights founded by Bunting just as it was getting under way. In 1931 Dimitrov's policy was universally enforced and the one man whom Africans unreservedly admired among the white communists, Bunting, was expelled from the Party[1] with

1. Bunting, though never reinstated, remained loyal to the Party until his death.

other 'right-wing deviationists' who had years of self-sacrificing work to their credit, while newcomers, doctrinaire 'Bolsheviks', Douglas and Molly Wolton and Lazar Bach, were empowered to purge the Party. Incidentally, Africans nicknamed Wolton 'Deepening Economic Crisis'. The African trade unions which communists had helped to establish were smashed, the night-schools in Johannesburg dwindled. By 1933, according to Dr Roux, the historian of this period and one of those expelled, communist activity had almost vanished; there were probably 150 members, most of them white. Whereupon the Woltons left South Africa and went to England.

As far as the A.N.C. was concerned, it was not on the best of terms with the Communist Party and had been referred to by certain communists as a lot of 'materialists', 'brigands', 'bastards'. The turbulence within the Party therefore only affected the handful of men who happened to be members of both organizations, some of them of mixed race, some African. The two who were significant in A.N.C. activities were J. B. Marks, a school teacher in Potchefstroom, strong in his convictions and popular, and Moses Kotane. While Marks remained within the fold beside the Woltons, Kotane took an independent line.

Kotane, born in 1905, of Bechuana parents in the Transvaal, had been brought up in a traditional household by a strict Lutheran grandfather. The boy tended cattle and worked for local farmers until he was fifteen and went to a Lutheran Bible school. But at seventeen, when he had to earn a living, he got a job with a photographer in Krugersdorp, cleaning his studio and milking the cow at £1. 10s. od. a month. When he asked for £2 he was dismissed. Next he was a cleaner in a boarding house where, with a dictionary, he read as much as he could. As he found pronunciation difficult, he paid a child 2s. a month to teach him, but the child was lazy and progress slow. After a spell in the mines he was back in another boarding house as waiter and cleaner. This time his hunger for learning took him to a night school, but he knew so much more than the others that he found himself teaching them so he left, to rely on a white woman in the boarding house who patiently answered his innumerable questions. When he observed that white people arrested in Potchefstroom location for protesting against injustices to Africans were communists, and asked her, 'Did this have something to do with communion in church?' – though it did not seem quite to fit into the context – she said, yes, she thought they *were* church people. 'Anyway,' he thought, 'they must be good as they were talking for the people.' It was not until he got a better job in a bakery that he had enough time to attend political meetings and join an organization.

He joined the A.N.C. It was 1927 and he soon felt 'when in Congress you learnt nothing. You went to meetings and you protested and they didn't *teach* you anything. They did not think about the ordinary fellow.' He joined the Bakers' Union, which in the vacuum left by I.C.U. splits was organized by the Communist Party, but he saw no reason to join the Party. However, he went to a branch meeting, where Bunting was in the chair. Kotane suddenly found himself being put up as a member, which he thought 'bloody dishonest'. In his experience, you went out and joined the A.N.C., you were *asked* to join a trade union, but the Communist Party 'hooked you in'. But what mattered to him was that here for the first time his craving for education was answered: there was a night school – 'now here is where I learnt something' – nor did he have to pay. He joined the Party.

As he lost interest in the A.N.C., 'down almost to nothing', with Seme 'collecting people in the street and getting them to vote for him', he became more and more absorbed in Communist Party activities, addressing their street meetings, organizing trade unions, helping in the night school, and becoming typesetter for one of their papers, *Inkululeko*, as well as editor of its African section, working in its shabby offices in Johannesburg.[1] In 1931 he was sent to Moscow. Twenty-six years old, he set out, not without apprehension. He spent two years in the U.S.S.R. learning Soviet history of the labour movement and political economy.

1. On a site now occupied by the Anglo-American Mining Corporation's new skyscraper.

He returned to South Africa to find that the 'Bolshevizing' carried out by the Woltons and Bach had broken the Party, that Bunting, a 'proper humanitarian', had been expelled and that when people asked why, they were expelled too. The Non-European Federation of Trade Unions, which, founded in 1928, had at one time played a useful part in organizing on the Rand, had been replaced by the one Party committee trying to do everything, with Bach making fantastic claims of successes, telling African organizers, for example, to say when five miners came to a meeting that a hundred had been recruited! Kotane protested, Bach attacked him for dangerously introducing a social democratic line, and his briefly held appointment as joint-secretary of the Party committee in Johannesburg came to an abrupt end. As he did not want to attack the Party nor to renounce the principles he had come to believe in, he decided to go to Cape Town.

Although Kotane and J. B. Marks were on different sides in these Party upheavals, both had been influenced in the early stages of their political growth by Bishop Brown Montgomery, a defrocked American Episcopalian, whose books on Christianity and capitalism contained such precepts as 'banish the gods from the skies and the capitalists from the earth'. But subsequent studies were more orthodox. The only comparable socialist influence elsewhere in Africa at the time was in Senegal where, in the late twenties, the Senegal Socialist Party had been founded.

By 1933, when left-wing activity was at its lowest, the extreme right-wing flourished. Pirow, newly appointed Minister of Defence, was in friendly contact with Hitler; and bitter anti-semitism soon surfaced in the Greyshirts and Blackshirts.

Against this background an economic crisis drove Hertzog and Smuts to form a coalition. Their Government took South Africa off the gold standard and the country once again thrived. Many more gold mines were opened and secondary industries expanded, while farmers prospered. Johannesburg grew more in four years than it had in the previous forty and there was a feeling of confidence and hope among white South Africans. Non-whites, for all the discrimination and disabilities, and the lower standard of living to which they were restricted by law, found much to appreciate in this industrialized society, as did thousands of Africans drawn to it from the poorer, rural, British and Portuguese colonies. Politically this had disadvantages, partly because migrant labourers usually remained barely educated and within a tribal fold, and because the urban Africans, having achieved a few small possessions, wanted exceedingly to protect such security as these represented. Besides there remained always the unmeasurable factor: the psychological result of prolonged oppression, of the oppressed coming to regard themselves as inferior. Nor did the influx of Africans from neighbouring countries make any political impact on Union inhabitants although in British and French colonial Africa the hitherto apathetic Imperial powers had begun to recognize Africans as capable of being educated and responsible.

However in the mid thirties the Italian attack on Ethiopia made all Africa sharply aware of being part of one great continent. For Africans in the Union, Italy's wanton invasion of the ancient African kingdom had a double significance: some, particularly Christians, believed that their race stemmed from Ethiopia and there was a legend that the Queen of Sheba who had visited King Solomon was a Hlubi woman; besides, the Ethiopian church was one of their most important churches. But apart from this, the black kingdom was standing against European invaders. Black pride was high and African newspapers, full of reports of the war and pictures of Ethiopian soldiers, had record sales. The defeat of Haile Selassie caused a sad relapse.

5 1936–9: The White Man's Path of Honourable Trusteeship

Hertzog had been promising the whites segregation since 1924, a promise that to the non-whites was a threat. In the late twenties he had begun to formulate the basic laws to achieve this, arousing widespread protests not only from African and other non-white leaders but also from the Anglican Archbishop, former Chief Justices and other notable white liberals, who warned of national disaster if the bills went through. However, at that time Hertzog had not had the two-thirds majority necessary to amend the entrenched clause that guarded Cape Africans on the common voters' roll. But by December 1934 he could move for he and Smuts fused to form the United Party, commanding some four-fifths of the seats in the Assembly, with the Afrikaner 'purified' Nationalists under Dr D. F. Malan forming the opposition.

Hertzog could not have chosen a better time to put forward his segregation bills. Twenty-five years after Union, non-white political activity was at its lowest ebb. The I.C.U. had almost petered out and its failure had damaged the movement for liberation by giving the rank and file a feeling that politicians were self-seeking and corrupt. Communist activity was intermittent and in 1935 further expulsions took place while their newspaper *Umsebenzi* was collapsing. As for the A.N.C. paper, *Abantu-Batho*, in its early days a fine achievement, after fighting to the end for better conditions, it was finally forced by competition from the white-owned *Bantu World* and by Congress weakness to close down. Seme's continued domination was a disaster. To add insult to injury he described the alliance of Smuts and Hertzog as 'really a very rare combination of the most powerful and capable people' and on behalf of Congress he expressed 'our hope and our faith in the members of the Government whose names have earned in our country, as well as in the whole world, the highest reputation'. The gulf between the desires of the ordinary people and the leadership had never been so deep.

One of Hertzog's bills laid down that no more Natives could register as voters; the 11,000 existing voters in the Cape would thus gradually disappear. Instead, Natives would indirectly elect four white senators through electoral colleges based on the pattern of chiefs. A Natives' Representative Council – purely advisory – comprised of Natives, including Chiefs, and Government officials, would be set up. The Native Trust and Land Bill deprived Cape Natives of their right to buy land outside reserves but provided for more land to be acquired for Natives; however the total proportion of the country thus allowed for would even so be only 13 per cent. Sir James Rose-Innes, a former Chief Justice, remarked on the 'full-blooded fascist flavour' of the proposals.

A crucial point in the history of South Africa had come.

As in 1910, so now all over the country Africans awaited a leader. But this time Seme, aged and involved in his own problems, did not respond though people urged him to call a mass conference. They turned to Professor D. D. T. Jabavu of Fort Hare Native College, the father figure of African education, and he agreed to collaborate with Seme in calling it.

On 16 December, Dingaan's Day, 1935, the All-African Convention (A.A.C.) met in Bloemfontein. The 500 delegates included Indians and Coloured people, the largest representative conference yet held among the non-whites, covering a wide range of political, social, religious, sporting and chiefly interests. The Mayor of Bloemfontein opened it, the Superintendent of the Native Administration Department was there, as well as a number of white liberals. A newcomer to African politics took the chair, Dr A. B. Xuma, a young medical doctor recently back from studying in America and Europe, who delighted delegates so often forced to listen to long-winded lectures from their

65

white guests, when he firmly but politely limited these visitors to five minutes each.

There was remarkable unanimity among former opponents – Jabavu, Seme, Kadalie, Champion. Black people of Africa must stand together. This was the theme. Mrs Charlotte Maxeke took it up; non-Europeans, she said, while thanking Europeans for their support, must go ahead themselves. In the midst of the indignation and bitter distress, speakers yet pointed out that the only way for South Africa was one of political identity, that history had disproved that granting political rights to Africans would be a menace to the whites: the wars and friction which had prevailed before the enfranchisement of the non-Europeans had only to be contrasted with the peaceful relations that had followed and had now lasted seventy-five years. They called for at least a qualified franchise for all Africans throughout the Union. Once again, in spite of the tight spot they themselves were in, they considered their neighbours in the High Commission Territories, who at the time were threatened by incorporation with South Africa. Once again they appealed to His Majesty and to the British Parliament.

When it came to action, the outcome of this, the most significant and representative conference yet held by the non-white majority of South Africa, was to override a minority call from militants wanting immediate demonstrations and strikes, and to decide to send a deputation to see the Prime Minister. An Afrikaner newspaper summarized the result on placards: NATURELLE BLY STIL (Natives Stay Quiet).

Against a background of considerable agitation, with Africans coming together with churchmen, trade unionists and representatives of many organizations, as well as distinguished liberals, the deputation arrived in Cape Town, led by Professor Jabavu and consisting of clergy and moderate men. They found themselves caught in the web of a plot.

It had become apparent that Hertzog could not quite get the two-thirds majority necessary to amend the entrenched clause because the Members of Parliament representing Eastern Cape constituencies would lose face among their Native voters if they agreed to the bill as it stood. These United Party M.P.s had therefore framed a 'compromise'. Instead of the Cape Native vote being abolished, in addition to the four senators to be chosen by Native electoral colleges, the Cape Natives would be put on a separate roll to vote for *three* white M.P.s. Not only was this a fantastic piece of treachery from the Eastern Cape M.P.s, but the compromise itself was considerably weaker than Hertzog's own proposal in 1927 and 1929 that *seven* seats be allocated for Natives; a proposal vociferously rejected by these very Cape M.P.s on the grounds that it violated the principle of common citizenship entrenched in the Cape Native franchise. But this was not all. The M.P.s wanted it to appear as if the Natives themselves had initiated the compromise; thus the United Party could present it as 'what Natives themselves ask for' and the Party's self-styled liberals could vote with a good conscience for the abolition of Cape Native voters from the common roll – a right enjoyed for nearly a hundred years; thus the Prime Minister could rely for his two-thirds majority on his own Party, and not have the humiliation of appealing to Malan's Nationalists.[1]

The Press played a leading part in the double talk that followed. The *Cape Times* (11 February 1936), while admitting that the Cape Natives had never abused their electoral privilege over eighty years and that it would be difficult to find a parallel anywhere for a proposal depriving people of franchise rights merely because of the colour of their skin, urged the Africans to accept the compromise! It warned the All-African Convention deputation that it would be 'calamitous' for them not to do so, that 'on their heads' responsibility rested.

Jabavu and his deputation were men anxious to see the best in others, quite unable to argue militantly on behalf of their people. Hertzog, when they saw him, powerfully persuaded them that he had no alternative. Meanwhile the Cape M.P.s were busy persuading them that they should suggest a compromise – that half a loaf might be better than none.

Rumours of the compromise had reached two doctors on the

1. Based on a statement by R. F. A. Hoernlé, O. D. Schreiner, W. H. Ramsbottom.

Executive of the A.A.C. Puzzled and angry they at once set out for Cape Town: A. B. Xuma hurrying from Johannesburg and James Moroka, from Thaba 'Nchu: representing Transvaal and Free State delegates to the A.A.C. They determined to retrieve whatever blunders Jabavu and the Cape delegates might have made. When they met they were all at loggerheads. For a week they argued while the Government excelled itself in hospitality to them and intermittently sent messages such as, 'Gentlemen, you must not disappoint the Prime Minister, he expects you to be reasonable.'

Hertzog's gambit was to impress on them that his Bills were for their own benefit, that if they did not accept them they were doomed. He told them: 'It is not that we hate you, but if we give you the right to vote, within a very short space of time the whole Parliament will be controlled by Natives. I must tell you point-blank I am not prepared for this.'

They came away with Jabavu and Mahabane still favouring the compromise, with Moroka insisting, 'We must have *nothing* to do with it. If they are going to take our rights away let them do the dirty job themselves!' Fortunately the committee of liberals who were assisting them and particularly Rose-Innes and Donald Molteno (a young barrister descendant of the Cape Colony's most liberal Prime Minister), were utterly opposed to the compromise. Moroka led the deputation in rejecting the compromise. One of them illustrated their feelings by telling the Press a fable: A man had many fowls. One day he sent word he wished to consult them. They were astonished for it was not his custom to consult the fowls. He said: 'My children, I want to consult you on an important matter. I want to make soup of you – a great deal of soup. I have therefore come to ask you: into what kind of soup would you like to be made?'

The Rev. Zaccheus Mahabane addressed a big African meeting. Obliquely replying to Hertzog, he said that the white man made much of the 'black menace', a thing which did not exist except in his own imagination; in introducing these laws he had started from a wrong premise, he was actuated by fear. The white man feared, said the reasonable black clergyman, that from preponderating numbers the black man might swamp him, attack him, or pounce on him.

Whereupon a voice from the back of the hall, no doubt a deep voice, remarked: 'He will one of these days.'

The Press was determined to carry on with the farce: the *Cape Argus* (17 February 1936) reported that 'dramatically the Prime Minister announced at the joint session of the two Houses of Parliament this afternoon that he had accepted the compromise on the Native vote'. As for Smuts, who had said in 1926 that to deprive the Cape Natives of the vote would be a direct violation of the constitution, just back from giving an address on 'Freedom' in Scotland, he fully backed Hertzog in what the Bloemfontein *Friend* called 'the coping stone' on one of the Prime Minister's 'most cherished ambitions'.

When Sir James Rose-Innes condemned the disenfranchising of Africans *en masse* as 'a step for which there is no precedent in history ... and which runs counter to the trend of civilized world opinion', and when he went on to point out that far from the whites being in danger of swamping by the Native vote, in 1933 of an electorate numbering 922,000, Africans numbered only 10,700, Hertzog had the answer to all such arguments. The final answer that, through the years, has never ceased to excite white South Africans: joint voting, he said, paved the way to miscegenation. The *Cape Argus* hastened to quote this brilliant conclusion. Indeed, it described the Prime Minister's speech in moving the second reading of the Bill as 'worthy of a great occasion'. The Bill was passed by 169 votes to 11. The honourable eleven included a member of the Cabinet, Jan Hofmeyr. Hertzog had persuaded a few Cape waverers to support him with the argument that all the remaining rights of Cape Africans would be preserved, a patently dishonest argument as it was inevitable that Cape Africans would come to lose land rights as well.

So ended a most disreputable transaction between two men, General Hertzog and General Smuts, for long political enemies. The *Cape Argus* enthused about the 'path of honourable trusteeship' along which Hertzog was leading the white man.[1]

1. 26 February 1936.

At least Hertzog's segregation laws had jerked Africans into greater political awareness. When the A.A.C. deputation reported back to the full Convention, in June 1936, they found a new mood of strength and of unity. The mood was short-lived. Should people collaborate and elect men to the Natives' Representative Council and to Parliament, or should they boycott?

After much argument it was agreed to 'give it a try'. Even the communists thought this; only a group led by Coloured Trotskyists quarrelled angrily with the decision. When it came to the elections to the N.R.C., several Congress leaders were voted in. Among them were Selope Thema, opportunist, well-informed and a good orator; Thomas Mapikela, still the Speaker of Congress, indeed its 'Grand Old Man'; and Dr Dube. In the first election of the three white Members of Parliament and four white senators to represent Natives, the A.N.C. joined with the A.A.C. and the Cape Native Voters' Association in asking Donald Molteno to stand, while Mrs Margaret Ballinger was amongst the other successful representatives. They were invited to become patrons of the Cape A.N.C., the only time whites became formally associated with Congress.

Another question that disrupted African unity was whether the All-African Convention should continue as a permanent organization. Despite hot opposition from A.N.C. leaders, Jabavu obtained majority support in advocating this, and became President with Dr Moroka, Treasurer.

The emergence of this rival organization, coming on top of the A.N.C.'s failure to lead the opposition to the Hertzog bills, shocked some of its members into a decision: Seme must go. But how to achieve this, when he had just got himself re-elected by a standing vote of confidence? Fortunately, at the same conference, he had appointed as Secretary-General the Rev. James A. Calata, whose characteristics might have seemed contradictory yet integrated: though restrained he had fire; a Christian, he was a patriot to the marrow of his bones; he also had a quality rare in A.N.C. leaders, he was *with* the people. The fact that he was a Xhosa living in the Eastern Cape represented the swing into purely African politics of people newly pushed off the common voters' roll.

Born in 1895, James, as a boy, had gone to St Matthew's, the Anglican Training College in the Cape, to become a teacher and musician before taking orders. Offered the principalship of St Matthew's school, he refused because he wanted to be amongst his people.

In 1928 he had been sent to the St James's Mission Church in Cradock, in the eastern Karroo, a perennially poor area. The location where he worked was a sprawl of flat-topped golden-brown clay houses, no drains, battered earth, roads rent by gullies – typical of most locations except that it had beauty with its church, large and simple, shaded by dark pine and peppercorn trees, a landmark for the whole village, and with a view across bare veld to strongly etched hills. Though Calata was especially keen on choral music, on youth work and education, and as Commissioner of the Pathfinders (African Boy Scouts), worked with friendly whites, he soon found himself deeply concerned with problems that were insoluble in socio-religious terms. During the depression of the early thirties he watched the outspans fill with Africans turned out by farmers who could no longer employ them. To fight for the needs and rights of these displaced persons he turned to the A.N.C. At this time, becoming seriously ill with tuberculosis, he had to go to a sanatorium, and while there had a vision of his mother urging him not only to save souls but to help his people in their plight. When he emerged from hospital, his church gave him two years' leave but as he had only £8 saved he and his wife stayed at home. Inactivity made him feel worse, a discovery that coincided with his appointment as Secretary-General of the A.N.C., and his anxiety to set about reorganizing Congress was so obvious that his doctor agreed. He invested part of his £8 in a visit to Mapikela, for he felt sure the Bloemfontein branch, as the centre for Congress conferences, must have cash in hand. But he and Mapikela found the balance to be one shilling and even that only on paper and not in the cash box! Whereupon local people made a collection to send him to Johannesburg.

Should the A.N.C. continue? In view of its decline and with the advent of the A.A.C., had it any future? These were the questions he asked as he went the rounds of men holding the remnant of Congress together. He believed it was imperative to revive it, and eventually the decision was taken: Congress should continue. The vital question was, who should replace Seme? Calata, eager to draw graduates in, wanted Dr Xuma, energetic and successful, but he was in England. Others wanted one of the 'old guard', someone esteemed and capable of uniting people. Eventually, the Rev. Zaccheus Mahabane was persuaded to resume the Presidency. So, in its Jubilee year, Congress had two clergymen at its head, both eager to ensure its revival, but both with pastoral work to do.

Calata's dedication to Congress was unremitting, but the fact remained that there were no funds in the kitty, and with African clergy notoriously ill paid, he simply had not got the cash to travel in order to raise funds from chiefs or townspeople to achieve the necessary reorganization. His awareness of the living conditions of rural Africans made the frustration the more intolerable. Not far from his home 40,000 Africans, according to a survey made by Professor W. M. Macmillan, had £3 per annum spending power and for half or more of this they depended on wage-earning away from their homes and families. Throughout the country almost two million Africans were working on white farms, completely subject to their masters, with no supervision, no education or religion. A good wage on a farm was £2 a month plus living, while some wages were 6s. a month, or even no wage at all with children also forced to work. Many were still forced to labour under such conditions to earn cash to pay poll tax, a fact openly stated in Parliament. The cost of living rose steadily for this was a time of spectacular prosperity. Meanwhile the Native reserves remained at 12·4 per cent of the land despite population increases, in other words the division of land equalled 370 acres for every white to 6 acres for every African. The reserves were almost denuded of able-bodied men gone to work elsewhere for cash wages, particularly in the mines, finding themselves in cruel competition with poor whites, who had been driven from the poverty of the *platteland* by the depression of the early thirties and who often were incapable of doing the skilled jobs reserved for whites.

And all the while the laws and their implementation at once increased people's bitterness while intimidating them and discouraging protest. One example was an innovation to implement more stringently the pass laws and the liquor laws: pick-up vans were introduced by the police. Prosecutions of Africans immediately increased as police drove arrogantly around the locations and urban areas at all hours, stopping Africans, demanding to see their passes, banging at doors, bursting into houses, tearing up floor boards in search of illicit liquor, humiliating parents in front of their children. All this provoked, in September 1937, one of the periodic small explosions that punctuate the country's history: in Vereeniging location, in a series of raids in search of liquor, police were stoned. Next day reinforced police drove into the location in one of their hated pick-up vans, to meet a defiant crowd which overturned the van and battered three policemen to death. Armed and bayoneted reinforcements rescued the other police and shot a number of Africans. The resulting inquiry typified Government reaction to such riots. Although the location Superintendent gave as one cause the 'harsh and oppressive laws' that young and inexperienced police had to administer, and although the Magistrate showed that the advent of pick-up vans had increased prosecutions, the Prime Minister's conclusion was: 'no punishment or means must be left untried' in ending the violence. The causes of the violence were left to fester.

One major obstacle Calata found in reorganizing was continuing division in the Provinces. In Natal the Zulu Paramount Chief's escape into being a simple tribal leader had left Dube and Champion competing like two bulls in one kraal for effective leadership of the Zulu people. And in the Cape Thaele refused to accept defeat in provincial elections. Calata, after trying tactfully to unite the branches, sadly remarked: 'I am afraid we are still very far from salvation as long as we have men who look more after their own interests than that of the nation.'

73

Moses Kotane was one of those concerned in the reorganization in Cape Town, but in 1938 he became more involved in communist activity as the Party revived, to initiate the National Liberation League in the Cape and the Non-European United Front. Like other communist-inspired united front organizations, these did not last long. In the trades union field, meanwhile, schism upon schism had left Max Gordon, a young Trotskyist, the one efficient organizer of several African unions in the Transvaal.

Militant demands remained the prerogative of the, left-wing and when the A.N.C. met in 1938, it was intent, as Calata put it, 'on closing our ranks behind our Parliamentary representatives and members of the Natives' Representative Council'. The N.R.C. was already proving ineffectual, with the Government taking no notice of its resolutions, while the white M.P.s representing Natives, though they got a fair enough hearing in the House, could never affect the voting.

Once again the A.N.C. decided to send a deputation to see the Minister of Native Affairs; this time to protest particularly against the pass laws. Mahabane and Calata were accompanied by Z. K. Matthews, a young academic, just back from studies in England and Germany, and one or two others. The Minister, H. A. Fagan, agreed that the pass laws should be abolished and promised to do his best to achieve this. Just before they left he asked Calata how many members Congress had that year.

Calata replied: '4,000.'

Fagan laughed and remarked, 'I knew you were only representing your jackets. How can an organization of 4,000 members claim to speak for 8 million?'

There was a good deal in this, and the All-African Convention continually mocked the A.N.C. for being moribund, but Congress might have retorted that non-whites had none of the facilities nor freedom of the whites to organize political parties. They might have added that the A.N.C. was the oldest and most consistent of African organizations, that while others had sprung up with a flourish, these had faded out; the Congress survived.

6 1939–43: The Ferment of War brings Hope

War broke out in Europe. In South Africa, General Smuts ousted Hertzog to become Prime Minister and to support Britain by declaring war by a narrow majority in Parliament. Among Africans, recruiting went slowly and Calata commented: 'If the Government of South Africa does not get Africans to volunteer for service they must examine the situation from within. I am afraid they are themselves to blame for the present attitude of mind of the Africans. Hitler had absolutely nothing to do with it.' However, soon recruiting picked up, and again Africans were digging, driving, fetching and carrying. They were also eagerly sought for the iron and steel works and the munition factories and other industries that proliferated.

The non-white contribution was all the more valuable in face of the violent pro-Hitler activities of such Afrikaner organizations as the Ossewabrandwag and Pirow's New Order: 'Under the Swastika'. Many Nationalists were vocal in support of the Nazis, and one newspaper editor, H. F. Verwoerd, made his newspaper their tool.[1] Policemen were among saboteurs.

The year 1940 was unique: no racially discriminating laws were introduced. A.N.C. members elected a new and promising President: Dr Alfred Bitini Xuma who, sophisticated, vital, widely travelled, enjoyed a successful career. As a child, like any young Xhosa, he had herded cattle in his home in the Transkei. His ambition had been fired when he heard about Seme, Dube and others who had studied abroad; he taught until he had saved enough to get to the United States where he worked his way through high school and qualified as a doctor in Chicago and St

1. Judgments (Transvaal Supreme Court), 13 July 1943.

Louis. His Negro wife became prominent in Y.W.C.A. affairs. Later he studied surgery and gynaecology in Hungary and Edinburgh.

Hitherto, apart from his part in the deputation to Hertzog in 1936, Xuma had believed that if he made his career a success that in itself would vindicate the rights of Africans to be treated as equals by the whites. But the leadership of the oldest of African organizations filled him with enthusiasm and he set about reorganizing Congress throughout the country with an added qualification – the private means to do so. He tore up the old constitution and drafted a new one with the help of Bram Fischer, a young lawyer, an Afrikaner, communist grandson of the fierce old reactionary, Abraham Fischer; a constitution which was more democratic and nearer to that of a political party. And Xuma generated optimism among younger more militant men, that he would lead the A.N.C., at last, into action.

In the country at large there were signs to justify an even deeper optimism for, with the fall of Singapore in 1942, white South Africa was gravely alarmed at the prospect of a Japanese invasion, and Smuts, set about on all sides by Afrikaner Nationalists who were jubilant at Hitler's advances, suddenly made the startling declaration: 'Isolation has gone and I am afraid segregation has fallen on evil days too.'[1] He and Xuma both quoted the Atlantic Charter produced by Churchill and Roosevelt on 14 August 1941. Smuts said that it should mean 'for all, improved labour standards, economic advancement and social security', while Xuma told an A.N.C. Conference that Africans should draw up their own Atlantic Charter; the world should know 'our hopes and our despairs directly from us'. He spoke about 'our men' who were 'dying up North', who were helping to take North Africa and Madagascar, who would have done even more 'if we had not been debarred from skilled trades for war production, and if we had arms as befits all brave men who have never betrayed their Government'.

Such being the influence of the remote but possibly imminent Japanese forces, there was a sudden relaxation of pass laws, with

1. Address to the S.A. Institute of Race Relations.

a startling drop in arrests – in Johannesburg, for example, they fell from 200 a day to 20. But soon the United States fleet engaged the Japanese. The pass laws were again intensified.

'To hell with the Pass Laws!' This was the slogan adopted by the Communist Party which promptly joined the A.N.C. in a decision to launch an anti-pass campaign. They began to plan action.

Then hopes were aroused by the Government's appointment of an Inter-departmental Committee of Inquiry, under Douglas Smit, into conditions in urban areas to which Xuma gave evidence on behalf of the A.N.C. Among the perennial representations about low wages, the pass laws and the need for more education, he made a powerful case for the hundreds of thousands of Africans flocking to the towns in response to the huge demand for cheap labour in wartime industries, to be immediately segregated into insanitary, over-crowded slums under the Natives (Urban Areas) Act. In Pimville, he pointed out, people had been living in iron half-tanks for forty years and were surrounded by a sewage farm. The locations had little if any street lighting, no house lighting, bad roads, often non-existent sanitation. They were many miles from the towns and Xuma reasoned that decent housing, at a fair distance from work, would make workers more competent. African wages might be £3 a month at a time when the breadline, as the Government's own Committee remarked, was £7 10s. od. As a result nearly half a million Africans a year were convicted for non-payment of tax and other statutory offences: as few could afford to pay the resulting fines they went to jail and the family lost its breadwinner. Nor, he added, was there any benefit for unemployed Africans as there was for Europeans, yet they were liable for tax.

The Smit Committee confirmed much of this, and Smuts's Government, strengthened by the good news from the North African front, and by a three-fold split in the Afrikaner Nationalist front, could certainly have fulfilled its promises of a better life for all. But when the frustration building up in African workers surfaced in a series of strikes along the Rand and in Natal, Smuts responded by passing War Measures rendering illegal 'all strikes by all Africans under all circumstances' and forbidding unauthorized meetings on mine property.

Not surprisingly there was a riot – in Marabastad, Pretoria – in which sixteen Africans and one European were killed and many wounded. A subsequent commission of inquiry found evidence of much discontent. And despite the prohibition there were some sixty illegal African strikes between 1942 and 1944.

In August 1943, in the African township of Alexandra, tucked away to one side of the main road out of Johannesburg to Pretoria, the local bus company raised its fare from 4d. a journey to 5d.: 2d. a day extra for people who, as the Smit Committee had found, had a probable average wage of £5. 2s. 11d. a month: a fifth of a wage on fares. Spontaneously the African people walked. It was mid-winter, and in the bleak cold of the highveld, Alexandra lay under a thin grey cloud of smoke from the braziers on which the night meal had been cooked. Every morning early from thousands of small, iron-roofed houses the people emerged and set out along the steep main road towards the city. 15,000 men and women trudged the nine or more miles to work; cleaners and messengers and clerks, washerwomen and maids. Some were given lifts but most of them walked. Again, in the chill of nightfall they walked the nine miles back home. A Bus Service Committee was quickly set up, led by an A.N.C. member, and including leaders of the community, representatives from Trade Unions, Vigilance Societies, the Communist Party, as well as certain white sympathizers. But the people of Alexandra had significantly shown that they were ahead of any organization and, militant and determined, for nine days they walked until the bus company gave in and reduced the fares to 4d. The Government set up a Bus Commission.

The second half of the year 1943 was full of momentous incidents. Smuts had won an election with a secure majority, though admittedly the election had been held under ideal conditions. The Allies were surging forward on all fronts against Germany and Japan. African optimism, always near the surface, rose again when the Lansdowne Commission was set up to investigate conditions on the mines, this in response to the demands of the newly inaugurated African Mine Workers' Union. Then at a meeting of the Natives' Representative Council, the Deputy Prime Minister intimated that the freedoms envisaged in the Atlantic Charter would be for Africans too. Non-whites recalled how in 1942 Smuts had said that, looking to the friendly relations that had grown up between white South Africans and brown and black soldiers in the war, old ideas on the colour question 'which had brought nothing but bitterness and strife' must change. Now once more, at the end of 1943, he spoke about the world needing 'the British system' with its goodwill, good government and human cooperation, 'a mission of Freedom and human happiness'. This surely signified that he subscribed to Britain's abhorrence of Nazi ideas of race and sympathized with her as yet vaguely held out promise of self-government for Africans. The new Deputy Prime Minister, furthermore, was Jan Hofmeyr, the most liberal of Ministers in the history of South Africa. The Government was even considering 'a people's charter' covering employment, social security, housing, public health, nutrition and education for all.

While Nnamdi Azikiwe was publishing an Atlantic Charter for British West Africa, in South Africa the cream of African intellectuals, under Z. K. Matthews, Reader in African law and languages at Fort Hare College, worked on their Bill of Rights based on the original Charter. They agreed that Africans desired the end of Nazi tyranny as promised in the Atlantic Charter but, they emphasized, Africans wanted *all* racial domination completely destroyed. The point that most deeply concerned them was the right of all peoples to choose the form of government under which they would live. The acid test of the good faith of the creators of the Charter lay, they declared, in the application of this point to Africa.

In this ferment of events and ideas militant young Africans were coming together: undergraduates from Fort Hare College expelled for taking part in strikes, and young men working in Johannesburg or studying at the University of the Witwatersrand, had simultaneously begun to take an interest in the A.N.C.

7 1943–5: African Nationalism and African Claims

Injustice in South Africa and ideas of freedom abroad fanned the flames of political discontent into a new and self-conscious nationalism among young Africans. They wanted to rid their people of the sense of inferiority that had insidiously grown over years of oppression. The aggressive entry into the war of the non-white power, Japan, stimulated them. The feelings and ideas thus generated took shape when a number of them came together in Johannesburg to meet, night after night, excitedly arguing and planning, evolving their concepts of nationalism and their tactics in the radical transformation of the A.N.C. that was urgently essential.

Two men, teachers, studying to become lawyers, both from the humblest of tribal backgrounds, were elected to lead the Youth League thus founded: Anton Muziwakhe Lembede, outstanding spokesman of the new nationalist philosophy, became its President, Oliver Tambo its Secretary.

Lembede's parents, Zulu farm labourers, had scraped together money to send him to primary school but after two years he had become kitchen-boy to an Indian family until he had saved enough to go back to school. Phenomenally industrious, in 1933 he had won a bursary to Adams Teacher Training College, the Congregational institution in Amanzimtoti, where among his tutors were the Principal, Dr Edgar Brookes, and Albert Lutuli and Z. K. Matthews. Lembede's manners were rough, an uncouthness that went oddly with his sensitivity and the passion for learning that drove him. While teaching he learnt Afrikaans and Sesotho, took his matriculation by correspondence, a distinction in Latin; then again by correspondence, took a B.A., majoring in Philosophy and Roman-Dutch law. When he moved to Johannesburg in 1943, at the age of thirty, he was articled to Dr Seme, an old man and delighted to have this remarkable student in his firm.

Lembede's friends found him an intriguing personality – arrogant and aggressive yet with an unusual ability to laugh at himself. Though not a fluent speaker, sometimes stammering, his swing from pedagogic to demagogic utterances could be spell-binding.

Oliver Tambo, younger than Lembede, so disliked school that he frequently played truant until his father, a Pondo peasant, sent him to the Holy Cross Mission in Pondoland where his fees were paid by two Englishwomen. The fun of going a long way from the tribal village to boarding school made him suddenly mad keen on education. When he was later accepted by St Peter's School with his stepbrother sharing the fees of twelve pounds a year with the Englishwomen, there was the double thrill of going to this renowned Anglican school and of going to Johannesburg. After two years, at the age of nineteen, he passed his Junior Certificate with a first class, which led to a scholarship that took him on to Fort Hare College. There his part in students' strikes led to expulsion. But his rebellion had been as much for spiritual as for political reasons: when a pledge was demanded of students regarding their conduct and spiritual life, he could not comply: 'An agreement with God written and signed?' Impossible. He returned to St Peter's in 1943, at the age of twenty-five, to become science master. But he hankered to do law, and it was through another member of the Youth League, Walter Sisulu, that he later became articled to a firm of attorneys in Johannesburg.

Walter Max Sisulu more than anyone in the Youth League knew just what it meant to be 'a native'; and although tens of thousands of Africans had gone through similar experiences, like tens of thousands of perfectly good oysters, they lacked the grain that would produce a pearl. An incongruous simile for Sisulu, whom some people saw as frustrated, unsuccessfully reaching for fulfilment and consequently bitter. Perhaps, but others knew him as trustworthy and generous.

Born in the Transkei in 1912, he had been strictly brought up by an uncle, a headman: prayers twice a day, with due respect – in the best Victorian tradition still prevailing among the older generation of the Xhosa – for the upper class, which meant the white missionaries and officials. But the uncomfortable grain was there and Walter was reproved for being rude to patronizing white visitors – 'I doubt whether you will be *allowed* to work for a white man' – a reproof which delighted him. At the Anglican school he relished stories of Moses and David and the struggle of the Jews to overthrow foreign rulers, while in the village he enjoyed the gossip about Wellington Butelezi, who had travelled about the Transkei, claiming to be American, educated at the 'University of Oxford and Cambridge', and promising liberation from oppression through the help of brother Negroes. Later it came out that Butelezi came from Natal where he was irreverently known as 'Bootlaces'. But legend is he collected thousands of half crowns before disappearing into obscurity.

Upon the death of his uncle, Walter left school at the age of sixteen to cope with the stocks and crops, but soon, having passed through tribal initiation to assert his ultimate manhood, he went to a Johannesburg mine, breaking rocks a mile underground, living in the celibate barracks of one of the innumerable compounds. From 'mine boy' to 'kitchen boy', working for a white family who took a personal interest in him, whose manners he studied, and the way in which they brought up their children. Meanwhile, though he attended I.C.U. meetings and was thrilled by Kadalie's speeches, he did not join.

He learnt his first political lesson when he had a job in a bakery at eighteen shillings a week. Having picked up a little about trade unions he led the workers out on strike for higher wages, whereupon the boss saw each man separately, persuaded him to resume work at the same wage, and sacked Sisulu. As he went through a succession of factory jobs, clashing repeatedly with white bosses, he sought relief in Xhosa history, writing articles about tribal heroes for the white-owned *Bantu World*. The clashes came not merely from personal revolt: in the train one evening, he saw a white ticket-collector, for no apparent reason, confiscating an African child's season ticket. He asked the collector why he had done this. The man hit him. He fought back, was arrested and imprisoned. He had never been in prison and it was 'the nastiest experience' of his life.

In all his experience the whites whom he and Africans most often encountered were the police, raiding locations for passes or liquor or for tax receipts, or pass officials dealing with queues of 'boys' like cattle, or jailers who beat up African prisoners and caused 'shocking misery'. All this aroused in him not fear of the white man, but contempt.

Yet his search for political expression remained vague during the thirties. As he went from job to job in Johannesburg, he studied for his Junior Certificate by correspondence. He took part in music and debating clubs, and his mother, who came to live with him in one of the small brick box houses in Orlando Township, took in washing for white families. In 1940 he joined the A.N.C. having been so impressed by a lucid presidential address by Xuma that he felt proud to find they came from the same birthplace.

At this time, when Sisulu was having a little success running an estate agency which dealt with such freehold land as existed, he was glad to assist a newcomer from the Transkei whom he believed to be a young man with a future: Nelson Rolihlahla Mandela.

Nelson Mandela, born into as privileged a society as an African could be – one of the Royal family of the Tembu – was eager from childhood for a wide and more adventurous life. At his home, near the Bashee river, a green-watered stream flowing through the lovely hills of the Transkei, he tended sheep, helped in the ploughing, and generally found life dull, envying the exploits of his more plebeian friends – such as stealing a pig and taking it to the forest to roast and eat. When he listened to his guardian and cousin, the Paramount Chief, trying cases in the tribal court, he dreamed of becoming a lawyer. So much did he long to see life that, when he attended a Methodist boarding school, he tried on several occasions to run away – unsuccessfully.

But from Fort Hare College – where he was suspended for taking part in a boycott of the Students' Representative Council, because it had been deprived of its powers by the authorities – he had more urgent motives for running away: partly that his cousin the Chief had ordered him to drop his boycott, mainly that he learned the Chief was planning a tribal marriage for him. He promptly fled to Johannesburg.

From then his life took on the anomalous character of any black aristocrat faced with making a living in a white-dominated society. He became a mine policeman, sitting at the compound gate, clutching his 'badges' of office – a whistle and a knob-kerrie. However, a telegram from the Chief tracked him down and again he had to hide. He thought he would like to become a clerk in the Native Affairs Department but had no idea how to achieve this, and when a friend suggested Sisulu might give advice he turned gratefully to this new acquaintance. It was through Sisulu's help that he became articled to a firm of lawyers, meanwhile completing his B.A. degree in 1942 by correspondence and going on to study law at the University of Witwatersrand. By this time he was twenty-five years old, a tall athletic young man with natural authority.

Two of the Youth Leaguers were medical students, others were teachers, young women too; one – Albertina, a nurse – became Walter Sisulu's wife in 1944. They would all meet appropriately enough, since they were planning a new policy for Congress, in the office of its founder, Seme, where Anton Lembede worked, or – in the same ramshackle building in the business area of Johannesburg – they met in the A.N.C. office, or perhaps in someone's home in Orlando, the expanding township crammed with innumerable identical little houses. Sometimes they talked all through the night. As their ideas caught on, new members were continually joining.

Lembede was proving creative and had a magnetic quality so that his roughness and sarcasm were seen as masculinity, and his rigid views were accepted as part of his passionate drive to free his people. His view on the basic principle of African nationalism was that the philosophical basis was neither that of communism which saw man as essentially an economic animal, nor of Nazism which made of man a beast of prey. The Youth League, he explained, believed that 'man is body, mind and spirit' and history was a record of humanity's striving for complete realization. He quoted Paul Kruger's words which he regarded to be 'deep human wisdom', that one who wanted to create the future must not forget the past, and he reminded Africans of their great leaders, Shaka, Moshoeshoe, Hintsa, Sikhukhuni, Khama, Sobuza and Mosilikaze. African nationalism's economic basis was, he said, socialism – 'our valuable legacy from our ancestors'. Another legacy was democracy, for in African society men were not assessed by wealth but all took part in khotlas, the tribal assemblies. As for the ethical basis, he urged Africans to 'retain and preserve the belief in the immortality of the spirits of our ancestors', on a foundation of Christian morals 'since there is nothing better anywhere in the world'.[1]

There were conflicts: over the emphasis on Africanism, for instance, or of personality; but their motto 'Africa's cause must triumph' carried them along. The League came to be known as the propagator of 'Africanism', yet the concept 'Africa for the Africans' formulated in the 1890s by an English Baptist missionary, James Booth, was not specifically expressed.

Their manifesto attacked past policies of the A.N.C. It had yielded to oppression, 'regarding itself as a body of gentlemen with clean hands', but now the Youth League must be the 'Brains Trust and Power Station' of the spirit of African nationalism and must give force, direction and vigour to the struggle for freedom by reinforcing the A.N.C. As the 'harshness' of white domination roused 'feelings of hatred' in the African of everything barring his way to full citizenship, the conflict had become one of race on one side and ideals on the other. 'The Whiteman,' said the Youth League, 'regards the universe as a gigantic machine hurtling through time and space to its final destruction: individuals in it are but tiny organisms with private lives that lead to private deaths.' White South Africans had acquired as absolute measures of values, as the things to

1. *Inyaniso* (Voice of African Youth).

live for – 'personal power, success and fame'; whereas African ideals could be understood in the African regard for the universe 'as one composite whole: an organic entity, progressively driving towards greater harmony and unity', its individual parts inter-dependent, realizing their fullest life in communal contentment.

Among the League's objectives was one which would become a point of great significance many years later. This would divide land among farmers and peasants of all nationalities in propor-tion to their numbers, with planned development and scientific methods taught to farmers and peasants towards achieving full industrialization and the raising of the living standard of all workers, with abolition of the colour bar in all fields.

The Youth League rejected 'foreign leadership' and though useful ideas might be borrowed from foreign ideologies, their wholesale importation into Africa was likewise rejected. Leaders should have high ethical standards, personifying and sym-bolizing 'popular aspirations and ideals'.

Patently fed up with the A.N.C.'s 'old guard' and with in-effectual tactics, they drew from Xuma warnings not to antag-onize people. But he accepted the inevitable: the Youth League was formally constituted. Lembede's insistence on Africans relying on themselves for their liberation, and the semi-mystical nationalism that he expressed, had thus found a channel. But for the time being the impatient young idealists must be content to work in the background, awaiting the right moment.

Their militant ideas were a foretaste of the rise of African nationalism in West and East Africa where the considerable part played by Africans in the war – serving in the Middle East and encountering other nationalisms and resistance movements – was a potent factor in stimulating political activity. But in South Africa for the time being the conditions created by the war set off a series of revolts with a pattern of mass action led, not by the A.N.C. or its Youth League, nor by the A.A.C., but by elemental indigenous leaders thrown up by the situation, and responding to basic human needs.

The greatest of such revolts began in 1944 when tens of thousands of Africans who had for so long been jammed into the dreadful slums around Johannesburg followed a demagogic township eccentric, James Mpanza, in a spontaneous trek from Orlando to vacant municipal land near by. There they squatted, setting up shanties of sack-cloth, old iron and mealie stalks. From the swarming slums of the Reef thousands more joined them. Mpanza's slogan, 'Sofasonke', 'we all die together', became his nickname. Inevitably in the chaotic situation the movements became corrupted.

One revolt with a constructive outcome took place in Alexandra Township, where once again the bus company put up the fare and once again the boycott was on. This time it lasted for seven weeks, with men, women and young people walking in mid-summer heat and sometimes heavy rain the eight or nine miles each way into Johannesburg. And this time their victory was more sure when, early in 1945, a Utility Company took over the bus service and reverted to the original fare.

The situation in South Africa would seem predictable and any observer would expect violence; yet when it erupted it somehow seemed unpredictable, like the event on a Sunday afternoon in November 1944 when a tram driven by a white knocked down and killed an African in the Western Areas of Johannesburg. In a moment a crowd had gathered and stoned the tram and passing cars, and white hooligans used the opportunity to destroy the near-by building of the *Bantu World*. Usually poverty and frustration found their outlet in faction fights between groups of men of different tribes or in the steadily spreading crime in the townships.

One leader who found himself faced daily with thousands of people homeless, ill-paid, without adequate transport, exposed to the ravages of disease and lawless elements and voiceless in the councils of state, was Paul Mosaka, a businesslike, articulate member of the Natives' Representative Council representing the urban areas of the Transvaal and Free State. These people caught, as he put it, in the 'maelstrom of industrialism', looked to him for relief and direction. He told them to join the A.N.C., to which he belonged, and to ask its branches to deal with their local problems. But Xuma's reorganization was more political than practical. The branches failed to help. Mosaka and Senator Hyman Basner, a barrister who had earned African confidence by fighting cases on their behalf and who, in 1942, was elected to the Senate as Native Representative, repeatedly appealed to Dr Xuma to galvanize them. When he did not respond, Mosaka and Basner launched the African Democratic Party, which they hoped could give mass backing to the Natives' Representatives in Parliament. Although Mosaka intended the A.D.P. to become an organization affiliated to the A.N.C., this was unprecedented, and his action was regarded as a treacherous weakening of the A.N.C. He therefore broke with Congress and, although the A.D.P. failed to make much progress and Basner's presence aroused suspicion of a 'foreign element', Mosaka himself remained a respected member of the N.R.C.

At this point in 1944, when the Allies were mounting the offensive for their last great onslaught on Hitler, Smuts's Government, rejecting a move in Parliament for a repeal of the pass laws, instigated mass arrests of pass offenders. The A.N.C. therefore launched the campaign against the pass laws – carefully planned with the help of other organizations over the past year. In Johannesburg Xuma chaired a spectacular conference of 600 delegates, representing 605,000 people. Afterwards many thousands marched in protest through the city. The Vice-National Chairman to Xuma was Dr Yusuf Dadoo, influential leader of the Transvaal Indians and a communist. Their secretary was the A.N.C.'s Transvaal Secretary, David Bopape, an exceptionally hard worker (who had even organized street hawkers), and a good psychologist, with crowd appeal. Out of all this activity, and a determination to do away with the passes such as had not been seen since the 1919 campaign, came the objective of a petition; the target a million signatures. Meetings were held all over the country except in Natal, where the examination of passes had been relaxed. The Natives' Representative Council, the Transkei Bunga and the Transkei African Voters' Association, supported the demand for abolition of the pass laws.

The great petition was due to be delivered to the Government in August 1944, but not until June 1945 did the National Anti-Pass Committee send a deputation to Cape Town, and then without having achieved anything like the hoped-for million signatures. And although the deputation had come to protest against the most anachronistic of South Africa's laws, Jan Hofmeyr, acting for Smuts, refused to see them. So they organized an immense demonstration along the Grand Parade. The veteran Selope Thema, Dadoo and others were promptly arrested for leading an illegal procession. Instead of relief, there was a threat that the pass laws would be extended to Africans in Cape Town. This set off a new flood of protests: from the N.R.C., from an all-race meeting in Cape Town's Cathedral Hall where the Anglican Bishop Lavis described the pass laws as 'disgusting' and as 'Hitler methods in a so-called democratic country'; from a deputation of the Institute of Race Relations, the newly formed Campaign for Right and Justice; and from the A.N.C., who met the Minister of Native Affairs, Major Piet van der Byl, only to be airily dismissed.

And so with every possible constitutional protest made, the National Anti-Pass Committee had achieved precisely nothing. Recriminations broke out with Xuma and Thema accusing communists of pushing their line, and communists accusing Xuma of playing safe. The Youth League, while agreeing with the strong criticisms of Xuma, were unremittingly hostile to the communists.

Many organizations in Johannesburg celebrated victory in Europe in May 1945: 20,000 Africans with people of other races followed the two brass bands and leaders carrying the flags – the A.N.C.'s black, green and gold flag waved alongside those of the victorious Allies. The slogan that day, with the Nazis defeated in Europe, was 'Let's finish the job'.

Since July 1943 the Russian army's series of victories transformed them overnight into glorious allies, and South African communists suddenly found themselves respectable. The open diplomatic relations between the South African Government and the Soviet Union brought many notabilities to the annual celebration of the October Revolution at the Soviet Embassy. South African communists, as well as Africans – this being the only Embassy to invite them to its functions – found themselves in a minority as they looked around the room and saw Hofmeyr, the Deputy Prime Minister, Colin Steyn, the Minister of Justice, senior diplomats and civil servants, among their fellow guests. Another reflection of this respectability was that Hilda Watts, a communist, had been elected by a white middle-class suburb to the Johannesburg City Council.

The unusual opening up of communications between the non-communist and communist worlds during the war years, which gave African nationalists throughout the continent an increased interest in Marx's modes of thought and methods of organization, was but part of the transformation as British Imperial Power was diminished and America and Russia became the two giants in world affairs. However, the fierce anti-colonialism increasingly goading the West Africans' political struggle, which had developed in some of them during their years of study in the United States, hardly affected Africans in the dissimilar situation in the Union.

For the first time since Plaatje's contact with West African leaders in 1919, the A.N.C. sent delegates to the Pan-African Congress – the fifth, in Manchester in October 1945, where they met many of Africa's young leaders, among them Kwame Nkrumah, Chief Akintola, and Jomo Kenyatta. This Congress, while demanding for Africa 'autonomy and independence', made a significant move when it endorsed Gandhi's passive resistance as the only effective way of persuading alien rulers to respect the rights of unarmed subject races. Once free, they would unite against restoration of any western imperialism as well as the dangers of communism.

In line with these aims were the 'African Claims' unanimously adopted at the A.N.C. conference on 16 December 1945. The delegates made the revolutionary claim of one man one vote, equal justice in the courts, freedom of land ownership, of residence and of movement, with of course repeal of the pass laws. They claimed freedom of the Press, and demanded equal opportunity in training and in work, and a share in material resources, equal pay, and the removal of the industrial colour bar. One important point was their rejection of the concept that 'there is any need for a special type of education for Africans as such', which showed apprehension of what might lie ahead; compulsory and equal education for all was what they claimed. Implicit in all this was the repeal of discriminatory legislation.

But how to set about achieving these claims? Xuma increasingly maddened the Youth League by his attitude, expressed in his foreword to the published 'Claims': 'We know that the Prime Minister . . . and his delegation to the Peace Conference will represent the interests of the people of our country.' And, although he remarked that Africans realized the Government would not grant their claims 'for the mere asking and there must be a long struggle entailing great sacrifice of time and means and even life itself', he proceeded to tell people to remember the 'wise and encouraging' advice of the Prime Minister that they should concentrate on such vital matters as native health and native food.

Even ordinary people took the Atlantic Charter seriously, and at a meeting in Cape Town in October 1945 some 8,000 Africans had called for its immediate implementation. One African speaker referred to the thousands of Africans who had joined up, many of whom had been killed and wounded in defending the freedom that had always been denied to them. Another speaker said that they should appeal to Smuts, when he returned from the United Nations, to abolish the pass laws, and maintained that he who had done so much for world freedom would surely listen sympathetically.

Smuts was at the United Nations busy drafting the Preamble to its Charter. In the Union during the war years, for all the excellent surveys that he had had made, his Government had failed to implement their main recommendations. Even Johannesburg's African housing problem – the result of twenty years of neglect, exacerbated by the wartime influx of Africans and the simultaneous shortage of materials – which the Johannesburg City Council (and a Labour Party Council at that) failed to cope with, was not treated by the Government as a national emergency; in 1946 there still remained a backlog of some 50,000 houses. A Campaign for Right and Justice was formed by a number of economic, social, political and religious organizations, under the chairmanship of a judge, to assure the Government that in any progressive measures it might institute it would have considerable backing. The Campaign believed that through a positive economic policy people could become so absorbed in constructively meeting the needs of the country that racialism might be overcome. But Smuts, the world statesman, remained incapable of thinking in large concepts about home affairs. He did not see that the Union had come to the end of an era.

8 1946: A Turbulent Year: Indians then African Miners lead the Struggle

In 1946 at the very time that India was leading Asia in the sweep towards freedom, Smuts, struggling to hold his weakening Government, allowed himself to be pressed by the largely English-speaking voters of Natal into enacting laws to segregate Indians in South Africa, just as Hertzog had segregated Africans ten years earlier. Lord Wavell, the Viceroy of India, and Lord Auchinleck, the Commander-in-Chief, were a party to the Indian Government's prompt threat to terminate trade with the Union Government. Gandhi, at the height of his influence in India, appealed to the 'great soldier-statesman', Smuts, not to take the whites down the precipice that this artificial protection of races would lead them to.[1]

Smuts was adamant. In May the 'Ghetto' Bill was passed. In June the Indian Government recalled its High Commissioner from South Africa, and the Indians in South Africa for the first time since Gandhi's days launched a passive resistance campaign. Smuts by this one act had incurred the wrath of a potentially powerful State and had paved the way for the outside world to condemn the Government's racial policies in the United Nations.

It was not as if the Indians were a threat. Their forebears had been brought to South Africa in 1860 to work on sugar plantations in response to the Natal Government's entreaties, its pledges of equality of treatment, and its blandishments about the rich land and bright prospects awaiting them. Their labour had so transformed Natal's economy that within two years sugar exports had risen by nearly 400 per cent. But since 1880 the

1. *Harijan*, 24 March 1946.

Natal British had played up the bogey of 'Asiatic domination' –
yet whereas until 1921 Asians had outnumbered whites by about
5,000, in 1946 they outnumbered Asians by 4,000, while in the
country at large the Indian population remained practically
stationary, fluctuating between 2·3 per cent and 2·5 per cent of
the total. Hardly a year had passed without some new anti-
Indian restriction. Gandhi had made patient efforts to negotiate
for reforms; failing, he had initiated passive resistance between
1906–14.

Now the leaders turned to these methods again. The Indians
might be an isolated community, rejected by both white and
black, divided among themselves into religious groups, but they
had a handful of remarkable individuals to lead them. The
resistance movement was headed by two doctors, the articulate
communist Yusuf Dadoo, from the Transvaal, and the thirty-
six-year-old Gandhian, Monty Naicker, from Natal. Other influential leaders were the Muslim, Maulvi Ismail Cachalia, and a
Gandhian, Nana Sita.

The Prime Minister might be devoid of vision, but there
were young South Africans who had a vision of a common
society, of what South Africa could and should become, and a
sparsely furnished flat in a block of Indian apartments in
Johannesburg's commercial centre had become the meeting
place for them and their friends. The flat belonged to Ismail
Meer, a law student, one of the organizers of the passive resistance campaign and editor of its journal, *The Passive Resister*.
As the son of a Muslim trader in midland Natal he had been
brought up to believe in the brotherhood of man, in a family
which always had African and white friends. He was one of those
young Indians agonized by their community's representatives:
conservative merchants and businessmen who believed in conciliation with the white authorities. It was not until the late
thirties that the Indian youth, through the extension of university education, got the intellectual impetus they needed. Many
were influenced by a remarkable old English woman, Dr Mabel
Palmer, a Fabian and friend of George Bernard Shaw, who
taught all races at the Sastri College in Durban, enriching the

lives of hundreds of young Indians by stimulating lectures and discussions on a variety of subjects, including socialism and Marxism. By the time Meer came to study at the university of the Witwatersrand, for him as for other Indian students the Communist Party provided a relevant political and economic philosophy, though more important than dialectics was its role as a meeting place for all races in complete equality.

Meer's best friend from Natal, and a fellow-student at the law school, was Jaydew Nazib Singh, who was teaching part-time to help him through college and lived in an African township near Johannesburg. Among their university friends was Ruth First, attractive if over-fierce in her pursuance of the ideals bred in her, for she had been born in a communist family from those Jewish immigrants from Latvia and Lithuania who provided some of the bravest campaigners for the Left.

Nelson Mandela had also become a friend of Meer's and frequently stayed in the flat. He was the best-dressed, meticulous and rather aloof. He was 'violently anti-communist' partly because he still believed in chieftaincy, partly because he had been told that communists were anti-Christ and his background was religious.

Although the resistance campaign was taking place in Durban, there was a constant going to and fro, and something of the spirit of exaltation that led more and more young Indians to compete for acceptance as resisters percolated to the youth in Johannesburg. Before long 600 volunteers had gone to jail and, under Dr Xuma's chairmanship, a conference of Africans in Johannesburg unanimously expressed support for the Indian people, while a branch of the A.N.C. joined the resistance in the belief that in time all non-European people would unite against common injustice. The Rev. Michael Scott, a friend of Meer's, went down to Durban with Yusuf Cachalia – younger brother of Maulvi Cachalia – and was moved to take part by the quiet steadfastness of the Indian resisters, including young girls, withstanding attacks from white hooligans. With the others, he was imprisoned.

Great days – and in Meer's flat over endless cups of tea and curry meals at any time of the day or night, they discussed and argued and planned, they studied and they listened to the gramophone. They could afford to feel optimistic: they were young and planning for a better world and, despite the obtuseness of the Government and its continual resort to restrictive legislation, they realized they were a part of the world at large, and had the assurance of knowing they were in step with what was happening in Asia and with what was likely to happen in the rest of Africa.

However this exhilarating understanding was as yet the fruit of a few personal friendships. The wider conflicts continued. Mandela and the A.N.C. Youth League were determined that Africans must lead themselves and were ever suspicious of 'foreign' influences. The Youth League and communists constantly clashed and heckled each other furiously. But though the Youth League urged the A.N.C. to act, it was a communist in Congress who took the lead.

That year, 1946, was one of unique opportunity for the Chamber of Mines. These leaders of the mining industry in Johannesburg – many of them blessed by a liberal education and therefore with considerable advantages over Afrikaners, and doubtless seeing themselves as upholders of western Christian civilization – were approached by the poorest of their employees, the African mineworkers, and were asked for a rise in pay.

The wretched situation of African miners was common knowledge; in Parliament in 1942 all the Members representing Native interests had warned Smuts of great unrest on the mines because of the low wages and had said that unless a cost of living allowance were granted, there would be trouble. No allowance was made and the miners had come out in sporadic strikes. In 1943 a cost of living allowance was granted to all African workers *except* those in mining and in agriculture. By 1946 the average cash earning of mineworkers who, as Donald Molteno, M.P. pointed out, were by far the most important body of workers in the country, was £3. 11s. 8d. per month, while the peasant income that this had to subsidize was £2. 10s. 0d. per month at the most. Bishop Lavis told the

Anglican Synod in the Cape about the 300,000 men in the mines separated from their families for all but a few years of their lives under the pernicious migrant labour system. He referred to the appalling infant mortality rate among African babies – never less than 150 and rising to 700 per thousand.

The Chamber of Mines suppressed a report from the chief nutrition expert of the Institute of Medical Research disclosing startling figures of malnutrition and disease in the Transkei, where more than a third of the people had no land and no income except what they earned in the mines, and where the soil was eroding and productivity constantly decreasing.[1]

During these years the African Mine Workers' Union, which had been initiated by leaders of the Transvaal A.N.C. in 1941, had developed into the first effective organization of African miners under the Presidency of J. B. Marks, the tough, kindly teacher who spoke the language of the people and could sway a crowd powerfully; and who, furthermore, as a member of the Communist Party had had some political and trade union education. The obstacles that had defeated several attempts to organize African mineworkers since 1920 still existed – the mine authorities imposed restrictions so that no outsider could enter the compound without a permit and a guide; besides, many of the miners who came on regular contracts from remote tribal areas were illiterate or disinterested. However, after the A.N.C. had successfully called a conference of miners, Marks and the Union Secretary, J. J. Majoro, a former miner, held huge meetings constantly at the compounds which were orderly and invariably attended by police.[2]

As a result of the Union's demand for reforms which followed on the spontaneous strikes in 1942, the Government had appointed the Lansdowne Commission of Inquiry into conditions of employment. A year later, the Commission recommended a cost of living and other allowances, paid leave and overtime, and increases in wages on each shift. The Government refused to implement the recommendations of allowances and only

1. Evidence by Senator H. Basner in subsequent trial.
2. Evidence given by police, 17 September 1946, in subsequent trial.

agreed to a lesser wage increase and overtime. The A.M.W.U. promptly called a conference to which more than a thousand African miners came and wanted an immediate strike. The Union dissuaded them on the grounds that the war effort should not be hindered. There followed Government intimidation with the arrests of Marks and other organizers and the total prohibition of meetings on mine property, a formidable obstacle for the Union.

Yet their work continued. Meetings were organized in townships to which mineworkers went on their weekends off. And there were clandestine meetings at night, in the shadow of the mine dumps, when Union organizers and the communists who were always ready to assist them would address an almost invisible audience, for the faces of the miners gathered around were lost in the darkness, and in the starlight only their helmets glistened faintly. If any speaker said something good he just heard an approving grunt, 'Hawu!', out of the dark.

Nevertheless the Government's embargo gravely handicapped the Union and its income from subscriptions dropped from £120 to £30 a month. And all the time the cost of living was rising with the war, and in the reserves there was a two years' drought. By 1946 Marks felt that the Union could no longer hold the workers from striking. He sent for Senator Basner and urged negotiations with the Government, but an interview with the Minister of Labour was fruitless. Basner went on to see the Secretary for Native Affairs. Nothing was done. He saw a representative of the Chamber of Mines. Nothing was done.

At the Union's annual conference in April 1946 the members clamoured to strike. They resolved to demand a minimum wage of 10s. per day, against the existing minimum of between 2s. 3d. and 2s. 5d.; 'in accordance with the new world's principles for an approved standard of living subscribed to by our Government at U.N.O.' When friends of the Union criticized this demand as excessive, it replied that the white trade union movement had long advocated this wage for unskilled work.

It was at this point that the Union approached the Chamber of Mines, writing three times to the Gold Producers' Committee to put the miners' grievances and demands and to ask for an interview. The committee did not reply. Even when a big meeting of mineworkers was told this by Marks, they still agreed that there should be one more appeal to the Chamber of Mines, but if at this eleventh hour it remained 'intransigent' they unanimously resolved 'the strike will begin'. Marks soberly warned them that they were challenging the cheap labour system of the country and they must 'be ready to sacrifice in the struggle for the right to live as human beings'. On 7 August the Union wrote again to the Chamber of Mines. There was no reply.

At 3 a.m. on Monday, 12 August, it was a cold clear night on the highveld. All along the Reef from hundreds of shaftheads African miners surfaced at the end of their shift and walked out in the wintry night, back to the compound. Some, as they tramped wearily along, passed others, waiting to go underground. But on seven mines they passed no one. The cages went down empty. The huge fly-wheels stopped. The great mine strike had begun.

50,000 Africans were out! A sixth of the miners. Soon 70,000 were out. The biggest strike in South Africa's history. Lorry-loads of police rushed to the East and West Rand. The Stock Exchange was soon in 'a mild panic' and, not far away from its solid edifice and from the fine modern offices of the mining houses, men in blankets and men in suits, went to an office in a decrepit arcade, asking for President Marks, making their reports and seeking instructions. In that shabby small office, through the bitter cold of midnight, the volunteers of all races produced leaflets from inadequate machinery. At 2 a.m. each morning the volunteers set off for the mines. The message on their leaflets was brief: 'Ikona Mali – Ikona Sebenza', 'No Money – No Work'. These were distributed to the miners coming off shift.

By the second day Press comments had begun. The *Rand Daily Mail* under the headline 'A Foolish Strike' spelled J. B. Marks's name Marx, described him as 'intemperate', making 'wild speeches and absurd demands', while the *Cape Times* spoke of the 'wicked irresponsibility' of agitators calling unfortunate natives out on strike. However it conceded that there

might be some justification. The word 'agitators' was thence-
forward freely used.

All the compounds were sealed off under armed guards. The
strikers were thus put out of touch with the Union organizers and
with no news from other mines or compounds. Marks was
arrested. The Council of Non-European Trade Unions (said to
represent 150,000 workers) promptly demanded a general strike
within two days. The Cabinet met. The police, with rifles and
with batons, began driving men back to work, and on one mine
where men stoned them, they fired and wounded ten, while
four Africans were trampled to death in the resulting panic.
The *Star* reported that the survivors 'decided to return to
work'. Altogether eighty-three men were injured that day. The
Stock Exchange made a slight recovery. However on one mine –
City Deep – the workers, after being driven out of their compound and forced underground, held a sit-down strike a mile
down under the earth. This was something new in South Africa's
history.

Smuts remarked that he was 'not unduly concerned', the
strike was not caused by legitimate grievances but by agitators.
Senator Basner and Mrs Margaret Ballinger, M.P. at once
wired him, expressing shock that such a remark should be made
when there were so many dead and injured. On the third morning of the strike, the Wednesday, the *Rand Daily Mail* in a four-
column headline announced '4,000 strikers tried to march on
Johannesburg', and it went on to say that they were 'armed with
choppers, iron bars, knives and an assortment of other dangerous
weapons – in a six-mile long procession. . . .' Having duly
panicked the whites of Johannesburg the report mentioned that
when the police cordoned off the road, the 4,000 'sat down and
there were cat calls and threats. Then, acting on instructions
from Pretoria (the Government), the police drew their batons
and charged.' Three strikers were seriously injured while scores
had minor injuries. The *Mail* editorial that day (a classic example of how a comparatively enlightened newspaper could obey
the unwritten law of the English-language press in South
Africa that the gold mining industry was sacred) expressed no

regret for the six now dead and the 400 injured, nor referred to the reasons for the strike. It asked 'the average Johannesburg citizen' to consider what would have happened if those 4,000 Natives, 'all of them armed with some weapon or other' had not been intercepted by the police. The police, it said, deserved the public gratitude for their courage and skill. The *Rand Daily Mail* hoped that the Cabinet would not be weak.[1]

The 'facts' reported by the *Mail* were challenged by an independent paper, the Labour Party's *Illustrated Bulletin*, edited by Colin Legum, which asked how it was humanly possible for any reporter to determine how many of 4,000 dangerous blanketed marching Natives who were stretched over six miles, were armed. It pointed out that the pictures of the event showed no arms, and further that this great threat was dealt with by forty policemen. But the *Bulletin* had a limited circulation.

At this stage in the mine strike, on 14 August, the Natives' Representative Council began its annual sitting in Pretoria, forty miles to the north of Johannesburg. The African elected members included some of the most respected men in A.N.C., A.A.C., or in urban or tribal affairs. They had all read their morning papers, they well knew the reality of the hardships that lay behind the strike and, as was the case for all Africans upon learning of the shooting and the baton charges, they identified with the strikers. They naturally expected that the Minister of Native Affairs, who usually attended the opening of the Council, would make a statement on this most serious situation. But he was not present, and nor was his deputy who had gone to Johannesburg; the Under-Secretary for Native Affairs took the chair and the proceedings opened in their usual formal leisurely way. A new member, elected from Natal on the recent death of Dr Dube, was welcomed; a heavy, pleasant-faced Chief – Albert Lutuli.

The Chairman made a speech. He did not refer to the crisis of the mine strike. Paul Mosaka, the leader of the African Democratic Party and the youngest member of the N.R.C., promptly pointed this out, called for a full statement, and asked whether

1. 14 August 1946.

the Government was negotiating with the African Mine Workers' Union – if not why not? The Chairman was evasive.

Professor Z. K. Matthews expressed distress at the lack of any statement on so alarming a state of affairs.

Dr James Moroka, the distinguished physician who had played a notable part in the 1936 deputation to Hertzog, emphasized that they regarded the situation as 'very serious'. 'We put the blame on the Government – they treat us like children,' he declared . . . 'we are not going to tolerate it.'

Selope Thema, now old, took up the theme: 'When we say we blame the Government . . . we mean what we say. The Press says that communists and agitators have started the strike, but 50,000 people will not leave their work because of agitation. The cause goes much deeper.' Mosaka underlined this: 'We hold the Government responsible for the wanton shooting which took place on the Reef.' The Under-Secretary for Native Affairs wanted to delete 'wanton' from the records. 'No,' insisted Mosaka, 'it expresses my own feelings.'

The strike went on. The Mine Workers' Union and its volunteers worked day and night but increasingly they were depleted by police raids, searches, confiscation of leaflets and arrests. Strikers were arrested and tried for refusing to work, and some had their contracts cancelled and were sent back to the Reserves. When the strike committee tried to hold a meeting, the hundreds of Africans who gathered were surrounded by police and given five minutes to disperse on orders from the Minister of Justice. When Coloured and Indian workers in tobacco factories wanted to express their sympathy and began to walk to a meeting, they were turned back by the police, and as they walked away they were baton charged. The procession scattered. Six women lay injured in the road. On the mines the casualties mounted.

Native Representatives and City Councillors tried to rally white opinion but not a single United Party 'liberal' would sign a protest against police brutality, and a request for the miners' right to negotiate with the Chamber of Mines. But from Durban the Indian passive resisters sent £100 for the strike fund.

The Minister of Justice, Harry Lawrence, had announced that refusal to go back to work might be countered by rifle fire. The Press reports assumed a certain monotony – 4,000 Africans on one mine, 5,000 on another, after clashes with the police, 'surrendered and said they would return to work' or 'went underground readily'. In one instance nearly 300 police, some with bayonets, moved into the dormitories of Pondo miners and drove them to work. On another mine 'they drove Natives stope by stope, level by level . . . afterwards the strikers indicated their intention of resuming work'. 500 men from one mine set out to walk from Benoni 'to see the Chamber of Mines', met the police and were 'routed' by a baton charge and sent 'scurrying over the veld'.

In the Natives' Representative Council, the debate went on with passion and with bitter sorrow. Moroka said that there was no doubt at all that the real cause of the trouble was the Native policy of South Africa; until it was changed 'things like this will continue to happen'. To the Government he said, 'You can do what you like, you can shoot us, arrest us, imprison us, but you are not going to break our spirit.'

African Councillors expressed the urgent wish to go to the Witwatersrand to see for themselves what was happening; they were after all supposed to represent eight million Africans and to advise the Government on their interests. The request was refused.

This was the last straw. All the mounting frustration of thirty-six years broke through in these temperate men. As Moroka later described it, 'You sat down there, you came with resolutions, you talked until your mouth was dry and that was the last you heard of it. It was a disgrace; tomfoolery out and out.' The Councillors knew perfectly well that the Government thought nothing of them. Mosaka bitterly pointed out that the Minister of Native Affairs, Piet van der Byl, seldom visited the Council, the Prime Minister had not been near for nine years, resolutions were continually ignored. Thema accused white South Africa of inventing Nazism. One Councillor called the N.R.C. a 'dismal failure'.

Paul Mosaka summed it up as 'a toy telephone'.

Towards the end of the second and last day of the Council's session, when feelings were high, Moroka rose and asked to put a resolution as a matter of urgency. Unsuspecting, the Chairman agreed. The dignified doctor proceeded, and as his quiet voice read on and the Government officials present realized what the Chairman had inadvertently allowed, there was a shocked silence. Moroka accused the Government of continuing 'a policy of fascism', the 'antithesis and negation of the letter and the spirit of the Atlantic Charter and the U.N. Charter'. He moved the immediate adjournment of the session and the abolition 'forthwith' of all discriminatory legislation.

The Chairman hurriedly refused the motion. Mosaka tersely interposed: 'How long must gold be rated above human values?'

The twelve elected African Councillors persisted. The motion was unanimously carried; even the three Government-appointed chiefs voted for it. The Natives' Representative Council adjourned.

This was yet one more, the most serious and the most prolonged, effort to be made by African leaders to use constitutional methods for redress of the injustice and wrongs that they suffered. It was the Thursday night. Few miners were still on strike. Press reports continued to mention their return to work; perhaps the most remarkable was one describing 'a general stampede' in which 'the police used their batons freely', and which concluded, 'not long afterwards, the Natives came to the gate and offered to return to work. They marched out and, in a happy mood, went underground.'

Still leaflets were going out under the noses of the police – in bundles of washing, in shopping bags under groceries, in shirt fronts. They called on the miners to keep courage, but courage had ebbed, and the strike committee had been incapacitated by the arrest of Marks and several other members. In the background trade unionists and A.N.C. quarrelled. Some of the A.N.C. felt the strike had been precipitate and should not have been called until the Union had achieved far greater strength, and for this blamed the influence of communists, while Lembede and the Youth League felt that Marks together with Xuma should have carefully organized a country-wide general strike, using the immense feeling generated by the anti-pass campaign. As it was, an attempt to call a general strike in Johannesburg by trade unions and the Transvaal A.N.C. fizzled out.

Africans had pitted themselves against the biggest industry in Africa and failed.

The Stock Exchange reported, 'prices rally'. At the weekend, the *Rand Daily Mail* exclaimed 'TOTAL DEFEAT' and commented: 'The Native strike has ended just as it was bound to do. Quite a number of strikers have sore heads; a few are dead; and not a single one of the points for which they struck has been gained.' A more constructive editorial was that of the *Sunday Express* pointing out that the present policy was to treat the Native worker rough and tell him nothing, an attitude which would merely ensure that every strike would automatically be a riot. 'Native industrial workers must eventually be trade unionists,' it argued, 'whether Europeans like this prospect or not.'

The Chamber of Mines was forced to declare something of its attitude in the subsequent trial of the alleged organizers of this strike, although even then it evaded certain awkward questions when minutes of its meetings relating to the A.M.W.U., promised to the court, were withheld.

The trial was the biggest political trial in the country's history and the fifty-two accused included not only J. B. Marks and other leaders of the African Mine Workers' Union, but Moses Kotane, Bram Fischer and other communists, and even Dr Dadoo who was brought from prison in Natal where he was still serving his sentence for passive resistance.

In the trial, the defence called the Secretary of the Chamber of Mines, A. J. Limebeer, as a witness and drew from him the evidence that although the Chamber had received letters from the Union dated 6 and 26 May, 24 June and 7 August, 'simply, I was told not to reply to them', though 'it was apparent' to the Chamber 'that there was serious resentment'. He admitted that in a recent strike of white miners there had been no prosecutions, nor any use of force.

To a court crowded with spectators, a detective-sergeant reported on J. B. Marks's actions. He admitted that Marks, in addressing a huge Union rally on 19 May, had said that the Union did not like strikes and the meeting had agreed that they should try to open negotiations with the Chamber of Mines and the Government, and that only after a subsequent meeting to discuss the complete failure of attempts to negotiate had workers in the crowd proposed a strike, with Marks warning that on no account must violence be used. This police witness also admitted that the Chamber of Mines used plain-clothes informers.

Subsequently several of the accused were given short terms of imprisonment while the charges against others were dropped, but for the communists involved this was not the end. On 21 September their hey-day was abruptly ended when offices and homes of party members, of trade unionists and of the *Guardian* newspaper were raided in nine cities. The police acted on instructions from H. G. Lawrence, Minister of Justice. The Acting Prime Minister, Jan Hofmeyr, and other members of the Cabinet said the raids had taken them by surprise. The Minister of Labour said he had no idea that the raids on trade unions were going to take place. Not long after, the Executive of the Communist Party, Kotane included, was arrested and charged with sedition. Although the case fell through, as happened in Pirow's day in the early thirties, the general impression had by this time been confirmed among whites that African discontent was caused by communist agitation.

However in the Cape and in Johannesburg academics, liberals and churchmen were protesting against the behaviour of the Government and the Chamber of Mines. The Rev. Michael Scott, who had worked with the African Miners' Union, and Father Lunniss of the Community of the Resurrection, succeeded in getting strong support from the Synod of the Anglican Church in Johannesburg for a resolution calling on the Government to recognize the Union and other African trade unions, and for immediate negotiations between the Chamber of Mines and the Africans. The Government refused to act. The Pretoria Synod also called on the Government to recognize African trade unions, to no effect. The *Rand Daily Mail* and the *Star* promptly commented that the affairs of the mining industry were outside the scope of the Church.

Meanwhile the Natives' Representative Council's powerful resolution had aroused widespread support from Africans, and Hofmeyr, Acting Prime Minister, wrote to Smuts, who was abroad, to say that even more serious than the mine strike was the attitude of the N.R.C. which meant 'that the (hitherto) moderate intellectuals of the Professor Matthews' type are now committed to an extreme line against colour discrimination' and, he added, they 'have carried the chiefs with them'. But, Hofmeyr told the Prime Minister, he could not see what they could do to satisfy Africans 'which would be tolerated by European public opinion'. A few weeks later he wrote again to report on a meeting with Matthews. He prophesied 'something in the nature of a climb down' and said 'it is clear that some of them at least are now frightened of the possible consequences of their action.'[1] What Matthews, as leader of the N.R.C. caucus, had said was that *if* there were a positive gesture from the Government towards abolishing colour discrimination, the N.R.C. might reconsider its resolution.

At the very time that Hofmeyr was writing the letter, early in October, the feelings of the African Councillors were being forcefully expressed to a crisis conference of the A.N.C. Among the 500 delegates the predominant feeling that emerged was one of rage: rage at the shootings and batonings, rage at the crushing of the miners' justified protests, rage at the contempt the Government consistently showed for the N.R.C. The crisis drew Lembede, the Africanist, together with Moses Kotane, the communist, in proposing a motion which met with overwhelming approval. This endorsed the N.R.C.'s adjournment, called on the Councillors to attend a meeting asked for by the Government in a month's time, and called for the boycott of elections to the N.R.C. and to Parliament of Native Representatives. Its urge that the African people struggle for full citizen rights met with wild applause. Then there was silence for two minutes, as

1. Letters of 8 September and 7 October 1946.

delegates remembered the nine miners killed and the 1,200 injured.

The repercussions from the breaking of the strike continued. The African Mine Workers' Union never recovered; it was defeated not only by the police brutalities but by the Chamber of Mines which considerably strengthened policing of the mines, while tribal segregation in the compounds was made strict.

Four days before the Government was due to reply to the N.R.C. resolution calling for the abolition of all discriminatory laws, the Chamber of Mines ran a three-column advertisement in each of the main daily and Sunday papers in Johannesburg, captioned 'TRIBAL NATIVES AND TRADE UNIONISM'. The policy of the Chamber of Mines, it declared, was one of Trusteeship. Trade unions at the Natives' 'present stage of development' would lead to abuses and irresponsible action. 'A trade union organization would not only be useless, but detrimental to the ordinary mine Native in his present stage of development.'

When the time came for the Government to meet the N.R.C., Smuts had gone to the U.N., and Hofmeyr again deputized for him. He told them he was surprised at their 'violent and exaggerated statements'. He claimed that many of the differential provisions in the laws protected Native interests. Changes, he said, must be 'gradual'. He spoke of Government goodwill and desire for African advancement. His remarks amounted to a flat refusal to accede to the N.R.C.'s resolution. Furthermore, he said that Government would not allow a trade union for Native mineworkers.

These were the conclusions which South Africa's most liberal statesman, a great scholar and a brilliant brain, put to the university professor, the medical doctor, and the other distinguished Africans with whom he met. Politely they thanked him. He left. They were given time in which to think over his words. He did not return to hear their reply.

Professor Matthews, as Chairman of the caucus, made the reply, his pleasant face grim. He said there had been no advance in Native policy beyond the thoughts of people in 1903; the

Acting Prime Minister's statement did not seem to show any intention on the part of the Government to recognize changed conditions. The N.R.C., he clearly stated, 'repudiate Mr Hofmeyr's suggestion of extremism and recklessness on our part'; on the contrary, he accused, 'these charges could more fittingly be applied to the methods of the Government in suppressing the mineworkers' strike by the unprovoked use of brute force'. He spoke of the intolerable conditions and of how the African people throughout the country had looked forward to the Government reply. But, he said, Hofmeyr's reply was 'apparently oblivious of the progressive forces at work' in the world in general and in South Africa. He concluded: 'It gives no hope for the future.'

Matthews moved that the Council be suspended until the Government could give a more reassuring reply. He was seconded by George Champion who enumerated all the discriminatory laws passed since 1909. It was a long list. One factor emerged distinctly: as Africans became more educated, more urbanized and westernized, so the restrictions against them were increased and harshened.

The debate went on for a week. The elderly Selope Thema was more in tune with the world at large than Hofmeyr: he said, 'The tide in the world is against the white man.' He asked the Government, 'Do you want us to join those forces that are outside, those forces which are out to destroy? If you drive us to that we shall know what to do; but we don't want to do that.'

Dr Moroka, a tall, almost elegant figure, a man with years of life in Edinburgh and in Vienna behind him, also brought realism to bear. The true reason for the Government's refusal, he said, was that it feared the opposition – the Nationalists who were due to fight the next election on the colour issue. 'Until the European people of this country,' he stated, 'realize that we must be given an opportunity to rule this country as they rule it, we will never, never, never have peace in this country.' Smuts had been partly responsible for the Atlantic Charter – 'How can he allow the colour bar?' Moroka asked. 'I just cannot understand it. I cannot get into his heart, and find out how after all he has done in the world, the big work he has done for humanity, he can now return to his own country and say that freedom cannot be given to the black people because they will murder the Europeans and want to marry Europeans.'

The Government's actions caused the turning-point in the attitude of African intellectuals.

In December Hofmeyr, who had been Acting Prime Minister during much of this turbulent, tragic time, wrote to a friend about how 'smoothly' things had gone in South Africa since June, adding: 'Our main troubles of late have been on the international stage.'[1]

1. *Hofmeyr* by Alan Paton.

9 1946–8: African Internationalism Confronts White Isolationism and the Electorate Chooses

Dr Xuma took the Africans' case to the United Nations. There he delivered the first petition from the Hereros and other tribes in South-West Africa, protesting against the South African Government's desire to incorporate the Mandated territory.

Although then, in 1946, there was no procedure under which he could make a direct petition, he lobbied effectively, helped by Senator Basner and a representative of the South African Indian Congress. It was hard work, with little known about South Africa and a preconception abroad that General Smuts could do no wrong. However they were helped by the lavish supply of ammunition provided by the South African Government: the handling of the mine strike, the regular imprisonment of passive resisters – more than a thousand had already gone to jail and served terms of several months with hard labour – and the scandal of the African housing shortage. All these events, backed by facts and figures (available in any Blue Book) on the restrictions binding the non-white majority in South Africa and in South-West Africa, made an unanswerable case for Xuma.

India took the lead in the debates, with Sir Maharaj Singh contributing valuable first-hand knowledge from his years as Indian High Commissioner in South Africa. Smuts argued persuasively for white 'civilization' but this was soon revealed as a euphemism for 'domination'. His tragic blind spot was never more apparent: he showed no understanding of the changing world, and of the abhorrence of racialism so deeply felt by many great nations and expressed by President Truman in his opening address, which envisaged justice for small nations and for individuals 'without distinction as to race, creed or colour'. Smuts found the Preamble to the U.N. Charter, which affirmed 'faith in the fundamental human rights, in the dignity and worth of the human person, in the equal rights of men and women and of nations large and small', which he had helped to draft and his Parliament had ratified, frequently quoted against him.

The United Nations' castigation of South Africa has frequently been blamed on the Afro–Asian powers, yet in 1946, when the organization consisted of only 54 nations and Afro–Asian votes totalled only 14, the General Assembly voted by 32 votes to 15 on a French–Mexican proposal advocating a settlement of the dispute over the treatment of the Indian community in South Africa; and by 36 votes to none, rejected Smuts's request to incorporate South-West Africa. Eric Louw, one of the Afrikaner Nationalist M.P.s in South Africa, not having the prescience to know that he would one day be repeatedly placed in even more uncomfortable positions than Smuts, mocked the Prime Minister for his defeat and said: 'Imagine a Boer General (and a British Field-Marshal to boot) employing such poor tactics. A Union Defence Force Corporal would have done better. . . .'[1]

Before Xuma left New York he attended a reception at which Smuts was present. Smuts's Secretary recognized him and asked, 'Have you met the Prime Minister?'

'No,' was the somewhat obvious answer from the leader of the A.N.C.

The Secretary took him over to meet the Field-Marshal. Smuts shook his hand and said, 'Zuma [sic], my dear man, what are you doing here?'

'Well, sir,' replied the doctor, 'I have had to fly 10,000 miles to meet my Prime Minister. He talks *about* us but he won't talk to us.'

To which Smuts replied, 'Man alive, let's get together! You know, Zuma, I am a most misunderstood man.'

He was about to discuss the Natives' Representative Council when his Secretary drew him away.

In South Africa, besides the role played by India at the U.N., the passive resistance campaign had impressed certain Africans

1. *The Struggle for Equality* by P. S. Joshi.

who, for the first time since the A.N.C. had led protests against the pass laws more than twenty years before, witnessed organized resistance to unjust laws. A pact to cement the understanding was drawn up on 9 March 1947, when Dr Xuma for the A.N.C., and Dr Naicker and Dr Dadoo, the Presidents of the Natal and Transvaal Indian Congresses, signed an agreement to work for full franchise rights and for equal economic and industrial rights and opportunities as well as other freedoms. Three days later Naicker and Dadoo flew to India to attend the first Inter-Asian Conference, carrying with them the good wishes of mass meetings of Africans and Indians. Soon after the largest demonstration ever held of non-whites took place in Johannesburg with Xuma presiding and the crowd unanimously supporting the pact and celebrating United Nations resolutions – which included the demand for U.N. trusteeship over South-West Africa. The great gathering was more immediately concerned with the desperate situation of the hundred thousand Africans by this time existing in the shanties that germinated from the overcrowded townships on the outskirts of Johannesburg.

Two months later Smuts sent for a Deputation from the Natives' Representative Council. He spoke vaguely about broadening the Council's powers and of the possibility of it having power to administer the African reserves and levy local taxes. He appealed to them to think about this, adding with a paternal smile, 'It is a point for the N.R.C. to chew over.' The Press began to expound on Smuts's 'new deal'. The deputation made it clear that it saw no new deal, no change in policy at all. Its scepticism was justified, a new law, the Industrial Conciliation (Natives) Act, laid down that there would be no trade unions for Africans in the mining, agriculture or domestic service fields; it would be a criminal offence for Africans to organize a union not registered and strikes would continue to be illegal. This was the death sentence for the African Mine Workers' Union and meant that existing multi-racial unions were segregated.

Anton Lembede promptly addressed a mass meeting in Vereeniging – attended by residents from Sharpeville and other locations – winning unanimous support for the call to boycott elections to the Natives' Representative Council and of white representatives to Parliament. It was his last public act; within a few weeks he died. He was thirty-three. Through his short life from farm labourer to politician he had fought illness, driving himself with such energy and carelessness of his body that he could hardly be persuaded to sleep or eat. As a lawyer, for all his theatrical manner, he had been popular, honest and carefully able. Although his close friends in the Youth League regarded him as a man of vision, they realized his moodiness and inflexibility would have been handicaps had he lived to lead the A.N.C. He was a mass of conflicts – abhorring pretension and with a direct sense of humour that won him friends among simple people and led him to dislike the new sophistication of urban society, yet with a racial pride that could obscure for him the virtues of someone of another colour. Suffering had sharpened his mind and increased his inner strength. His death aroused great sorrow.

What was the significance of Lembede's role in the liberation movement? In terms of action it was small, in terms of influence large. He has been called the 'architect of African nationalism in South Africa', and 'undoubtedly the greatest future leader the Africans have ever had'.[1] After his death, some of his contemporaries were to claim him as the first 'Africanist', insisting that he would have taken their rigid line had he lived. Perhaps, but it is as conceivable that he might have matured otherwise, as did others in the Youth League who in those days vied with him in a narrow nationalism. But his philosophical leadership was undoubted, and he was nearer than any other African leader in South Africa to the 'charismatic' leaders becoming popular in West Africa.

At the time of Lembede's death, a less spectacular but remarkable leader was coming forward in the A.N.C. – Gert Sibande, born in Ermelo, a Transvaal village, in 1901, and like Lembede the child of farm labourers and a labourer himself. But whereas Lembede, with his hunger for knowledge, finally

1. *Drum*, January 1954.

achieved legal success and a Master of Arts Degree on a thesis concerning 'The conception of God as expounded by Descartes and subsequent philosophers', Sibande remained a farm labourer. He was brought up in the harsh conditions of the Eastern Transvaal. Unable to go to school, he taught himself to write and read 'up to a point', and was fluent only in Zulu. He was a lay preacher in the South African Apostolic Church of Zion and, activated by Hertzog's Segregation Act and by other farm labourers who brought their troubles to him, he formed a Farm Workers' Organization. He was by this time living in Bethal, the labour recruiting centre in the intensively farmed maize triangle where the conditions for labourers were so intolerable that only illegal immigrants from Rhodesia and Nyasaland or drafted labour would go there. Sibande took their many problems to the Native Commissioner who simply blamed the laws. And so he decided there was nothing for it but to get the backing of a national organization. He joined the A.N.C. During the early forties his A.N.C. branch held many meetings in the Bethal location and on the farms where the labourers were known to be ill-treated – the latter had to be secret meetings at night. Sibande found that farmers took away the labourers' ordinary clothes, forcing them to wear sacks even in winter. They worked till long after nightfall and often were locked into the compounds at night and had to eat their food from the floor like pigs.

Some deserted. Sibande came across a group of deserters. 'What really touched me was this,' he said: 'on this particular day it was very cold. Those people who had deserted were found dead alongside the road. Four of them.'

On the same day ninety-nine people on one farm were caught in the rain and had to sleep in their clothes. It was so cold that they could not work afterwards. The farmer had them arrested and six of them were charged. The farmer then conceded that they were in a bad building, said he would build another, and the case was withdrawn. Sibande would report cases of the ill-treatment of people who deserted to the Native Commissioner but he found that they were promptly arrested, and he would protest again. Eventually he was forced to try other tactics.

It was midwinter, in June 1947, that Sibande, the peasant, took a journalist and a priest round the Bethal farms and showed them what his friends and neighbours were suffering. The effects of this tour were to rock the country.

When Ruth First and Michael Scott arrived in Bethal's main street they were met by this big vigorous slow-speaking man who cocked his head slightly to concentrate on the unaccustomed English they spoke. Yet he did not seem surprised that they had come and seemed to know at once what they wanted and how to get it. Obstacles did not exist for him. 'You want to meet farm workers? All right,' and into a smoke-filled compound he took them.

They came out with a story by Scott that was sympathetically headlined in the *Rand Daily Mail* and throughout the country – Bethal was after all an Afrikaner dorp. The *Cape Times* referred to Scott's 'striking disclosures'; what gave them 'utmost significance' in Government eyes was the U.N. Session looming up. It was not only Scott who had made the allegations but a succession of magistrates, one of whom had described the conditions as 'tantamount to slavery'.

Smuts promptly promised investigations of the allegations of ill-treatment of natives. His Minister of Justice, Lawrence, sent squads of police to Bethal. They got complaints from only seven of the ninety-one farms and a handful of white foremen and native boss boys were charged with assault. Lawrence announced that the inquiry had vindicated the Bethal district. He promised the farmers to consider supplying them with convict labour and to improve the system of bringing back deserters to the farms. When Sibande and Bopape, the Transvaal A.N.C. leader, addressed a meeting of several thousand Africans in the Bethal location, people in the crowd pointed out that the police investigation was unsatisfactory because Africans feared the police, that indeed conditions were even worse than Scott had reported. The gathering called for a Commission of Inquiry into labour conditions. The Government took no notice.

Now Bethal was a United Party seat – a shaky one at that. Besides, since 1943, the United Party had lost four of eight by-elections to the Nationalists. It seemed suddenly to dawn upon Smuts that he had been rash to hurry police into the area and antagonize the farmers, so although he himself had roundly condemned the compound labour system in 1945, his Minister of Native Affairs, Piet van der Byl, now warmly defended it. The Government took no further action in Bethal.

But, in October, just in time for the United Nations Session, Smuts published his 'New Deal for Natives'. This suggested that instead of twelve natives being elected to the Natives' Representative Council there should be fifty, who would discuss 'tentative proposals'. The N.R.C.'s reaction was quick and sharp: it accused the Government of a breach of faith, while Professor Matthews said the Prime Minister was 'pulling a fast one'. However, when the A.N.C. came to consider the matter, caution won: they decided to give Smuts another chance, and elect men to the enlarged Council. It was the All-African Convention which called for a boycott and under Professor Jabavu rejected Smuts's proposals outright.

The A.N.C. had just sent delegates to the latest Pan-African Congress at Dakar, while Smuts's hope that he would convince the U.N. that Africans were getting a new deal was dashed when representatives of the non-white people of South-West Africa and the Union – Michael Scott and members of the South African Indian Congress – once again could produce more than enough facts and figures of what was taking place in South Africa to win support for their cause.

Back in South Africa the two white parties were shaping up for the imminent elections. J. G. Strijdom, Afrikaner Nationalist leader, significantly chose Bethal for a *Stryddag* (struggle day), when he announced that the white man should always be master in every sphere of public life in South Africa. Smuts was saying that United Party policy was leadership by the European race. To the black bogey the red bogey was added and for the third time since the war the Executive of the Communist Party was arrested for sedition, but despite this gesture on Smuts's part, Nationalists announced: 'A vote for Jan Smuts is a vote for Joe Stalin.'

George Bernard Shaw, who had twice visited South Africa in the thirties, at this time described Smuts's policy as having 'standards of shallow and irresponsible democracy' and, as for 'White Africans', Shaw thought them 'very imperfectly civilized' and 'mentally lazy and snobbish'.[1]

All the same Smuts had appointed a Commission of Inquiry into the conditions of the non-whites, under Mr Justice Fagan, himself a former Minister of Native Affairs. Among authorities who gave evidence was a leading liberal academic, Mrs Winifred Hoernlé, who spoke of the extreme weariness of the African people: in Moroka, one of the enormities in the Reef housing problem, the women were tired out, she said, and the overcrowding of 60,000 people was a symptom of widespread social evil which should have been dealt with as a national emergency. There had been riots, with police firing on the crowd, during recent violent resistance to enforced removals of squatters, and three policemen had been killed. Fagan and his Commission made the most careful investigation in the history of the country. It remained to be seen what would come of this.

There were warnings enough for white South Africa – in the growing interest taken in its policies at the United Nations, and from Gandhi in India who said that if the so-called whites retained their prejudice and kept themselves in purdah their 'attitude of unreason' would mean a third war. This was recalled at the time of Gandhi's assassination – a sad blow to the passive resisters in South Africa. Gandhi in a last message to them had said: 'What the Government of South Africa has done deliberately is not going to be changed suddenly, even for the sufferings of the brave men and women. This is said not to damp the zeal of the fighters but to steel them for long and greater suffering. They must not expect the struggle to close quickly.' And *The Passive Resister* recalled that in 1910 Tolstoy had written to Gandhi, then in the Transvaal, to say that the passive resistance in South Africa 'is the most important activity the world can at present take part in, and in which not Christendom alone but all the peoples of the earth will participate'.

1. *The Passive Resister*, December 1947.

The 1948 election would be the test of the civilization of white South Africans, with many of the young men just back from defending freedom and defeating fascism in North Africa and in Europe. Would they see that freedom was indivisible? The A.N.C. had planned a campaign on the eve of the white elections, calling for full franchise rights for the non-whites to culminate with a People's Assembly for Votes for All. It promised to be the one note of sanity, but by the time it came about it had been disrupted by the usual quarrels between nationalists and communists. However 322 delegates unanimously adopted a People's Charter which proclaimed a 'burning belief in the ideals of democracy' and introduced a civilized note in the election campaign by quoting Lincoln's ideal of government of, by and for the people, as well as the U.N. Charter and a smattering of Marxist slogans.

It was not only the non-whites – whether left- or right-wing – and Gandhi and the U.N. and the militant left-wing ex-servicemen's 'Springbok Legion' that were warning white South Africa; the Roman Catholic Bishop of Natal, the Rt Rev. Denis Hurley, declared that South Africa was doomed to strife and bloodshed unless the European population gracefully accepted an end to white supremacy and accepted equality of all races.

But the United Party were set on their path of segregation and the Afrikaner Nationalists on their ossified version of segregation – apartheid. This had been defined over many years, promising separation not only between white and non-white but between the various non-white groups, and prohibiting marriage between races. Natives in the urban areas would be regarded forever as 'visitors', allowed no political or social rights in the 87 per cent of the country that could virtually be described as European areas.[1] Representation of Natives in Parliament would be abolished as

1. Population then was: approximately 2½ million Whites, 8½ million Africans, over 1 million Coloured people, under ½ million Indians. Total: 12½ million.

Numbers at school (1945): 438,000 whites, 596,000 Africans, 215,800 Coloured people and Indians; with £16,500,000 spent on white education, £2,300,000 on African, £2,200,000 on others. In 1947 there were 951 non-whites at University.

would the Natives' Representative Council. From these major acts of subjugation, many minor discriminations and restrictions would flow. All this dressed up as being in line with 'the Christian basis of our National life' and backed by warnings that churches and societies which undermined the policy of apartheid and propagated doctrines foreign to the nation, would be checked, while the Nationalist Party would not tolerate interference from the outside world.

It was on this platform of apartheid that Dr Malan and the Nationalists[1] won the election. Afrikaner nationalism, cultivated over fifty years, nurtured in the hot-house of isolationism, fertilized with reminders of past defeats, watered by bitter tears of mourning for the excruciating loss of 26,000 Afrikaner women and children who died in British concentration camps in the Boer War – had won its ultimate victory. On the day of the election, the far-Right Ossewabrandwag advocated a powerful totalitarian administration and the reserving of southern Africa for the development of Afrikaner western culture only.[2]

This was the logical outcome of the British Government's handover of power to the white minority in 1910. The tragedy was that the Afrikaner tribe, which had fought so bravely for freedom, had neither the vision nor the daring to conceive that freedom *is* indivisible and to act on that conception. To preserve their inbred tribalism then, against all the world, would require a unique combination of cruel ruthlessness and silliness.

African leaders, so many of them imbued with humanitarian ideals, did not apprehend the power of the conviction that drove the Afrikaner Nationalists, a conviction in their inherent racial superiority which steeled them against the world and its revolutionary ideas of freedom and justice. As for the English-speaking whites, preoccupied with making money, they comforted themselves with the hope that the Nationalists must surely modify their anti-British and anti-Semitic tendencies now that they had power and the country's economy to consider. The business

1. Strictly speaking the National Party but commonly known as the Nationalists or Nats.
2. *Cape Argus.*

community advised, and their advice was listened to by the British and American Governments, 'Don't harden the hearts of the Nationalists.' It might have been expected that after the British Government's experience of the Boer War and the Act of Union it would have known that British generosity and diplomacy would at best be regarded as patronage and something to be exploited, but governments seem indifferent to the lessons of history. The few white liberals continued to think in terms of piecemeal reforms and, like the communists, were powerless to instigate change.

The Minister of Justice, C. R. Swart, gave English-speaking people their first severe jolt when he released convicted war criminals and repealed the National Security Regulations which had hitherto banned the 'Storm Troopers' – the Ossewabrandwag, and the Afrikaners' secret society – the Broederbond, from being state employees. Though the Ossewabrandwag did not last long, the far more sinister and powerful Broederbond soon permeated the Civil Service, the police, the armed forces, and the Cabinet itself. The bell was tolling all right but only the leaders of the non-whites and their friends in the white community were aware that it tolled for all men.

The first assault in restrictive legislation came when the new Minister of Labour, Ben Schoeman, announced the abandonment of the proposed recognition of certain Native trade unions and the suspension of training of Natives as building artisans because they were a threat to white builders – an obvious sop to the Afrikaner voter who feared competition with the African whose aptitude had been proved since he had been welcomed into more skilled occupations in the wartime industries. The Government quickly rejected the Fagan Report with its recommendations for the amelioration of the evils of the migrant labour system and reform of the pass laws. But most inhuman of all its acts was the suspension of school feeding for African children – by far the poorest, indeed often wholly dependent on this one meal a day for sustenance.[1] Soon bursaries for African medical students were stopped. Segregation

1. Costing about half a million pounds annually.

was enforced on Cape suburban railways. The policy of buying land for Africans was reversed and the reserves became static at 12·4 per cent of the countryside – 3¼ million morgen short even of the area earmarked under the 1936 Act.

In October 1948 the grimness of the outlook brought Africans together: A.N.C., A.A.C., Natives' Representative Councillors, Non-European Council of Trade Unions, and members of the Communist Party gathered in Bloemfontein to hear Dr Xuma gravely addressing them. South Africa stood at the cross-roads, he said, one leading to a greater, united and progressive country through inter-racial cooperation and mutual association, while the other led to national suicide – race and colour conflict arising from race bigotry. There was a new note in the speeches which J. B. Marks initiated when he pointed out that there would soon be 400 million people in Asia 'to come to our aid and apartheid will then be a thing of the past'. But calls for action were dissipated in procedural quarrels and rivalries and by the time the conference ended it was in disorder.

The All-African Convention and the A.N.C. had always been at loggerheads. The A.A.C. was still led by Professor Jabavu, and had been strengthened by notable African intellectuals and teachers in the Western Cape and Transkei: I. Tabata, A. C. Jordan and N. I. Honono. But it had virtually been taken over by Coloured teachers in the Cape, with pronounced Trotskyist leanings, whose organization – the Anti-Coloured Affairs Department – joined with the A.A.C. to become ultimately the (Trotskyist) Unity Movement. In print their record was powerful: militant resolutions repeatedly called for total boycotts. In practice they achieved little. It was as if the extremity of their programme on paper and in their journal, *Torch*, psychologically satisfied the need for action.

The A.N.C. was left to call for a mass struggle for national freedom. All differential institutions, including the N.R.C. and the Native Advisory Boards, must be abolished and the right of direct representation achieved – this would be done through a programme of action.

But for the moment this was mere talk and in January 1949

when the Natives' Representative Council eventually met again, it was to hear the new Government's reply to the Council's 1946 resolution calling for the abolition of discriminatory laws. The Government replied: the laws would continue; the N.R.C. would be abolished. The Council adjourned itself.

The U.N. Session was just over. The Government as always had been angered by the criticism of South Africa abroad. Xuma said people who 'state true facts' were said by white South Africans to misrepresent facts; the best way to stop this was for the Government to do away with inequalities based on colour. Eric Louw, South Africa's new Minister for External Affairs, who had taunted Smuts when he had been humiliated at the U.N., having himself set off with the bold announcement that South Africa would not stand as the accused at the U.N. but as the accuser, was just back, having listened to endless castigation of South Africa's policy from most of the nations of the world, both in its treatment of Indians and of the Africans of South-West Africa. Dr Dadoo had been an able lobbyist at the U.N. But the understanding so far built up between a few of the African and Indian leaders in the Union had not yet percolated to the ordinary people.

In Durban on Thursday, 13 January, as Africans and Indians were queuing for homeward-bound buses at the end of the day, an African boy and a young Indian quarrelled in the Indian market near by. The African slapped the Indian; the latter complained to his employer who followed the boy into the street and assaulted him. In the tussle the African's head accidentally crashed through a shop window and blood flowed. From the street crowded with bus queues Africans saw an Indian adult assaulting an African child, and they saw blood. They went berserk: all the years of oppression and of poverty that had packed frustration and rage tight down in the Zulu people reached bursting point and they turned on the nearest and easiest target, the Indians – who were the traders of the area and who felt superior to Africans, so that pin-pricks resulting from these incongruous relations had accumulated into bitter anger at Indian exploitation. Infuriated Africans burnt Indian houses by the score, clubbed their owners to death, raped their wives and daughters. Thousands of Indians fled. Arson and looting continued until police with army and naval forces moved in and began to put down the spreading riots.

Xuma, Marks, Dadoo and Maulvi Cachalia hastened to Durban, where they found Dr Naicker with the Meers, the Singhs and other Indian Congress leaders, already working in the distressed areas. There was deepest suspicion to break down on both sides, and the leaders set up a joint committee calling upon their people to devise ways of achieving mutual understanding and closer cooperation in their fight for freedom. Even during the height of the riots individual African and Indian families had helped and protected each other, and now, encouraged by their leaders, when tens of thousands of Indians sought refuge in temporary camps, African nurses helped them.

142 people had been killed – 50 Indians and, largely as a result of police and military action, 87 Africans, with one white and four people whose race could not be determined. More than a thousand were injured of whom 58 died, and hundreds of stores and homes were damaged or destroyed. These riots, therefore, were more terrible than the race riot in Chicago in 1919 when 15 whites and 23 Negroes were killed and several hundred injured, or than the Gold Coast riots in 1948 when 29 people were killed. Yet the Durban riots met with smug complacency from the authorities. Only the A.N.C., the Indian Congress, the Native Locations Advisory Boards, and a handful of academic, liberal, and left-wing whites, drew attention to the grievousness of the situation and to the underlying causes – poverty, lack of homes, inadequate transport, lack of opportunity. The Government's Commission of Inquiry admitted that 70 per cent of Natal's Indians lived below the bread-line and 'the slum areas on the fringes of Durban are a disgrace to any community which calls itself civilized'; that 23,000 Natives were living 'under the most sordid conditions'; yet it declared the Native was quite content with his lot, that certain Europeans told him he had grievances so he said he had, but really he was happy! It rejected the suggestion that recent speeches made by Dr Malan and other Ministers

propagated racial hatred. Instead it claimed: 'One of the most unsettling influences upon the Native mind is the fact that South Africa has a hostile Press abroad.' It rejected allegations that the police failed to suppress vigorously the initial outbreak of violence and that they failed to use tear-gas which would have considerably reduced the casualties. It agreed that while the riots were in progress 'certain Europeans actively incited the Natives to further acts of violence', and regarded the European women 'who went dancing up the street' urging the Natives to 'hit the coolies' as 'degraded specimens of their race'.

Among the causes of the disaster the Commission listed lack of discipline among urban Natives, bad precepts from Indian passive resisters and the racial characteristics of Indians and Africans, with resulting tension. Having indulged in some sarcastic asides against 'intellectuals' and the 'publicist, especially of British stock', who regarded the vote as the panacea for all evils, the Commission recommended 'constant vigilance'. It made no reference to past warnings from responsible officials and citizens that Durban was 'sitting on a volcano' of African slums and discontent. It said: 'Unfortunately South Africa is full of grave and exceedingly interesting problems, many of which are insoluble.'[1]

The Nationalists found proof in the disaster of their belief in the mutual antagonism of different races. The average white's opinion was that the riots showed how 'kaffirs' hated 'coolies', with general sympathy going to the 'kaffirs'. All the more remarkable was the magnanimity of Indian leaders throughout. And when an apprehensive calm had been restored, these men and women in the Indian Congress, shaken into a greater awareness of the complexity of race relations, recognized that understanding must be campaigned for; it could not simply grow on its own. The various leaders, Indian and African, addressed meetings at the International Club, and made joint declarations condemning violence. Out of this gradually came closer cooperation, and in both Natal and the Transvaal the

1. *The Durban Riots and After* by Kenneth Kirkwood. S.A. Institute of Race Relations.

A.N.C. was to acquire knowledge of Gandhian technique and benefit from Indian experience in organizing and fund-raising, while the Indians' movement gained in importance.

The shock of this tragedy might have brought the Government to consider the poverty of the people. Its own Commission had spoken frankly about this, and in Parliament Senator Brookes, the Ballingers and Sam Kahn, a communist lawyer recently elected as a Native Representative, regularly warned about the unrest that was rapidly building up because of the malnutrition, poverty and the resentment against recent laws providing even wider powers of deportation and detention of 'idle' or 'undesirable' Natives. In two years 345 policemen had been found guilty of assault on Non-Europeans under arrest, and another 52 were punished departmentally. But the Government was busy prohibiting mixed marriages and forcibly drawing South-West Africa within the orbit of apartheid by virtually incorporating the Mandated territory. Then it was rumoured that African women would have to carry passes, and in the mining town of Krugersdorp a riot was sparked off, to be followed by two further riots – one provoked by a police liquor raid, and the other by increased tram fares for Africans – all in the vicinity of Johannesburg. Six Africans were killed, a number of others injured and about three score policemen were injured.

Xuma declared: After a year of Nationalist rule, 'South Africa has chosen the road that leads to national suicide and racial clashes.'

10 1949–51: Action: The Youth Take Over

The Youth League decided the mood of the people was ripe. For too long the A.N.C. had been a talking shop for intellectuals, passing splendid resolutions, dispersing and returning the following year to find out whether the resolutions had been implemented, getting satisfaction out of the knowledge that they were discussing national affairs and enjoying the social get-together.

The question was, who should supplant Xuma?

They gave him one last chance. Sisulu, Mandela and Tambo called on him to discover his attitude. They gave the ultimatum that the Youth would only adopt him as a candidate if he accepted their Programme of Action with its clear concept of African Nationalism. He warned against isolationism. Tambo urged that they should be able to 'go it alone'. Xuma was anyway opposed to boycott and the interview ended with his angry repudiation: 'I don't want your vote. I won't be dictated to by any clique.'

They turned to the distinguished academic, Z. K. Matthews, who had played a considerable role behind the scenes in A.N.C. policy-making. He wished to concentrate on the Cape Congress. As the role of President-General required prestige and authority, reluctantly they reconsidered Xuma. Perhaps this inspired him in his rousing speech on Dingaan's Day, or perhaps it was the knowledge that away to the north, in Pretoria, the Nationalist Government and tens of thousands of Afrikaners were celebrating the Voortrekker victory over Dingaan and the Zulus, as they dedicated their massive monument to the past. In Bloemfontein, Xuma and Selope Thema solemnly led a singing procession of delegates along the dusty location roads to the Market Square. Then Xuma referred to the whites' celebration of the crushing of Dingaan, Dingaan who was a hero to Africans. At Blood River the Zulus, he said, had died like heroes for the freedom of their people, and the struggle should never be allowed to languish; it must be continued until Africans had a voice in their own affairs. When the true history of the country was written, he declared, Dingaan and his men would not be shown as murderers but as honest defenders of African freedom.[1]

The A.N.C. conference opened. The usual excitement of an election conference was intensified by the delegates' experience of eighteen months of Nationalist rule. Through the day they considered conditions. Among the guests in the audience was Dr James Moroka, who had so strongly defended African interests when Hertzog put through his Colour Bar law, and who was still a leader in the A.A.C. When the conference discussed the Programme of Action he warmly supported the boycott of the N.R.C. which, he said, was an illusion; people must not think they could depend on it. He approved the Programme of Action. His speech met the mood of the people, and Youth Leaguers felt he was just the man they were looking for. There was one question – whether he would agree. That night they put it to him. He was unwilling as Xuma was an old friend, but eventually he came to the conclusion that he must think only of the African people, and it was his duty to serve. By this time it was late at night and the conference was seething with excitement. Two names were put forward: Dr Xuma and Dr Moroka. The old men voted for Xuma, and the young – who by this time had come to be in the majority – for Moroka. The Youth League's *coup* had come off.

James Sebebuijwasegokgobontharile Moroka – his names meant 'I have come last, having been criminally enslaved, but will bring rain, peace and freedom to my people' – at fifty-eight years was a busy, successful doctor and land-owner. A great-grandson of Chief Moroka of Thaba 'Nchu, benefactor of Voortrekkers, James had attended the village school, but so

1. *Rand Daily Mail*, 17 December 1949.

backward was education in the Free State that he was already eighteen when he went on in 1909 to complete his primary school course at Lovedale College. His parents then sent him to the Royal High School in Edinburgh and within seven years he had qualified as a doctor. Back in Thaba 'Nchu, his expanding practice soon included Afrikaner patients. He worked in the Moroka Missionary Hospital for which he, a Wesleyan, had helped provide the land. It was the only African hospital with training facilities in the Free State; it also provided the only high school for boys. In 1930 he had studied surgery in Vienna, but back in South Africa, he found himself prevented by colour bar from using the only operating facilities existing in the Bloemfontein hospital.

Hertzog's Bills finally shook him into action, and the Youth had also noted his speeches in the N.R.C. at the time of the mine strike. They were willing to overlook his failure to boycott the Council. Both the left and right wings of Congress felt him to be the most suitable man for the Presidency: sincere and determined, if without much personality.

There had been so much concentration on the Presidency that the election of the Secretary-General was virtually overlooked and came as an anti-climax. When Calata adamantly declined to be re-elected, regarding the Programme of Action as too 'drastic', Walter Sisulu was suggested, and was elected by one vote.

The new Executive, a mixture of moderates, Youth League and communists, was sworn to vigorous execution of the Programme of Action. There must be total boycott of elections under the Act of 1936, and 'strikes, civil disobedience, non-cooperation' to bring about realization of African aspirations.[1] A Council of Action was set up.

No longer would the A.N.C. have Mayors and Bishops opening its annual conference. The Minister of Justice, C. R. Swart,

1. In the same year, 1949, Kwame Nkrumah defined techniques of ' positive action' for the Gold Coast which included ' the constitutional application of strikes, boycotts and non-cooperation, based on the principle of absolute non-violence'. (Speech on the Tenth Anniversary of the Convention People's Party.)

announced he was studying the natives' speeches and that, in company with Sir Percy Sillitoe, the chief of the British Secret Service, he was going into the question of the growth of communism. Africans saw Sillitoe's presence as one more act of collaboration between the British Government and the Nationalists.

Walter Sisulu decided he must give up his living as an estate agent; there could be only one task before him. His wife, Albertina, agreed; they would henceforth depend on her wages as a nurse, for although Congress offered him five pounds a month, this was soon in arrears. Sisulu was its first full-time Secretary-General. He found a cheap office – a poorly furnished dilapidated room reached through a dark entrance in the business area of Johannesburg. He found a typist and threw himself into the work, bringing to it a dogged drive and his experience of life which made up for what he had missed in formal education.

The A.N.C.'s first step in implementing the Programme of Action – a one day stoppage of work – was to be on 1 May. In March Dr Moroka visited Johannesburg, to be greeted with ovations and driven through the streets in a coach drawn by Sofasonke Mpanza's white horses as part of a Defend Free Speech Convention, organized by the Transvaal A.N.C. and the Communist Party. But no sooner was this successful occasion over than the Youth League were angered to find that the communists had virtually taken over their call for 1 May. In a series of furious clashes they broke up communist meetings. Their bulletin, *African Lodestar*, equated the doctrines of the Communist Party with the Ossewabrandwag, the Broederbond and the Sons of England, in a rejection of all foreign ideologies. It declared that since the workers were Africans and were oppressed primarily because they were African and only secondarily because they were workers, 'it is clear that the exotic plan of communism cannot flourish on African soil'.

On 1 May – in spite of Youth League opposition, of a Government ban on demonstrations and meetings, and of the arrival of 2,000 police in the Johannesburg area – more than half the African workers stayed at home, while in several areas people disregarded the ban on meetings. The police broke up gatherings and in the subsequent riots fired on the crowds and baton-charged. Sisulu and Mandela, who were hastening around the African townships trying to persuade people to go home, were almost shot. Eighteen Africans were killed and more than thirty, including three children, were injured. In the outburst of public protest, the greatest shock was expressed at the police failure to use tear-gas. Only two days after the shootings was it announced that the Rand police would be issued with it. In Pretoria police broke up an African wedding reception and broke into a funeral to drive away people condoling with relatives; one of the Africans turned to an English clergyman and remarked: 'They treat us like wild animals. Perhaps after all we can get nothing by peaceable means.'[1]

The common sorrow and rage brought about a hitherto unimaginable *rapprochement*: the Youth League decided to join with the Communist Party in a demonstration of mourning and protest. There were other hard-headed factors: laws intended to drive people apart were in fact driving them together. One was the Group Areas Act which divided race from race and tribe from tribe and particularly hit the Indians. The Population Registration Act hurt the Coloured people most; but above all there was the Suppression of Communism Bill, which, as the Youth League immediately realized, was in fact directed at a far greater target than the two thousand odd communists; its object was to crush the struggle for liberty.

All the same, when the A.N.C. and its Youth League came together with the Indian Congress and the Communist Party on 14 May, it was in an atmosphere of cool mutual suspicion. They formed a coordinating committee with Sisulu and Yusuf Cachalia as joint Secretaries and on the following Sunday, from Dr Moroka's house in Thaba 'Nchu, the A.N.C. sent out the first call in its history for a national stoppage of work. It was to be held on Monday, 26 June.

The Nationalists were stepping up their scare campaign. They

1. The *Star*. Interview with the Rev. J. A. A. Maund, subsequently Bishop of Basutoland.

had conveniently forgotten that in 1913 and again in 1919 Dr Malan had praised Marx and Lenin and said that 'socialism is but a passionate demand for justice' Since 1936 they had been urging that communism should be made a criminal offence. On 14 June, the Minister of Justice, Mr Swart, announced in the House of Assembly with 'a feeling of trepidation', that under communist leaders, 'a secret organization amongst the natives' on 'a particular day' would poison 'the people's water supplies' and see that there was no power and light. Others, he added, were being taught 'to be in such a position that they can murder people' on that day. But the *last* thing he wanted to do, he assured the House, was to make people 'panicky'.

On 26 June the response was tremendous. Scores of thousands of Africans with Indians protested against apartheid. In Johannesburg, despite intensive police patrolling, nearly three-quarters of the African workers stopped work, Indian shop-keepers closed their shops, location schools were almost empty, and nearly half the African bus drivers stayed at home. In Durban the Indians led the way; many factories and schools closed; even Indian waiters stayed at home, and although a number were dismissed and replaced by Africans – a punishment calculated to worsen relations – the good response diminished African suspicion that Indians were simply opportunists. In other cities there were token demonstrations and in Port Elizabeth the achievement was spectacular. All cargo work was halted, businesses closed, shops, restaurants, hotels, garages and hospitals were short-staffed. Three-quarters of the railway staff stayed away. As one African housewife said, 'You could only see a donkey in the streets.'

Three men were responsible for thus putting the Eastern Cape – strong in Kadalie's day – back on the map: Z. K. Matthews, James Njongwe and Robert Matji. Matthews's life story encompassed the experience of Eastern Cape intellectuals from the Boer War to the advent of the Nationalist Government. Born in 1901 in Kimberley, son of a mineworker who subsequently owned a tea-room in the location, Zachariah Keodirelang, ('What do I do for Him?') Matthews had been brought up to serve God and his people. As a teenager he had proudly accompanied Sol Plaatje, who was a cousin, to the meetings protesting against the Land Act. But for the next twenty years he concentrated on learning, and accomplished a series of 'firsts': the first African to graduate *in* South Africa from Fort Hare College in 1923; the first African Headmaster at Adams College in Natal; and (through private study) in 1930 first Bachelor of Laws in South Africa. While at Adams he married Freda Bokwe, a fellow teacher from a family of ministers, musicians and doctors. Life was austere on a salary of thirteen pounds a month and in a three-roomed iron house they brought up the first of their five children – Joseph, who was to become the politician of the family.

So far Matthews's desire to help his people had found its outlet in leading the African Teachers' Organization, along with a friend and fellow-teacher, Albert Lutuli. Then, from Adams in the steamy village of Amanzimtoti on the Indian Ocean, he went to Yale University, getting an M.A. with a thesis on Bantu Law and Western Civilization. Next he read Anthropology under Malinowski at the London School of Economics. He returned to South Africa after touring Europe and knew he was back when he set foot in Cape Town: it took him an hour to find a tea-room that was not for 'Europeans only'.

Hertzog deprived him of his vote at the very time when he was appointed Research Fellow of the International Institute of African Languages and Cultures in London. The Secretary of State for the Colonies put him on the Commission on Higher Education for Africans in East Africa and the Sudan. Though Matthews had joined the All-African Convention to campaign against Hertzog's Bills, his first fully political act lay in response to Xuma and Calata when they appealed to intellectuals to join the A.N.C. He was then a lecturer at Fort Hare College in Social Anthropology, Native Law and Administration; by 1949 he was Vice-Chairman of the Senate of Fort Hare.

Fort Hare – the African College comparatively isolated from other nationalities and from the life of cities – was fast breeding African nationalists: Joe Matthews and Duma Nokwe, both influenced by Oliver Tambo at St Peter's School, and Robert Sobukwe, were prominent in its Youth League. It was the Fort Hare Branch that evolved the A.N.C. salute – four fingers clenched to signify unity, determination, solidarity and militancy, with the thumb up for the horn of Africa – Cape Guardafui – symbolizing Africans in South Africa as part of the Continent. Professor Matthews was teaching students who would lead nationalist movements from Cape Town to Uganda. Many of them regarded him as annoyingly conservative. Both his personal and academic training caused him to recognize that there are two sides to most questions, and one of his friends, a poet, said he was like an essay by T. S. Eliot – full of buts, ifs and ands, because he was trying to be extremely truthful. All the same, he had helped to frame the Programme of Action, and his record could speak for itself.

In Port Elizabeth he encouraged a fine team. Its President was Dr Jimmy Njongwe who, as a medical student at the University of the Witwatersrand, had been an early member of the Youth League. A mercurial young man, some mistook his self-confidence for arrogance. He was an extremely hard worker both in his practice and in organizing the local A.N.C., in which he worked closely with the Secretary of the New Brighton branch, Robert Matji, who had had little schooling. Matji found in his home town, Pretoria, that the only education offered in trade unions or political organizations came from a white communist. From 1947 he had worked hard in a factory in Port Elizabeth, where he was proving to be a brilliant A.N.C. organizer.

New Brighton, where Matji and Njongwe lived, was the main African township with about 100,000 inhabitants. Lying about six miles outside Port Elizabeth, it had become the true centre of Xhosa political life since Umtata (seat of the Transkei Tribal Council) virtually provided a rubber stamp for the Government. Port Elizabeth was an expanding factory town with the highest concentration of industrialized Africans in the country. The resulting potential political strength was intensified by the fact that they were one people, the Xhosa, with a long history of struggle. Unlike the Zulus and Bapedi they had not been militaristic nor were their chiefs ever dictators. Their society, like that of the Bechuana and Basuto, had been administered through a democratic tribal gathering, the Nkundla. For a century their élite had been well educated in the missionary colleges of the Eastern Cape. However, although fine leaders such as Rubusana had emerged in the past, in the Cape they had, generally speaking, been lulled politically by the comparatively liberal atmosphere. As a result Xhosa leadership had found more scope in the Johannesburg activities of the A.N.C. With the formation of Youth League branches in Port Elizabeth from 1947, the radical leadership for which the people were now ripe had emerged and soon showed distinctive qualities, often passionately religious, with a deep sense of being part of the people, and self-effacing, yet including strong personalities among men and women.

By early July 1950, the Suppression of Communism Act had been driven through Parliament, becoming law on the last day of the Session; rendering the Communist Party illegal (it had already dissolved itself); throwing together any who tried to bring about a social, political or economic change in the country under the definition of 'Communist'; and empowering the Minister of Justice to 'name' any whom he thought communist, and to ban them from organizations, meetings or areas. The penalty was drastic: up to ten years' imprisonment for furthering the interests of a banned organization, up to three years for defying the Minister's ukase. Protests though hot and widespread were ineffectual.

Men who had previously belonged both to the Communist Party and the A.N.C. now concentrated on the latter. Meanwhile neither Moroka nor Matthews had yet resigned from the Natives' Representative Council. With other members they awaited an explanation of the policy of apartheid from the new Minister of Native Affairs. Dr H. F. Verwoerd made his debut before the Council at a time of a new incidence of police shooting. In the Witzieshoek Reserve, near Basutoland, land hunger and cattle culling had driven people to angry protest since 1947, protests which had reached a climax in inter-tribal fighting;

when police intervened, sixteen Africans were killed and forty injured. Dr Verwoerd addressed the Council aggrievedly about the bloodshed after the Government had in its kindness tried to provide services for the welfare of the people. He went on to lecture about apartheid. Did the Councillors want to collaborate, or did they want to lead the Bantu and the whites 'to a fate which will lead to a fight to the death?' The Government, he said, 'believes in the rule or mastery of the European in his area but believes equally in the rule or mastery of the Bantu in his area.' His concluding remark implied that the N.R.C. was not to be allowed to discuss matters of political policy. When he had gone the Council, after a long procedural wrangle with his deputy, unanimously adjourned *sine die*.

All this was academic: the Government had already announced its intention to abolish the Council. When Moroka and Matthews finally complied with the long-promised boycott, at the end of 1950, their protest had entirely lost its point. However they staged it just before Parliament actually abolished the N.R.C. in 1951.

On the death of General Smuts in September 1950, Moroka had said that in the heat of the bitterest political battles which Africans had ceaselessly waged against him, they had been 'irresistibly and continually conscious of the giant nature of his mind and soul'. Moroka and Matthews were consistent in emphasizing the A.N.C.'s desire for people of all races to remain in South Africa and to have freedom. But, as Matthews told a Youth Rally, 'We hate injustice. Injustice must be rooted out of this land.' Moroka was addressing packed meetings in the long quiescent Western Cape; Africans, particularly women, were flocking to gatherings in Bloemfontein; Sibande was slogging away on behalf of Bethal farm labourers and, after a useless exchange of correspondence with Verwoerd, was taking new visitors round the farms – this time a reporter and photographer from *Drum* magazine whose sensational report at last provoked a Commission of Inquiry. Along the Reef, Marks and Bopape were busy. In the Youth League's branches nationalism flourished.

Only in Natal was the new spirit of determination blocked.

The equivocal Champion, who for so long had rivalled Dube, would give no scope to young men. The Youth League determined to challenge him and chose as suitable replacement as President, Albert Lutuli, a popular Chief and an efficient teacher, who besides was consistent, an appealing quality after Champion's instability. He had the added attraction of being a newcomer to Congress politics; an idealist, a change from self-seekers. The view of one young man, that he was a 'good boy' of missionaries, was over-ridden.

However Lutuli was unwilling to stand because he did not want to displace Selby Msimang, a founder member of the A.N.C., long active in Natal, who was in the running. Nor did he want to set off any more of the personality quarrels that had for so long debilitated Natal. When Msimang said he was ready to stand down, Lutuli made one further point: 'I am only a greenhorn and not keen on involving myself when I know so little about politics.' The Youth League assured him of support. He was anxious to serve his people and so, he told them, 'If this is how you feel, I will try and do what I can.'

On the following day the election took place. Lutuli was elected by a small majority. Msimang was re-elected Secretary.

In Johannesburg meanwhile Walter Sisulu was busy with the Programme of Action. In considering what form the civil disobedience would take, not being a Gandhian he wanted it to be 'typically South African and militant'. He talked it over with Mandela, suggesting all races should be invited to join in the action. Mandela disliked this, fearing that Africans would be dominated by other races, but in time he came to agree.

On 17 June 1951, members of the A.N.C. Executive attended the huge funeral of Dr Seme, the founder of their Congress. The service was taken by the new and as yet untried Bishop of Johannesburg, Ambrose Reeves. As soon as it was over, the Congress Executive hurried from the cemetery. Forty years earlier Seme had planned an organization to 'defend' the African people's 'rights and privileges'. Now Moroka, Sisulu and their colleagues were planning to fight for those rights by non-violent methods. That afternoon they approved the outline of their coming campaign, and agreed to invite the South African Indian Congress to join them.

By December the Provincial Congresses had studied the blueprint – all but Natal where Champion, who had received the plans just before his defeat, had kept them to himself. Lutuli only learnt of the proposed campaign as he set off for the A.N.C.'s annual conference. All he could do was discuss it with other Natal delegates as they drove to Bloemfontein.

Once again a location hall was the scene of drama. But first, typically, the conference took its leisurely course, with only the Press arriving on time. The next two hours passed in delegates strolling or driving up until all 300, with a handful of reporters, packed themselves into the hot hall. Dr R. Bokwe, the Speaker of Congress, was ill, and the delegates elected Chief Lutuli to act for him. This was his first public appearance as an A.N.C. leader and he made a good impression.

The conference began with the anthem *Nkosi Sikelel' i-Afrika*. The dingy hall was transformed by the rich, solemn singing. A young English visitor, Anthony Sampson, representing *Drum* magazine, studied the passionate faces around him – a delicate little clergyman, straining his thin throat with singing; a ragged old man, swinging his arms to the rhythm, gazing rapturously at the rafters; a bulging woman shouting every syllable with indignation . . .

> *Lord Bless us,*
> *Us Your Children*

As the singing died away, Moroka rose quietly, lifted his hand, in the Congress salute, and shouted, 'Mayibuye' with a long rumble on the last sound 'Boo-Yáa' and the crowd roared back – 'Afriká!'[1]

After the formalities, the proposal was put: mass protests on 6 April 1952, Van Riebeeck Day, when white South Africans would celebrate 300 years of white rule. Unless the Government repealed six particular unjust laws, country-wide passive resistance would be launched to defy those laws.

1. *Drum.* A. Sampson.

The response was clamorous. It was hard for Lutuli to stand up and explain Natal's unreadiness. One angry woman yelled at him 'Coward!' In the overwhelming agreement that the campaign should be on, it was conceded that Natal should join in as soon as it was ready.

The news went round the world. The Africans of South Africa planned to defy the law.

Overseas it was observed that they had emphasized that their struggle was not directed against any race but 'against the unjust laws which keep in perpetual subjection and misery vast sections of the population'. Overseas it was recognized that the non-whites were struggling 'for the transformation of conditions which will restore human dignity, equality, and freedom to every South African'. But in South Africa the whites – even liberals, condemned the decision. Xuma, the anti-Indian Selope Thema, and Manilal Gandhi (the Mahatma's son who pursued an independent way in Natal), all expressed foreboding. The latter said: 'Congress leaders haven't got the true spirit of sacrifice.' The foretellers of disaster found support for their arguments a few days later when, at the height of the crime wave on the overcrowded, frustration-ridden Witwatersrand, riots broke out between law-abiding Africans and gangs, and between tribal groups; these resulted in the death of forty-one people and injury to hundreds.

Through 1951 the Government had piled one abuse of freedom upon another: making the Suppression of Communism Law retroactive, attacking trade unionists, withdrawing passports, setting up Bantu Authorities in a perversion of tribalism, initiating the prolonged legal onslaught on the entrenched clauses of the constitution with the object of removing Coloured people from the voters' roll, and mocking both the widespread protests of the non-whites and the vast Torch Commando protests of white citizens against violation of the constitution.

In this situation how could the leaders of the A.N.C. prove equal to their formidable task of maintaining non-violence?

11 1952: Defiance

From the A.N.C.'s shabby office in Johannesburg and from numerous small township houses there and in the main towns, the organizing began. The leaders would go from house to house in the African townships, explaining the plan, sometimes talking all through the night. As always there were the problems of being black in towns catering only for whites. As they travelled about the country perhaps the only train they could catch arrived late at night in a strange town – there would be no hotel for non-whites, no taxis for them, and no telephones in the majority of African houses in the outlying locations. So they would walk the miles out to the location, knock on a likely-looking door, sometimes to find themselves welcomed by an enthusiastic householder, sometimes rebuffed by the cautious. There were. occasions when Mandela or Tambo – sophisticated young lawyers – would find themselves literally stranded in the streets.

Moroka was studying Gandhi's writings. He practically abandoned his medical practice to travel from place to place. He firmly believed: 'I was doing the work not only for the African people but *everybody* in South Africa, irrespective of whether they liked it or not.' Congress had chosen non-violence because it recognized that the proportions of the different races and their permanence were of such a nature that violence would not solve the country's problems. 'We believe that a violent revolution would leave such an aftermath of bitterness and resentment,' Professor Matthews later explained, 'that indeed the country would be unstable.' He also gave as an historical reason, 'the example of the bitterness which has existed between the Afrikaners and the English-speaking people as a result of the

Boer War',[1] and added that Congress had many Christians among its members.

The leaders were aware that the Government would probably react with force. But the alternative – to resign themselves to the position – was unthinkable and they were heartened by the practical and moral effectiveness of Gandhi's struggle. Although disillusioned by white liberal leadership they hoped also that by choosing democratic and humane methods, white democrats would be encouraged to join them. But perhaps most important of all they aimed to rouse the spirit of their own people and give them confidence in their ability to destroy oppression through a direct challenge to the Government.

On 21 January 1952, Dr Moroka and Walter Sisulu wrote to the Prime Minister, Dr Malan, pointing to the long history of Congress's endeavour by constitutional methods to achieve the legitimate demands of the African people. Instead of responding to their desire for cooperation, the Government had increased repression to the point where it was 'a matter of life and death to the people'. For the A.N.C. to remain quiet would be a betrayal of trust. Among the laws that had aggravated the tense situation were the Pass Laws, Group Areas Act, Suppression of Communism Act, Separate Representation of Voters Act, Bantu Authorities Act, and Stock Limitation regulations. If the Government did not repeal these by 29 February, Congress would hold demonstrations on Van Riebeeck day as a prelude to implementing the plan to defy unjust laws.

A week later the Prime Minister's Secretary wrote to Sisulu reproaching him for writing to the Prime Minister rather than the Minister of Native Affairs, and questioning his claim to speak authoritatively on behalf of the body known to the Government as the A.N.C. 'It was self-contradictory,' he said, to claim that Bantu should be regarded as no different from Europeans, 'especially when it is borne in mind that these differences are permanent and not man made.' The Government had no intention of repealing the laws – in any event they were not 'oppressive and degrading', they were 'protective'. If Congress pursued the

1. Treason Trial Record.

course indicated, the Government would 'make full use of the machinery at its disposal to quell any disturbances and thereafter deal adequately with those responsible for initiating subversive activity'.

On 11 February, Moroka and Sisulu wrote again to the Prime Minister, remarking that the A.N.C. had never accepted the Native Affairs Department as the correct channel. The point at issue was not, they declared, a biological question but one of citizenship rights. They added there was no alternative for the African people but to embark on the campaign. They re-emphasized the intention to conduct it in a peaceful manner. If disturbances occurred, they said, they 'will not be of our making'.

On 6 April the whites, still locked in an angry constitutional and legal struggle over the entrenched clauses, uneasily united to celebrate the tercentenary of Van Riebeeck's arrival in the Cape. Dr Moroka compared their view of South Africa with that of the blacks. The whites, he said, saw a vast land they had opened up, the mineral wealth extracted, the granaries filled, the factories, the thousands of schools, universities, churches which daily called on the God of Christ; and they saw thousands upon thousands of black men who for three hundred years had ministered to them and by whose labour they had achieved this dazzling progress. 'But as we look back we see a picture of a different background and colour': how Christian Europeans took land from non-Christian non-Europeans; how the Fish River was made a bar between black and white in 1779; the first pass laws passed in 1809; Africans barred from skilled occupations in 1911; from land in 1913. 'We are forcibly reminded that politically we do not exist.'

In Freedom Square in Fordsburg, the Indian centre of Johannesburg, Moroka and Dadoo addressed a vast crowd. Behind them banners were thrust high – VOTES FOR ALL, MALAN REMEMBER HOW HITLER FELL, AWAY WITH PASSES. Under a bright autumn sun the crowd listened intently for five hours. Moroka frankly expressed the Africans' disillusionment with the Christianity of Europeans: 'To you was preached a religion of love and mutual trust', he told the crowd, and having 'trusted your neighbours', this very religion which came from Europeans 'has torn you asunder'. Government efforts to redivide the people into ethnic groups – this must be resisted – 'you are one race' – and the white man's oppression that had caused Africans to look on the Coloured people and the Indians as foreigners, while they in turn had been made to look down on Africans – this must be resisted and 'we must come together or we will not live to see the dawn of the day of freedom'.

Sisulu outlined the plan of action. Moroka called for 'a solemn oath that we will muster all our forces of mind, body and soul to see that this state of affairs, these crushing conditions under which we live, shall not continue any longer'. He called for 10,000 volunteers. And when he appealed for silence at the end of the meeting, immediately the people were quiet and went away.

All over the country people came together that day – in Port Elizabeth there was the greatest gathering when tens of thousands met in a religious service to pray for freedom. The Bloemfontein *Friend* commented that the country 'breathed a sigh of relief' at the peaceful nature of all these passionately felt demonstrations.

Nelson Mandela, who with Oliver Tambo had just set up a law practice in Johannesburg, was appointed National Volunteer-in-Chief, with Maulvi Cachalia his chief assistant. In Port Elizabeth at public meetings the leaders encouraged people to come forward and almost every street in New Brighton soon had someone to lead it, and enough small donations had been raised for Robert Matji to give up his job in a factory and do full-time secretarial work.

26 June, the anniversary of the A.N.C.'s first call for a stoppage of work in 1950, was chosen for the day.

On 31 May the A.N.C. held a banquet in Korsten – a non-white area of Port Elizabeth – to combine this announcement with a welcome to National leaders – among them Moroka, Sisulu and Naicker. The banquet was also a farewell to Matthews who was about to go to New York as Henry Luce Visiting Professor to the Union Theological Seminary.

The world Press took up the announcement that the Defiance

Campaign would begin on 26 June and reported the prayer meeting in New Brighton that followed on the Sunday, when 3,000 Africans met – other races could not go into the 'location'. There were no bands, no uniforms, no marching to whip up the masses. The black, green and gold Congress flag blew in a strong cold wind. Women led the singing until the leaders arrived and then all solemnly sang *'Nkosi Sikelel' i-Afrika'*. Old bearded men were there, small children in rags watched, and a praise singer, dressed in skins with a cowtail whip and a small assegai, chanted traditional praises to the leaders. From cars the police watched.

Professor Matthews told the crowd: 'Fighting for freedom is not a picnic . . . it is a very painful process and in that fight there is going to be suffering and even death.'

J. B. Marks, in a recorded speech, because the Government had both banned him from gatherings and restricted him to the Johannesburg area, said that the Government had placed Non-Europeans in a position from which there was no alternative but to fight back. And Moroka led the people in taking the pledge: to fight for freedom even though it brought them suffering and death. 'We solemnly pledge that we shall exert all our moral, physical and financial effort to attain our objective – the freedom of the oppressed peoples of South Africa.' He reiterated: 'We do not hate the Dutch or the English, but we hate the oppressive laws under which we are compelled to live.' There was a crying need, he said, to evangelize the Europeans. 'Our struggle is a mortal one, but it is waged on the principle of non-violence.'

At sunset the crowd dispersed and went home.

Among the gatherings about the country when Congress leaders and their followers took the pledge, was a small meeting in the bare rooms of the A.N.C. office in Durban in the busy Indian shopping centre. The new President of the Natal Congress, Chief Lutuli, was about to make his first political act. He said to his Executive, 'Look, we will be calling upon people to make very important demonstrations and unless we are sure of the road and prepared to travel along it ourselves, we have no right to call other people along it.' M. B. Yengwa, a Youth Leaguer who had just become Secretary of Natal and who had been inspired as a boy by his father's imprisonment in the 1919 anti-pass campaign, described what happened after that: 'We all said we were prepared and he said he too was prepared, and he asked us to pray. We gave our pledge and we prayed.' Lutuli at that moment was transformed from being chief into a political leader. Previously over-conscious of his duties as a Chief, after that night-long session of discussion, dedication and planning, he was, according to Yengwa who worked closely with him, 'not irresponsible, but prepared to damn the consequences as long as he was advancing the cause of the movement'. Lutuli's conscious decision to take part in the Defiance Campaign had become the turning point in his life.

All this time the forces of opposition were building up, not only from the Government and the United Party but from white liberals who continued to try to dissuade Congress leaders, arguing that their plans were too ambitious and were inviting the Government's fierce retaliation. And there was strenuous opposition from certain groups of Africans. Selope Thema led a short-lived splinter movement, the National-Minded Bloc, which denounced the campaign as a capitulation to foreign left-wing elements and declared that Africans were not organized for civil disobedience. But he was old, increasingly unreliable, the editor of a white-owned newspaper, and his influence was negligible. The Non-European Unity Movement, which might have been expected to back this call to action if its own belligerent words were to be taken seriously, automatically opposed anything the A.N.C. initiated. But its membership was small, largely confined to the Cape, and its opposition had little if any effect. Then to the enchantment of the Government, a 'Bantu National Congress' was formed. It too rejected the African National Congress campaign and allied itself approvingly with the Government. One Nationalist member of Parliament claimed that it had two million Bantu members. The House of Assembly was not told that this group of Native herbalists had held one meeting at which its audience consisted of six Africans and one white; nor was the House told when its leader was imprisoned for theft and forgery.

The most serious handicap to the campaign was the Government's naming of 500 people under the Suppression of Communism Act. The first to suffer were Marks, Bopape, Kotane and Johnston Ngwevela, President of the Cape Western Congress and a stalwart since the early twenties, all of whom were banned for life from membership of the A.N.C. Dr Dadoo was similarly banned from the Indian Congress.

Government action might handicap; it did not hinder. These men promptly volunteered to be the first defiers. During June they addressed meetings, were promptly arrested and imprisoned for several weeks. And in June, Mandela, having toured the country, went through the enrolment of volunteers with Maulvi Cachalia. A code of discipline in remaining non-violent was put to each volunteer, as well as a code of conduct – volunteers should be erect and alert, with a high standard of cleanliness and the avoidance of rowdiness or any semblance of drunkenness. In Port Elizabeth, Dr Njongwe appealed to the public not to participate spontaneously because the campaign must be carried out by disciplined volunteers, who would 'submit to arrest willingly and with gladness in their hearts, knowing that ours is a fight against malnutrition, high infantile mortality, landlessness, deprivation, humiliation, oppression, and against destruction of family life and faith in Christianity as a way of life.'

The Parliamentary session ended – a session turbulent from the Government's persistent attacks on the constitution, condemned for the ousting of former communists from various councils, including Sam Kahn from Parliament, and the banning of *The Guardian*,[1] the left-wing newspaper.

On 25 June, in Port Elizabeth, African women held prayers through the day and night. This was in the tradition of women meeting to pray for their husbands and sons before they went out to action.

Very early on 26 June, a cold, midwinter morning, the first

---

1. *The Guardian* was promptly succeeded by *The Clarion*, while Kahn was promptly succeeded by Brian Bunting (son of Sidney), similarly elected by a big majority by non-whites; and when the Government ousted him, Ray Alexander, another former communist, was elected, and likewise ousted.

batch of volunteers moved out of New Brighton township, accompanied by a crowd singing 'What have we done, we the African people?' The twenty-five men and three women all wore Congress armbands and, shouting 'Mayibuye, Afrika!' went through the EUROPEANS ONLY entrance to the New Brighton railway station. Most of them were young – in their twenties – but two were over forty. Florence Matomela, a reviver of the Women's League, mother of five, a militant house-wife, was amongst them. As soon as they went through the entrance a white police sergeant came and told their leader, Raymond Mhlaba, A.N.C. official and also a communist trade-union organizer, that they were contravening the law. He replied that it was a political act and deliberate. The police arrested them and escorted them to the other side of the station which, they noted with satisfaction, meant using the EUROPEANS ONLY bridge. A trainload of Africans drawn up at a platform shouted encouragement and gave the thumbs up sign. Mhlaba was sentenced to thirty days' imprisonment and the others to fifteen days.

The campaign had begun. In the Transvaal Nana Sita, the gentle Gandhian President of the Transvaal Indian Congress, led forty-two Africans and ten Indians into Boksburg location, entering it without permits. They sang 'Jan van Riebeeck has stolen our freedom' as they approached the waiting police. They were arrested. That night in Johannesburg the A.N.C. held a meeting which dispersed at eleven o'clock, the curfew hour after which Africans required 'special' passes. The volunteers moved into the streets of the city's commercial area. Police, tensely waiting, came forward to arrest them. Willingly, singing 'Nkosi Sikelel' i-Afrika', they clambered into the police vans and were driven off to the cells. Altogether 106 people were arrested that day in the Transvaal.

During July more than 1,500 men and women defied – volunteers whom the historian Eric Walker described[1] as being generally decent church-going people, who preceded their act of defiance by prayer-meetings. In Bethal, Sibande led volunteers

1. In *A History of Southern Africa.*

to jail and was imprisoned for a month. Leaders' wives took part and went to prison – for instance Mrs Njongwe, a nurse about to have a baby; while in Cradock, Mrs Calata, leader of the Mothers' Union of Loyal African Women, led women praying on a street corner. As ever, there were lamentable gaps in organizing in the Transkei and the mines. Although Sisulu had visited the Transkei, it was under the influence of notoriously cautious chiefs and teachers, either a-political or members of the moderate Voters' Association or the Unity Movement.

But elsewhere the campaign mounted, stimulated by Government threats but also by events in other parts of the continent: in Central Africa the recently formed African National Congresses and the chiefs were hotly opposing Federation, and in West Africa countries moved towards self-government.

During August more than 2,000 volunteers went to jail, including Cape Town's first batch.

The arrest of the national leaders of the campaign was a great spur for volunteers. Moroka, Sisulu, Mandela, together with Dadoo, the Cachalias, Marks, Bopape and several others, were accused of defying bans under the Suppression of Communism Act. They appeared for the preparatory examination in a court crowded out and surrounded by people singing Defiance Campaign songs. The case was adjourned for several months.

September found 2,358 resisters going to jail and the Eastern Cape's leaders – Njongwe, Matji, and Mrs Matomela, among them – arrested under the Suppression of Communism Act and sentenced to nine months' hard labour, suspended for three years. The news of their arrest set hundreds more defying. Port Elizabeth and East London were responding magnificently, women as well as men.

The discipline and humour, the rich singing of the volunteers as they went into the EUROPEANS ONLY sections of railways stations and post offices, and from there were driven off to prison, won the spontaneous admiration of the outside world. The *New York Times*,[1] in doubting whether the saintly method of passive resistance could be applied for long, warned

1. 23 August 1952.

that under the Nationalist Government South Africa was headed for 'shipwreck', and that a solution to the country's problems based on pure racialism was 'false, immoral and repugnant'. The *Economist*[1] commented that 'the dispossessed have found a powerful totem: nationalism.' But most significant was the report in the London *Times*[2] that delegates of the Asian and Arab States in the United Nations had unanimously called for a debate on the racial policy of the South African Government for its 'flagrant violations of human rights involving the arrest of 4,000 people engaged in passive resistance against the segregation laws'.

Lutuli was ready to lead Natal into the campaign by the end of September. Preliminary meetings had been held separately from the Natal Indian Congress out of uncertainty as to whether Zulus were yet ready to cooperate with Indians. Caution was confounded by the great attendance of Africans at meetings and processions, led by Zulus and Indians, although the actual number of volunteers was not high. Their technique in Durban was that used in the 1946 passive resistance: meetings were held in the Indian part of the city as people left their offices at the end of the day. On a platform made of two lorries backed together, Lutuli would lead the singing in his mellow baritone: 'Thina Sizwe! Thina sizwe esinsundu' – We Africans! We Africans! –

> *We cry for our land*
> *They took it. They took it,*
> *Europeans*
> *They must let our country go. . . .*

Or Yengwa, his face lit up, led them in singing –

> *Hey! Malan, open the jail doors, we want to enter,*
> *we volunteers . . .*

with the chanting pronunciation of 'voluntiya'! These folk songs had become a part of the campaign and often were composed in jail. The rhythm and the mime that went with them was infectious, and some were sung to familiar hymn tunes or, like

1. 16 August 1952.   2. 13 September 1952.

Mayibuye Afrika, to a popular tune like *Clementine*. In Durban they aroused people to an exultant mood as they escorted volunteers through the main streets to the railway station. When the municipality prohibited meetings there, Lutuli and Naicker promptly announced a gathering, and with some supporters were arrested; not for the first time in the campaign police had to seek their help in dispersing the surrounding crowd. But after being charged in court, the case was adjourned indefinitely, the accused released.

Not long after, Lutuli was sent for by the Secretary of Native Affairs, Dr W. W. M. Eiselen, who politely asked him, as a Chief, to account for his participation in the campaign – for 'asking people to break the law'.

Lutuli firmly opposed this interpretation: 'Not to *break* the law,' he declared. 'To signify in this way our rejection of a particular *kind* of law.'

But Eiselen rejected his explanation that he had kept Congress politics apart from his duties as a Chief. 'You can't be a Jekyll and Hyde,' was his retort as he told Lutuli to decide: he must resign from Congress or from the chieftainship.

Lutuli's reply was to go as guest of honour to the Transvaal A.N.C.'s Annual Conference in Lady Selborne township, Pretoria. From a platform draped with the Congress flag, under posters proclaiming FREEDOM FROM WANT, FREEDOM OF THE PRESS, APARTHEID TO H . . ., he addressed a cheering crowd of thousands.

Early in October the Campaign was intensified to focus United Nations attention on South Africa. The A.N.C. was at its strongest – 100,000 paid-up members, whereas a few months earlier there had been only 7,000. The white-owned African Press, usually critical of the A.N.C., had switched from scepticism to encouragement as it found messages of support for the Campaign pouring in from all over the world. In servants' quarters, in factories, in villages, Africans excitedly discussed it. The Afrikaans Press sometimes verged on hysteria; the English-speaking newspapers increasingly carried pictures and reasonable reports.

The Government, finding that their attempt to cut off the head of the resistance by arresting the leaders did not have the desired effect, were discussing new laws to enable them more easily to get at the instigators. But a hopeful rift in the white front was apparent when, in Johannesburg, the new Anglican Bishop, Ambrose Reeves, joined with the four Members of Parliament representing Natives and with academics and other liberals, in calling for a return to the old Cape liberal policy.

October was the peak of the Campaign. For the first time in the history of modern South Africa the Africans' militant achievement had kept the initiative in their hands, initiative hard-won through discipline and self-sacrifice. Only one thing could rob them of such initiative: violence.

On 18 October, at New Brighton railway station near Port Elizabeth, two Africans who were alleged to have stolen a pot of paint were shot at by a white policeman. After firing twenty-one shots the policeman withdrew, leaving an enraged crowd attacking the station. In the subsequent riot seven Africans and four Europeans were killed (none of them police), and twenty-seven people were injured and much property damaged. The A.N.C. immediately condemned the violence, expressing sympathy for all the families who had suffered, and demanding a judicial inquiry, while Sisulu went down to make a personal investigation. Government refused the demand. Everywhere in the Eastern Cape the police were reinforced. One section of the A.N.C. in New Brighton called for an indefinite strike. The authorities' immediate reaction was to ban meetings in a wide area, to enforce a stricter curfew and – a most provocative act – for the first time in those parts to enforce influx control and the pass laws. Throughout the country protest meetings were held. Meanwhile Moroka and Njongwe ordered that the A.N.C. strike call be modified to a one-day strike; this turned out to be a remarkable success – a 90 per cent stay-away according to the most restrained among the white newspapers. Important employers – the South African Railways and the Municipality – promptly dismissed thousands of African workers.

Near by, in East London, the ban on meetings set off a new

and more ghastly riot. A prayer meeting was charged by the police, the crowd flung stones, the police fired and, leaving several dead and many wounded, drove away through the location, firing indiscriminately as they went. In a paroxysm of fury the crowd turned and killed the first whites they saw – a nun who was a doctor coming to help the wounded, and an insurance agent. Once again the A.N.C. demanded a judicial inquiry, but the Government even snubbed a similar demand from the Parliamentary Opposition.

On 8 November, in Kimberley, new riots occurred. Fourteen Africans, including two women, were shot dead by the police, and thirty-five wounded. In the thick of helping to alleviate the chaos and suffering that followed were two local Congress leaders – Arthur Letele, a doctor (the only one for 30,000 people) and Mr Sesedi, a butcher and an old man. It was a horrifying experience as they drove around seeing the injured people. People looked mad, with a fire in their eyes; even people Letele knew quite well looked crazy, and he had to tell them to keep away so that he could get to the injured and the corpses. The bullets were whizzing past. Teenagers were milling around saying, 'They killed about ten of ours, let's get theirs.' Then they turned to attack the clinic and the new crêche, the Municipal beer hall and the Administration Offices. What added to Letele's misery was that this should happen in the middle of the Defiance Campaign, destroying much of the A.N.C.'s work just as they had won so much support. On the day after the riot a convoy of police drove into the location armed to the teeth. Letele was among those arrested. He was charged under the Suppression of Communism Act as well as with incitement to public violence. The police tried to prove that the A.N.C. was involved in the rioting, and failed totally. The second charge against Dr Letele was dropped; on the first charge he was sentenced to nine months' imprisonment, suspended for two years.

In an inquiry made by the Kimberley City Council, several witnesses spoke of low wages, restriction on movement, denial of the right to sell their labour in the best market and the need for traditional home brewing rather than recourse to beer halls and illicit shebeens, as causes of the frustration driving people to take the law into their own hands.[1]

Government refusal to appoint a judicial Commission of Inquiry into all these riots – including one on the Rand – strengthened a growing belief that *agents provocateurs* had set the Port Elizabeth and Kimberley riots off to provide a pretext for suppressing the passive resistance and to alienate sympathy for the Defiance Campaign.

African support for the Campaign continued despite harsher sentences which included some defiers being sentenced to strokes as well as imprisonment. In October 2,254 went to jail. In London distinguished men appealed for funds to assist the families of the defiers. At the U.N., despite angry repudiation by the South African Government, a resolution was passed setting up a Commission to inquire into apartheid: the first direct international onslaught on apartheid as such, a fresh encouragement to the defiers.

Another source of encouragement was Lutuli's reaction when the Government announced his dismissal from the chieftainship. Declaring that he would remain in the struggle, he added that he had embraced the non-violent technique because 'I am convinced it is the only non-revolutionary, legitimate and human way that could be used'. He only prayed that his resolve should be strengthened and that he should not be deterred by 'ridicule, imprisonment, concentration camp, flogging, banishment and even death'; for the future might bring any of these.

Although Lutuli's statement had a profound effect on certain liberals – on Alan Paton, the author, for instance – a Congress appeal for white support in its campaign aroused only a few left-wingers in Johannesburg and Cape Town, among them Bettie du Toit, a young Afrikaner trade unionist; Albie Sachs, a law student and son of the trade unionist Solly Sachs; Freda Troup, daughter of a respected Pretoria family and author of a book on the Hereros' cases before the United Nations; and also Patrick Duncan, son of the former Governor-General.

1. The *Star*, 23 January 1953.

Their action in defying together with Africans and Indians – who now included Gandhi's son, Manilal – gave a new lift to the Campaign.

Even when the Government proclaimed penalties of up to a £300 fine or three years' imprisonment with lashes for incitement to break the law, volunteers were ready to test the Proclamation. One was Lilian Ngoyi, a forty-year-old widow, whose whole life had been a struggle against poverty. After only a year in high school she had been compelled to get a job to support her asthmatic father, her mother and brother. She could remember, as a child, delivering washing for her mother to a white family, who refused to let her and her baby brother come into the house; later she saw the woman take her dog into the house. This haunted Lilian. 'Why could an African child not get into this woman's house and there is a dog in her house?' During her family's frequent prayers she wondered, 'Something is wrong. The more we pray the more poor we are.' Years later when the Defiance Campaign began she felt inspired; but when she wanted to offer to defy her daughter was in hospital and her mother asked, 'How can you when your child is ill?' So Lilian, thinking back to Abraham and Isaac, called her mother outside and showed her all the lights in Orlando East where they lived and said, 'If all the children in those lights can be saved and my one dies, which would be better?' Her mother replied: 'Even if yours dies, if the rest are saved.'

So Lilian went with four other women into the European section of the Johannesburg Post Office to test the new Proclamation. There she wrote a telegram to the Minister of Justice saying he must remember that South Africa had been a peaceful place and would he please withdraw his proclamations; if not, he should remember what happened in Germany to Hitler and in Italy to Mussolini.

A white man who was standing alongside said, 'Annie, I think you are in the wrong department. Natives don't come this side.'

So she explained, 'It is because I am sending a telegram to the Minister of Justice and because of his apartheid I must do it this side.'

The others were doing the same. A policeman took her roughly by the shoulder, and said, 'You are under arrest.'

She said, 'You need not mishandle me, because I know I am.'

He ordered them all into a van and they were taken to the cells. They had never been in jail before and it was a horrible evening. In court they were defended by Oliver Tambo, but after three remands they were discharged. Her daughter recovered.

At the beginning of December, 280 defiers were jailed. On 2 December, Moroka, Sisulu, Mandela and others were tried under the Suppression of Communism Act for their leadership of the Campaign. What should have been the climax to the resistance was soured by a serious disagreement between Moroka and the others. As he objected to the inclusion of former communists among the lawyers assisting the A.N.C., he had independently engaged a defence counsel. In a campaign of this nature such an action was unheard of. The younger A.N.C. leaders attributed his action to lack of political awareness and believed that he had overestimated A.N.C. power and his own security as an eminent doctor whom the Government would never touch, so that once he was arrested the wind was taken out of his sails. He maintained it was due to his uneasiness over communist influences from the Indian Congress.

He was the only leader to take the witness stand. He pointed out that he was totally against communism, that his aim throughout his career had been to bring about harmonious relations between the races, that he had even contributed funds to enable needy white students to train as doctors and, finally, that he had cancelled the indefinite strike in the Eastern Cape as he had feared it would cause friction and possibly bloodshed. His appearance in the witness box was another blow, for his fellow accused had understood that in conformity with the Campaign procedure he would not give evidence. Nor did he achieve any mitigation.

The judgment contained some significant remarks: Mr Justice Rumpff said the charge had 'nothing to do with communism as it is commonly known' and, in sentencing all twenty men to nine months' imprisonment with hard labour, suspended for two years, added: 'I accept the evidence that you have consistently advised your followers to follow a peaceful course of action and to avoid violence in any shape or form. . . .'

On top of this sentence the Government issued a spate of orders banning leaders – fifty-two of them, including some of the ablest organizers. This meant that for the rest of their lives they were banned from taking any part in the A.N.C.'s activities or, in the case of people of other races, in activities of their respective organizations. Penalties for infringement were up to ten years' imprisonment. In addition there were other equally harsh restrictions: Nelson Mandela was confined to the Johannesburg district for two years and was banned from gatherings. Bopape was restricted nightly to Brakpan and could only be in Johannesburg during business hours to carry on the estate agency that he and J. B. Marks had established since they had both been banned from political activities. 'Gatherings' was a term increasingly widely interpreted.

The campaign ground to a halt. Time was needed to reorganize. In any event the annual conference was imminent; five replacements were needed for banned Executive members, but most important was the generally acknowledged desire for Dr Moroka's replacement.

12 1953–5: Police Persecution but Talk of Freedom

Somewhat to everyone's surprise, the comparatively obscure Albert Lutuli was elected. During the lobbying and counter-lobbying his Natal supporters had determinedly pushed his qualities. His maturity and natural authority and his firmness in withstanding Government pressure were great assets.

Moroka, with good grace, was to say: 'Nothing shapes a man better than the A.N.C. I became quite a new man after I became a member. I had more interest in the welfare of the people. The A.N.C. makes life really worth living. You feel that you are alive.'

Lutuli came into the leadership as his people faced yet more draconian laws: Africans in Sophiatown, a suburb of Johannesburg, were threatened with enforced removal from their homes, the Government was forcing through Bantu Education, a perversion of education, new bans were clearly imminent. People were asking how Lutuli would do and whether he was just a figure-head.

As for his own feelings, apart from the honour, he knew he was in for a policy of militancy. He later recalled: 'I had already been hit hard by the Government but I felt this was a task one had to undertake in the interests of what is right. If you are physically able to carry on, you can't say "no" to a liberation task. It was an overwhelming call of the people and the voice of the people is sometimes the voice of God.'

One thing was certain – he fully endorsed the Programme of Action and regarded the Defiance Campaign as a 'sensible form of struggle'. Had Congress followed a rigid racialist line he would never have been a member; but he was happy to follow its non-racial, non-violent policy.

Albert John Mvumbi ('continuous rain') Lutuli at fifty-five was a solid, imposing man. Born in Rhodesia, where his father had been on an evangelical mission, he had been brought up in the Lutuli family's ancestral home at Groutville in the heart of Natal's sugar plantations. Although his uncle, Chief Martin Lutuli, had led the Natal Congress early in the century, Albert's own background was remote from politics. From absorbing Zulu traditions in the household of his uncle the Chief, he had become one of the first three African instructors in the Teacher Training College at Adams, in Natal, and with Dr Edgar Brookes, the Principal, had helped establish a music school. At Adams he married a fellow-teacher, Nokukhanya Bhengu. They had seven children. In the thirties tribal elders lobbied him to accept the Groutville chieftainship but he loved teaching and at first resisted, but after two years he gave in, for he felt it might be a call of the people; certainly it was even more meagrely paid a job than teaching. He took over in lean years when sugar farming was hard hit, and he proved himself a conscientious chief who revived and led the Groutville Cane-growers Association. He had visited India and the United States to attend missionary conferences, was on the South African Christian Council, and had the brief experience of being a member of the Natives' Representative Council.

He thus brought to Congress the qualities of a reflective man of some authority. What he lacked in experience of urban society he made up by his real contact with rural people. And he had a good team of young men in Natal.

Walter Sisulu was re-elected Secretary-General. His success in organizing the Defiance Campaign had increased his self-confidence and he was more mellow; apart from him, Tambo, Njongwe and Mandela and others of the Youth League's effective members, were now on the Executive. However, enthusiasm for the Defiance Campaign was dissipating. Yet in Port Elizabeth 15,000 people met Lutuli and assured him that their spirit was still strong, and there the M Plan which Mandela had conceived, which meant street to street and house to house canvassing and organizing, was being carefully implemented.

As soon as the parliamentary session opened, Swart enacted the Public Safety Act and the Criminal Law Amendment Act, empowering him to suspend all but a few laws whenever he regarded any part of the country in danger, and making it an offence for anyone to take part in defiance of the law. The law embraced an editor of a newspaper reporting an incident inciting people to break the law; likewise anyone giving financial aid to defiance organizations. The penalties were up to three or five years' imprisonment, or fines of £300 or £500, possibly with ten lashes.

The United Party opposition approved these laws in principle. As in the case of Hertzog's Riotous Assemblies Act of 1930 and Malan's Suppression of Communism Act of 1950, the majority of parliament approved the extension of Nationalist tyranny.

Thus ended the Defiance Campaign.

The Campaign had been an amazing success: of the 10,000 volunteers called for, more than 8,500 had gone voluntarily to jail despite the intimidating effect of police action, of dismissal by employers, and the propaganda of the bulk of the Press and of the radio; some teachers who had done little before had thrown up their jobs to defy; the United Nations had been inspired to discuss apartheid and the Press of the world had taken the non-white challenge to oppression more seriously than ever before. Even the Government – instead of talking about *Baasskap* – began to talk about Bantustans and self-government for the Bantu. Congress prestige was enhanced; its membership greatly multiplied to more than 100,000. Yet the unjust laws remained intact: indeed, they had been augmented.

Perhaps the most significant gain was the immensé lift in Africans' self-respect. While Congress leaders had learnt that the ordinary working people were the salt of the movement and were politically conscious, the people for their part felt, as one of them put it, Congress had 'shown itself like a lion'. Yet, by the ruthlessness of the Government, the lion had been curbed.

At least some whites had been moved to identification with the Congress. Towards the end of 1952 Oliver Tambo and Yusuf Cachalia, representing their respective organizations, with Cecil

Williams, a theatre producer active in the left-wing Springbok Legion, had invited white sympathizers to a meeting held in the Johannesburg Cathedral hall. They hoped for an organization to educate white opinion and work alongside the A.N.C. but soon a division was precipitated when the left-wing raised the issue of the A.N.C.'s call for universal franchise. There were those not yet prepared to support this, who later helped to found the Liberal Party, which affirmed the dignity of every human being, his right to develop, and his right to participate in political activities, but with certain qualifications attached to a common franchise. The others, many but not all former communists, formed the Congress of Democrats (C.O.D.). Their constitution was based on the Universal Declaration of Human Rights. The A.N.C. resisted a move by one of them to form a united, non-racial organization, believing that at this stage each race could better work among its own community, but ready to work alongside the others. On the other hand, though they also welcomed the formation of the Liberal Party, its qualified franchise aroused suspicions.

The Nationalists, meanwhile, had been returned to power with an increased majority.

They promptly slapped bans on Lutuli and other leaders. He was restricted for a year. After the high confidence generated by the Defiance Campaign, demoralization caused petty divisions. At this moment Professor Matthews returned from New York. He felt constructive, unifying action was imperative, and to a crowded conference in the Cape he made what was to be a historic suggestion, that the A.N.C. call a 'National Convention, a Congress of the People, representing all the people of this country, irrespective of race or colour, to draw up a Freedom Charter for the Democratic South Africa of the future'. Thus people would turn from 'sterile and negative struggles to a positive programme of freedom for all in our lifetime'.

From division and despondency the conference was lifted to an exultant mood – responding not only to Matthews's concept but to the singing of James Calata's choir of young people he had trained and for whom he composed the songs. As the delegates joined in, the crowded hall was filled with music. People offered themselves for action then and there.

Soon after, in November 1953, there was further cause for rejoicing. Johnston Ngwevela, the Cape Town leader, challenged the sentence imposed when he had defied his ban under the Suppression of Communism Act. Having lost in the Cape Supreme Court, he went to Appeal in Bloemfontein, and won. As the Minister of Justice had not given him the opportunity to make representations before being banned, the conviction could not stand.

Throughout the country all banned leaders were suddenly free! Meetings celebrated the victory and the hitherto-banned made jubilant speeches, knowing they could safely do so until Parliament met in 1954 when it would amend the law.

At the A.N.C.'s annual conference, held in the pleasant Eastern Cape town of Queenstown, Chief Lutuli, free to utter again, was cheered. Delegates excitedly agreed to call an early Congress of the People to work out a Freedom Charter.

A great stir was caused by the appearance of Walter Sisulu and Duma Nokwe back from five months' visit to communist countries; Sisulu wearing a high-buttoned Chinese jacket and Nokwe in a 'peace' cap. Sisulu had been to China and to the Soviet Union. His report aroused various emotions: one said it was 'full of fabrications about the benefits Africans would get'. another described it as a straightforward report on conditions· Duma Nokwe – a former teacher studying to become an advocate – described his visit to Poland and the Festival of Youth, The general reaction was more tolerant than twenty-five years earlier, in Gumede's day. Some felt it useful for leaders to visit foreign capitals, while those knowledgeable about international politics were divided between appreciation of the Soviet Union's role at the United Nations and the feeling that Russia's help was of limited effect even at the U.N.

Sisulu has described how in Israel, their first stop, for the first time they were able to go into hotels and tea-rooms and to meet 'big people'. They were interested in the *kibbutzim*. In Rumania he was a guest of Government ministers. It was China that affected him most profoundly. He felt the peasants were the same as many Africans, 'even the type of building was like those in Vrededorp or Sophiatown'. People would say, 'This is where we used to live and this is where we live now and this is the new life we are now leading.' This excited him when he thought of the slums around Johannesburg; he felt people were working for the type of life they wanted to live. The tremendous industrialization was 'not like tribal chiefs ordering regimental labour, people were building it up because they believed in it.' Underlining his impressions was the fact that, 'you hear propaganda in South Africa and then you get there and see it's different and you get disgusted with people distorting the picture'. He had misgivings about the 'personality cult'; Congress had always tried to avoid it. He felt there was in the Soviet 'too much of Stalin in everything'.[1]

He returned to South Africa via London knowing that the greater part of the world was on the side of his people and that a country like China, overcrowded and far poorer than Africa, was working its way to prosperity. At the age of forty-one for the first time in his life he had been consistently treated as a dignified human being instead of as a 'native'.

Those whites who had experienced his suspicion were conscious of a change: he had come to realize that an African nationalist's tendency to assert himself to prove he was not inferior to the white man was in itself an inferiority complex. Friends who had arranged his tour were pleased with his increased political maturity. They would have liked to send Nelson Mandela to the United States – there had after all been a thread of American influence on Congress in its formation in 1912 and the impact of President Wilson's Fourteen Points in 1919. But there was the difficulty of getting a visa. Besides the Americans had shown no disposition to invite Congress leaders.

The readiness of communist countries to provide opportunities for travel, for South Africans as well as French Africans, as Dr Ruth Schachter has pointed out, meant increased awareness of international events. But whereas in French Africa the

1. *The Treason Cage* by A. Sampson.

communist influence hastened a process of consolidation,[1] in South Africa, while uniting different races, it had a divisive effect among Africans when it came to ideology. In the Transvaal for instance the left- and right-wing in some of the Youth League branches kept up a running quarrel. Ironically not only the left-wing borrowed language from Marxist sources, attacking the right-wing as 'disgruntled, self-seeking, politically bankcrupt [sic] and inconsistent weathercocks' in its journal *Lodestar*, but the right-wing in their bulletin, *The Africanist*, also used the jargon, attacking the leadership for a superfluous multiplicity of pacts with insignificant organizations, 'lackeys, flunkeys and functionaries of non-African minorities'. *Isizwe*, the New Brighton bulletin, quoted sayings by Diogenes, Howard Fast, Emerson, Steinbeck and Koestler. Just as elsewhere in Africa, African parties proved essentially eclectic, taking over, in Thomas Hodgkin's words, 'methods of thoughts, ideas and terms . . . not only from revolutionary democrats and Marxists, but also from Gandhist, Islamic and Christian, as well as from indigenous African sources',[2] all fused to form a new, nationalist ideology, which though it varied according to local conditions, possessed a certain underlying unity.

Pursuing the comparison it is interesting to find that, despite the Government's attempt to isolate Africans in South Africa, the A.N.C. had many things in common with movements elsewhere in Africa. Its structure had the same chain of authority from central executive to branches and party members, with the still larger body of sympathizers who attended mass meetings and who felt themselves part of the movement even if not formally members. It also had its working committee discussing major questions of policy and meeting frequently. It had the women's section, and the youth covering a wide age-range and tending to independent action and radicalism. Trade union activity, however, remained separate, with certain A.N.C. members also working in various unions. It also had developed from

1. *The Development of Political Parties in French West Africa* by Ruth Schachter.
2. *African Political Parties.*

an élite party of middle-class intellectuals to a mass party. In doing so it had acquired symbols such as the thumbs up sign and slogans like 'Mayibuye'. The flag, the blouses the women wore, the caps the men wore, the folk songs, the hymns and prayers, all these could be found from West Africa to East Africa to the North. There was pride too in 'prison graduates'. Conferences also – with the ritual from the opening anthem through fraternal greetings, executive reports and long discussions, to slogans, songs and public celebrations. One important weakness of the A.N.C. compared with many organizations in Africa was its failure to maintain its newspaper.

To its credit was consistency over fifty years in holding its annual conference when comparable organizations elsewhere, with a much shorter life, met irregularly. The A.N.C. could also claim to be singularly democratic, disliking charismatic leadership popular elsewhere however much this would make for a strong driving and uniting force.

Two vital factors made all the difference between the situation in other parts of Africa, where nationalism triumphed, and South Africa. One was the large, long-settled white population together with the mainly a-political Asian and Coloured populations which altogether numbered half the African population. The other factor was that in South Africa the white Government controlled a heavily armed, highly industrialized state. Furthermore, although the non-whites of South Africa undoubtedly had increasing sympathy from the outside world, they lacked the direct pressure of parliamentary and public opinion from Britain or France which could be exerted on behalf of the colonial peoples.

Had the Defiance Campaign taken part in a British or French-controlled country in East, West or Central Africa, the outcome would have been very different.

A corollary of this was that though the A.N.C. and parties in West Africa had similar organizational problems – lack of transport, funds, and restrictions – in South Africa these were exacerbated by the inexorable force of the laws and the ubiquitous police. Whereas in Nigeria, for instance, the main party could make an eight-month tour of the country, accompanied by brass bands, dancers, speakers, so that they 'touched the lives of hundreds of isolated communities in a way never known before',[1] in South Africa freedom of movement had not only been severely restricted for decades by the pass laws, but movement and freedom to meet and to organize were restricted by the Urban Areas Act, the Native Administration Act and the Suppression of Communism Act.

Thus, while its fellows elsewhere in Africa were taking part in developing legislatures, the grim South African situation restrained the rational and mature A.N.C. Yet it seldom became negative.[2]

One unique factor for a time in South Africa was the role of certain priests (incidentally Anglicans) who became identified with the non-whites' struggle in a way that caught the imagination of the outside world. Michael Scott, declared a prohibited immigrant by the Government in 1951, had to pursue the struggle abroad. Meanwhile Father Trevor Huddleston, C.R. was finding that a love of justice logically involved him in people's daily lives.

So it was that one Sunday in 1953, he hurried from mass to the Odin Cinema in Sophiatown. It was packed with 1,200 people, protesting against the threatened removal of 58,000 inhabitants from Sophiatown and the other Western Areas of Johannesburg. In near-by locations tens of thousands of Africans were still living in shanties and in tin tanks, yet the Government ruled not only that those Sophiatown people living in overcrowded slum conditions must move, but also the thousands living in solid decent houses. The area was almost unique in having freehold tenure for Africans and a white suburb was encroaching on it: therefore it must go.

Sophiatown's significance lay in its being a real community – with a heart and life and a spontaneous gaiety of its own – quite unlike the characterless monotony of the endless little barracks of houses stretching for miles in the 'locations', now known as

1. *Nigeria, Background to Nationalism* by James Coleman.
2. Comparisons based on *African Political Parties* by Thomas Hodgkin.

'townships'. Many of its threatened residents were in the audience that Sunday morning. As Huddleston addressed them police, armed with sten guns, rifles and assegais, drew up outside. Yusuf Cachalia was about to speak when the chief of the Special Branch of the C.I.D. entered the hall with detectives who grabbed Cachalia and roughly marched him off. The provocative action aroused the audience to a high pitch of anger but A.N.C. leaders at once calmed them. Huddleston argued with the detectives only to be warned not to interfere. 'The fierce breath of totalitarianism and tyranny in every attitude, every movement of the police', triggered off in him the determination to use every means open to him to tell the truth, at home and abroad, about the 'fearful lengths to which we have already gone in the suppression of personal liberties'.[1] He became Chairman of the Western Areas Protest Committee, alongside representatives of the A.N.C. and the C.O.D.

Such behaviour by the police had become commonplace. Wherever the A.N.C. initiated action the police would move to crush it.

In Port Elizabeth early in 1954 the New Brighton branch organized a successful boycott of several local shops where African customers were badly treated or where Africans were not employed. Outside a shop an African picket in a battered military coat would wait, and if anyone moved towards the door, would hurl the word 'Akungenwa!' – 'Don't enter!' – at him. Or a woman who appeared to be window-shopping, or a bunch of kids who seemed to be playing a game, if they saw anyone entering the shop, would bawl 'A 'Ngenwa!'

Major-General Brink, Commissioner of Police, announced: 'I take a very serious view of the matter.' He met senior police from all over the Eastern Cape and the Transkei to discuss the A.N.C.'s moves. Police raids, bannings, banishments, prohibition of meetings: these were the weapons of the Government. Walter Sisulu, like Mandela declared a statutory communist, was forced to resign from the A.N.C. Yet they and other banned people, of all races, did continue to work behind the

1. *Naught for Your Comfort* by T. Huddleston.

scenes, regardless of the considerable risks and the handicaps, a fact that can only be recorded long after the event.

In Johannesburg when the Congress called a conference with its allies – the Indian Congress and the C.O.D. – to 'resist apartheid', which Father Huddleston opened and which included in the 1,200 present his Superior, Father Raymond Raynes, C.R., and representatives of the Liberal Party, a hundred police armed with sten guns and rifles raided them. A senior officer announced: treason was being investigated.

There were occasions when the police were outwitted to the loud delight of the Africans. At one conference when the Special Branch arrived the organizers hurriedly sought a ruling from the Supreme Court. Wild cheers followed Mr Justice Blackwell's order to the detectives to leave. At another the A.N.C. arranged a public reception and, while the police attentively watched the crowds, the actual delegates slipped away to a secret meeting-place where they deliberated through the night. On another occasion Congress members from Cape Town decided to meet several hundred miles away in George – a sleepy town inhabited by retired English people – in the belief they would escape interference. However they were followed all the way by the Special Branch, and arrested for failing to produce tax receipts or driving passengers without permits. While awaiting trial, as one of them subsequently reported, 'We were all, very fortunately, locked into one cell in jail. Was it not a golden opportunity for us to get down to business!!!'

But these could be but feints in face of the force that Government could put into its body blows.

Nearly 600 people of all races had been named as communists. Among eighty-six men and women ordered to resign from their organizations were Njongwe, Matji, Joe Matthews, several Natal and East London leaders, as well as leaders of the Indian Congress and Congress of Democrats. Many others were banned from meetings or confined to certain areas.

Lutuli flew from Durban to Johannesburg to speak at a great Western Areas protest demonstration in Sophiatown. As he descended from the plane, police served him with a new banning order, confining him to a small area around his home for two years and forbidding him to attend meetings. Before the confinement took effect he went to Sophiatown; the people marched in thousands past the house where he was staying; he waved to them from the gateway. The glimpse was enough for mutual inspiration and encouragement to flash between him and the people.

Professor Matthews said of him: 'It has been said that it is the tallest trees that have to bear the force of the strongest blast of the wind.' Of Njongwe and Matji he said: 'One day when the story of the Freedom Movement in Africa is fully told . . . their names will rank high among those who by their selfless devotion and their undoubted gift for leadership advanced our cause by an appreciable amount.' Their name was 'written indelibly not on bits of paper which can be confiscated but in the hearts of their people where they are beyond the reach of governmental interference'. Njongwe, ill and on the verge of ruin, had to sell his car and livestock and start again in a small village in the Transkei. M. B. Yengwa, banished to a country district in Zululand, was forced to break his law articles in Durban. Sibande, by this time known as the 'lion of the East', was banished from Bethal. He asked the Native Commissioner, 'Where should I go to?' The official replied, 'I want to tell you this, there is not a single European on the farms who will accept you. The only thing I can advise you to do is to buy a little cart and a trolley and inspan donkeys and keep on moving . . . .'[1] The Government refused a passport to Professor Matthews to enable him to attend a conference sponsored by the Universities of Chicago, California, and Hawaii.

Not only the police and Government were adept at persecution: the Rev. James Calata was restricted by a local authority from marrying people and ordered to renew his permit for sacramental wine each month, while his Minister's railway concession was withdrawn. The Transvaal Law Society petitioned to have Nelson Mandela struck off the roll for having been convicted in the Defiance Campaign. Walter Pollock, Q.C., a

1. Treason Trial Record.

distinguished advocate and Chairman of the Johannesburg Bar, appeared *pro amico* on his behalf. The Supreme Court gave judgment for Mandela and deprived the Law Society of costs. Pollock's action was another factor in Mandela's accumulating experience of the generosity of individual whites which persuaded him to work with other races. The Cape Bar tried to have Joe Matthews, newly qualified in Port Elizabeth, struck off the roll. Donald Molteno, Q.C., successfully defended him on appeal.

1955 opened with Chief Lutuli gravely ill and confined to hospital for many months. The A.N.C. was gravely depleted, not only in leadership but financially: Natal's income in 1954 was £88; one Transvaal branch with 52 members had £2. 19s. od. in hand; a national organizer could only be paid £15 a month. And the A.N.C. faced a Government led by a new and more relentless Prime Minister, J. G. Strijdom.

The Western Areas removals were due to start in mid-February. As ever the Minister of Justice was ready with his horror stories. On 10 February he told Parliament the A.N.C. would oppose the removals by 'attacks with firearms; explosive in old motor tyres that would be rolled towards the police; old cars loaded with explosives which would be crashed into the police cars or lorries.' He assured the country: 'the police had reliable information that the natives of Sophiatown were in possession of a few machine-guns and revolvers and pistols, hand grenades and home-made bombs.' The imagination boggles at the mentality of the Government advisers who, over the years, have concocted such gems.

At least this added to the growing interest of the world Press which had begun to respond to eighteen months of protest against the removals not only from residents and Congress but from the Citizens' Housing League led by the Bishop of Johannesburg. Many protests had been overrun by the police, enhancing their news value. '*Asi hambi*' – 'we won't go' – was the defiant slogan Congress popularized. Some of the Press found the issue confusing when they compared the overcrowded squalor of much of Sophiatown with the tidy newness of Meadowlands, the area some ten miles farther on to which

people were to be moved. Perhaps they had not studied author-
itative statements from the Bishop and the Institute of Race
Relations condemning the removals because they ignored far
worse slums in existence since 1904 and because they not only
deprived people of freehold, but would place them under
arbitrary control of township superintendents. Nor could visitors,
in a brief descent on Johannesburg, sense the living organism
that was Sophiatown.

Among leaders of the Congress campaign was Robert Resha,
a Youth Leaguer who had lived in Sophiatown since 1940. From
being a miner he had become a sports journalist. He was frank in
admitting that, incensed by police abuse, he sometimes doubted
Congress's wisdom in insisting on non-violence. But though he
made furious speeches, when he calmed down he conceded that
non-violence was the wise policy.

Certainly there was not much African people could produce,
other than their bodies, when, as at Sophiatown, two thousand
police armed with sten guns, rifles and knobkerries, virtually in-
vaded the place two days before the removals were due to take
place, at dawn in drenching rain. Resha was on the scene in a
moment, Huddleston quickly joined him; the *Daily Telegraph*
and *New York Times* correspondents rushed out to be joined by
the other pressmen and photographers. Military lorries drew up.
Armed police moved into a few houses and stood over the
families as pathetic possessions were removed. Families, soaked
through, were huddled with their bundles and bits of furniture
on the lorries and driven away to Meadowlands. Congress
leaders exhorted people to stay. Forty families did stay despite
the threatening forces. But Congress had failed dismally both in
fulfilling its own calls for action – no matter what the sacrifice –
and in calculating that the authorities might use surprise tactics.
110 families went.

The exuberant community that was Sophiatown began gradually to be torn apart. Over several years it was dispersed until
rank weeds grew in its place; only the beautiful Church of
Christ the King stood among the weeds; on one edge the neat
bungalow that had been Dr Xuma's home was left standing,

occupied by a white family. Then new tidy houses were built. The whites moved in. Sophiatown was renamed: Triomf.

At least the public outcry and the attention of people overseas had ensured that the Government, instead of moving people to bare land as had originally been intended, put them into houses. Besides, it had been delayed from doing so for two years. In a negative way it was an achievement on the part of Congress and its allies that the Government needed 2,000 armed men to move 110 humble families. But the overall failure of the campaign brought fierce recriminations within the A.N.C. It was a serious setback not only in South Africa but abroad.

The right to own land and a home near a town – these were denied Africans because of their race. The right to education in the true sense of the word was about to be assaulted through the Bantu Education Act. Overseas condemnation of the South African Government had seldom been so persistently expressed as over these two examples of its fanatical determination to drive the 'Bantu' out and away from white society to the perversion of tribalism fabricated by the Minister for Native Affairs. Bantu education, as Dr Verwoerd made clear in a series of statements, would ensure 'that education should stand with both feet in the reserves and have its roots in the spirit and being of Bantu society.' There was to be 'no place for him [the Bantu] in the European community above the level of certain forms of labour.'[1] Africans would henceforth receive primary education largely in the vernacular; manual subjects such as tree-planting would be substituted for more academic lessons in primary forms; parents and children would have to clean and maintain classrooms; school hours for pupils in sub-standards would be shortened to three a day with teachers doing a double shift (an advantage in that more children would be accommodated but a disadvantage in that they would get inadequate lessons). African education had always depended on missions for the finest schools; this being a considerable saving in Government expenditure, Government made financial grants to the missions. Verwoerd was frank in his intention that he was withdrawing these

1. *Bantu Education: Policy for the immediate future.*

grants to oust the missions who created 'wrong expectations on the part of the native'.[1] The Western Areas removals in mid-February. Bantu education in April.

The A.N.C.'s Annual Conference in December 1954 had called upon the African people to withdraw their children from school when Bantu education was implemented. The dilemma was cruel. Parents were haunted by the dread of Bantu education which, as the Congress Women's League put it, was intended to 'dwarf' the minds of the children, but they also dreaded their children being on the streets. They asked the A.N.C.: What alternative are you offering us? What alternative could it offer with resources so thin? Nor could teachers be relied on to boycott the new system; only a few like Ezekiel Mphahlele, an A.N.C. member, were prepared to sacrifice their jobs and pay. Furthermore, provincial and local branches had only three months in which to organize before Bantu education was implemented. So the boycott was only carried through in half a dozen towns on the Reef and in the Eastern Cape. More than 7,000 children stayed away from school. Verwoerd promptly announced they would never be allowed in school again. Their teachers were dismissed.

Meanwhile the churches also were tragically divided. Only the Roman Catholic Church and the Seventh Day Adventists proposed to raise funds to maintain their own schools. A split among Anglican bishops left the Bishop of Johannesburg and his Synod almost alone in refusing to allow their school buildings to be used for Bantu education; a policy the Bishop regarded as 'morally indefensible'. Though others condemned Bantu education, most of them sold or leased the schools under their jurisdiction to the department of Native Affairs. In Britain Bishop Reeves addressed a series of immense public meetings, and the public responded to his appeal for funds for family centres to be started in school buildings, so that children at least could have recreation and be off the streets. Although St Peter's School and Adams College were briefly maintained, Bantu education virtually meant an end to the fine tradition of missionary education in South Africa.

1. *Hansard,* v.10. 1953.

To try to offset this great evil, the A.N.C. and its allies founded the African Education Movement which, helped by funds raised by the Africa Bureau in London, set up a handful of cultural clubs in the boycott areas. With pathetically limited tools and equipment, club 'leaders' (teachers who opposed Bantu education) taught children. It was a last desperate struggle for true education, made under the impossible condition of teaching while pretending not to teach. Many and frequent were the arrests of the 'leaders'. In one trial a policeman who arrested the teacher admitted pointing his revolver at the children. Despite all the obstacles some of the clubs managed to keep going for two or three years.

Professor Matthews warned Africans who had opposed A.N.C. policy on Bantu education or who had too easily given in to Government intimidation that as the years passed they would come to realize that 'education for ignorance and inferiority' was worse than no education. He feared that this device of the Government to condition the African – to make 'baasskap acceptable to him' – might succeed just as in Nazi Germany, Fascist Italy and Spain, where mass media had successfully been used to destroy freedom of opinion, speech and action.

At this time Moses Kotane and Maulvi Cachalia were in Bandung at the Conference of twenty-nine Asian-African States. Although they and the Algerian F.L.N. could not formally represent states, they were seated among the delegates. Pandit Nehru and Colonel Abdul Nasser were among the Prime Ministers with whom they had discussions. The conference signified once more that the vast majority of the peoples of the world supported the struggle in South Africa against discrimination and oppression.

The Government was destructive; the A.N.C. strove to be creative. The Congress of the People was about to take place. The A.N.C., forming an Alliance with the S.A. Indian Congress, the C.O.D., the recently founded S.A. Coloured People's Organization, and the non-racial S.A. Congress of Trade Unions, had invited not only other non-white organizations but a wide

173

range of white parties to take part – even the United Party in the hope that its supporters – largely English-speaking-whites – might learn they could never return to power by trying to beat the Nationalists at their own game. The United Party did not trouble to reply; even the Liberal Party did not accept the invitation. Of the whites only the Congress of Democrats with a few independent Christians – Father Huddleston, the Rev. Arthur Blaxall, another Anglican, and the Rev. D. C. Thompson, a Methodist – and one or two others took part.

Lutuli, banned from participation, envisaged the gathering as a practical demonstration of what the National Convention in 1910 should have been – a means of thinking creatively about South Africa, of defining more clearly the goal the liberation movement was aiming at. Circulars had gone out for months past asking people in cities, and villages, in kraals and locations: *'If you could make the laws . . . what would you do? How would you set about making South Africa a happy place for all the people who live in it?'* A typical reply came from the Rustenburg Inter-Tribal Farmers Association condemning Bantu education, the pass laws and the Bantu Authorities Act, and asking for 'more facilities re cultivation and grazing', 'to be directly represented in Parliament by own people', and 'to be given equal education for all races'. The urbanized people of Sophiatown demanded the right to be elected to state, provincial and municipal bodies, for full opportunity of employment and equal pay for equal work as well as the banning of hydrogen and atomic bombs. The most frequent demands were for better or 'adequate' wages, for abolition of passes, and for decent education. After that came better houses and food.

Surprisingly the authorities did not ban the Congress of the People. There were harassing tactics – withdrawal of some of the buses taking delegates from distant places, occasional road blocks, the arrest of drivers. The white Press gave it virtually no advance publicity, being preoccupied with a big demonstration by the Black Sash, the organization of white women who had begun their prolonged protest against the Government's latest assault on the constitution. The Congress Alliance had their own advance publicity – innumerable cyclostyled circulars which included a long Walt Whitman-type poem:

WE CALL THE FARMERS OF THE RESERVES AND TRUST LANDS!
Let us speak of the wide lands and the narrow strips on which we toil.
Let us speak of the brothers without land and the children without schooling.
Let us speak of taxes and of cattle and of famine.
LET US SPEAK OF FREEDOM!

WE CALL THE MINERS OF COAL, GOLD AND DIAMONDS!
Let us speak of the dark shafts and the cold compounds far from our families.
Let us speak of heavy labour and long hours and of men sent home to die.
Let us speak of rich masters and poor wages.
LET US SPEAK OF FREEDOM! . . .

On Saturday, 25 June 1955, on a battered patch of veld in Kliptown village near Johannesburg, 3,000 delegates responded to this 'call'. Just over 2,000 were Africans, with two to three hundred each of Indians, Coloured people and whites. Along the roadside, stalls sold bright soft drinks and mixed confections. One visitor from England thought it more like a black Derby Day than a solemn conclave of revolutionaries, as the crowd rolled up singing, laughing, shouting, wearing gay clothes – men in vivid Basuto blankets and straw hats, women in brilliant saris or in Congress blouses, with a variety of scarves and doeks. It was like South Africa in miniature – doctors and peasants, labourers and shopkeepers, ministers and domestic servants, students and city workers, teachers and housewives; and all the races in due proportion. The A.N.C. colours dominated the scene.

Banners announced the identity of branches or carried slogans – FREEDOM IN OUR LIFETIME, LONG LIVE THE STRUGGLE. Behind the platform was a great green freedom wheel with four spokes: the A.N.C. – the African elephant; the S.A. Indian Congress – the Indian fox; the S.A. Coloured People's Organization – the Coloured horse; the Congress of Democrats – the

European owl; and the S.A. Congress of Trade Unions included people of all races.

The Special Branch, large men in lounge suits, stood at the entrance to the wired-in enclosure of the gathering, taking photographs of all *white* arrivals. As the meeting proceeded they recorded every word – no matter what – and stared fixedly at the platform through binoculars, though it was no great distance away. There was grist for their mill in fraternal greetings from other parts of the world which came largely from communist countries and the left.

The most inspiring leaders were absent under bans; when the chairman, Piet Beyleveld, of the C.O.D., announced that the *Isitwalandwe* – the feather worn by the heroes of the people symbolizing the highest distinction in African society – would be presented to three men, Chief Lutuli, Father Huddleston and Dr Dadoo, only Huddleston was there to hear the people's cheers.

Throughout that day and the Sunday morning the delegates listened intently to a Freedom Charter read in English, Sesotho and Xhosa, drafted by the National Action Council representing the Congress Alliance. Lutuli had sent a message: the Charter was 'a torchlight in whatever dark skies may overcast the path to freedom'.

The Charter began: 'We, the People of South Africa declare for all our country and the world to know: that South Africa belongs to all who live in it, black and white, and that no government can justly claim authority unless it is based on the will of all the people.' Its aims were: the people shall govern, all national groups shall have equal rights; the people shall share in the country's wealth; the land shall be shared among those who work it; all shall be equal before the law; all shall enjoy equal human rights; there shall be work and security; the doors of learning and of culture shall be opened; there shall be houses, security and comfort; and there shall be peace and friendship.

At one point the amplifier broke down. Delegates cheerfully began to sway and shuffle round the arena in dancing groups, waving their brief cases and their black trilbys or Basuto hats in time to the rhythm. 'A-*way* with Bantu education! A-*way*!' they chanted.

Some of the Charter's aims arose out of daily experience – for instance 'the privacy of the house from police raids shall be protected by the law'; 'all shall be free to travel without restriction from countryside to town, from province to province and from South Africa abroad' or, 'miners, domestic workers, farm workers and civil servants, shall have the same rights as all others to work'. Some were typical of a social welfare state – 'the aged, the orphans, the disabled and the sick shall be cared for by the State'. Some were socialist – 'the mineral wealth beneath the soil, the banks and monopoly industry shall be transferred to the ownership of the people as a whole'. Most of the aims embodied human rights that in many countries had come to be taken for granted. The crowd approved each section with shouts of 'Afrika! Mayibuye!'

Meanwhile policemen slouched about, eating oranges, smoking cigarettes and swinging their rifles. The impact on a man who had observed the cold dignity of the police in Nazi Germany was that this unbuttoned, free-and-easy display of force was somehow worse. These young Afrikaners seemed to be showing, not simply the carefree confidence of the armed in the presence of the unarmed, but an appalling contempt for the 'kaffirs, coolies and kaffir boeties'[1] whom they surrounded. He felt that on the slightest provocation they would open fire – and not stop grinning.

Interleaved in the discussions was the singing, powerfully led by Ida Mntwana, the Transvaal A.N.C. Women's leader. There were new songs in the repertoire – one about Bantu education, one about Sisulu's visit abroad, and one, deploring the banning of a leader, which was adapted to each victim in turn.

On the Sunday afternoon the people were absorbed in the proceedings when there came a sound of tramping feet. They looked round to see police, armed with guns, marching towards them. A shout went up from the Congress – the crowds rose to their feet, hands raised in the Congress salute, thumbs pointing at the

1. Friends of kaffirs – abuse for whites seen with blacks.

police; and burst into singing '*Mayibuye*' to its cheerful tune of *Clementine*.

The Police Commandant went up to the Chairman, Beyleveld. The crowd watched and did not stop singing. When Beyleveld had heard what he had to say, he signalled to them to sit; they complied in a silence that could be felt. Beyleveld announced that he had authorized the removal of all papers and documents. He appealed to people not to make trouble. The police removed all posters and banners, including two notices at the food-stall – SOUP WITH MEAT and SOUP WITHOUT MEAT, and the people herded past tables where the Special Branch took their papers.

Under the pale clear sky of a Transvaal winter evening, the meeting went on. As Special Branch men crowded the platform and rifled the pockets and handbags of the speakers, the addresses went on – whites speaking with a new emotional intensity; an Indian with high-strung truculence; but the Africans seemed joyful, almost triumphant. Instead of shouting 'Afrika!' they now stood and sang '*Nkosi Sikelel' i-Afrika*'. The singers beamed. A young African girl, addressing the policemen with rifles at the foot of the platform, said into the microphone: 'It's a pleasure for us to have the police in this gathering.' To an outside observer it seemed that in the incongruous tension, the jeering policemen and the laughing Africans were teetering on the edge of violence. Once, the African band in its shabby uniforms with its battered instruments began banging out a compulsive rhythm – the crowd started to sway in a way that looked as if it could only have one climax. But the band changed its tune – the moment passed.

Darkness was coming. The delegates dispersed. The band played gay African songs; then it packed up its dented tubas and its drums and went home.

13 1955–6: The Women Knock on Strijdom's Door

'I have started the campaign of the women against passes, we have been holding meetings outside Bloemfontein in towns such as Ficksburg, Arlington, Bethlehem. . . . I hope you people shall not let us down at our Head Office, if there is anything new in the campaign please let us know early not last minute.' So the leader of the Free State women wrote eagerly to the A.N.C. National Women's League, proving herself a true inheritor of the spirit of her forebears in the Free State thirty and more years ago.

The Government had announced that from 1956 African women must carry passes, the '*verdomde*' – accursed – 'dompass' that more than any other law in South Africa tormented Africans and that since 1952 had been extended even to boys between the ages of sixteen and eighteen. Strijdom's Government was grimly pursuing the extension of its police state with the Criminal Procedure and Evidence Amendment Act, Native Administration Amendment Act, Natives Urban Areas Amendment Act and Group Areas Further Amendment Act – which not only intensified the suffering of the non-whites but symbolized the absurdity of apartheid and the inefficiency of a Government that year after year had to pass amending legislation to retrieve mistakes or close loopholes. To isolate South Africa further, the Departure from the Union Regulations Act was passed; the Minister of the Interior declaring it would prevent named communists from leaving the Union without a passport to visit communist countries and then to return armed for 'their devil's work'. He promptly refused a passport to Mrs Jessie McPherson, former Labour Party Mayor of Johannesburg, who wanted to visit her daughter in Britain, and to an African school-boy who had been offered a scholarship to an exclusive school in New England.

Lilian Ngoyi, President of the A.N.C. Women's League, was abroad representing the recently formed Federation of South African Women. Lilian, after living all her life in the slums and regimented locations of Johannesburg, has vividly described her tour. At London Airport she was warmly welcomed by friends. When she travelled in a full underground train and two well-dressed Englishmen stood up for her it was 'a miracle', as was the sight of white men with shirts off, digging up roads. In many encounters she felt she was respected as a human being. It was the beginning.

After two and a half months in London she visited East Germany where, on the tenth anniversary of 'liberation', she was taken to Buchenwald. When she saw in the museum the lamp-shades made of human flesh and pictures of men in the concentration camps, her thoughts went back to South Africa and she thought – if this is the curse of war, then it really was necessary for the A.N.C. to talk about peace. She wrote to a friend: 'Even if I know Dr Malan was against us as Africans I would never have wished him to be treated as the Germans ill-treated people. If this was European to European how much more if it was European to black.' Another question struck her: 'Europeans brought Christianity to us – how was it possible they should not respect humanity in Buchenwald?'

She went to China, feeling a bit scared as she remembered her father used to tell her the Chinese eat people. But 'it was the direct opposite; the warmth of people with their round faces was most wonderful.' Like Sisulu she was impressed because she could see the two things together: the old conditions and how they were building themselves up after liberation. In a village she met a woman who said: 'Delegate from South Africa, we are free in this country. There used to be placards saying – NO CHINESE AND DOGS.' She told the woman, 'We don't have that in South Africa but wherever there is something nice you see a sign – EUROPEANS ONLY.'

Her impression of Russia was that it was too advanced to have anything practical to say for Africa. What most struck her was Moscow library with thousands of people, even old people, reading.

Her last stop was in Lausanne for the World Conference of Mothers on the theme of disarmament. She told about conditions in South Africa: 'We have no peace, though no real war. We have apartheid which starves us and then lets us have little bits.' And she told them about the Bantu Education Act 'designed to put Africans in an inferior position.' She said: 'Our children have never had compulsory education,' and only 35 per cent went to school. But, she assured the women, her people were continuously struggling for a better life.

When she got back to South Africa she felt: 'I will fight for freedom to the bitter end.' She no longer feared jail. 'Lenin was banished ten times. I am determined. It does not matter what. I am determined to fight for a multi-racial South Africa where we can live in peace.'

She returned to Johannesburg as the Special Branch[1] was making fresh and more thorough raids throughout the Union – hundreds and hundreds of raids – African, Indian and white Congresses, the Central Indian High School in Johannesburg, Dr Moroka's home in Thaba'Nchu, Father Huddleston's quarters in the Priory at Rosettenville, many individuals – all were searched. The warrants declared the police were looking for evidence 'as to the commission of the offence of Treason or Sedition'.

Undaunted the women went on, organizing protests against the threat of the pass laws. Many wives of A.N.C. leaders were in the Women's League – Professor Matthews's wife, Freda, Albertina Sisulu, Maggie Resha, both nurses, and Tiny Nokwe, a teacher.

In 1954 the Federation of South African Women had been formed. During the few months of freedom the Ngwevela judgment had provided, Ray Alexander – who had done so much to organize trade unions in the Cape – took the initiative in calling

1. The political police, also known as Security Police.

the conference. From every part of the Union African women came, and a few Indians and whites. As had happened before, the left-wing initiators suggested a multi-racial organization of individuals, but the A.N.C. insisted that people should join as representatives of affiliated bodies. Thus Africans could work closely with other groups without being dominated by them. The first big protest against the pass laws was planned for October 1955, in Pretoria, in the Transvaal. One of the African women referred to the earlier demonstration of 1,000 women of the Black Sash: 'The [European women went to the Union Buildings and did not invite us. Now we will go and we will invite everybody.'

Two days before the Women's Federation protest was due, the Transportation Board refused licences for the buses engaged to drive them to the capital city. Desperately Helen Joseph, a social worker, one of the Federation leaders, drove with Robert Resha to all the centres of organization, telling people to go by train and somehow to raise the much higher fares. In Brakpan, a small mining town, for example, two hundred pounds had immediately to be raised for train tickets. Yet on the day, two thousand women, most of them Africans, from all over the Transvaal converged on the beautiful terraced gardens and the world-famous government buildings. Pretoria City Council had refused permission for a meeting – the women therefore simply sat in the amphitheatre until the leaders felt it was time to go, when they at once followed.

Africans are undemonstrative in public but when the Brakpan women got home, and as they got out of the train, their waiting menfolk flung their arms around them while a band played a welcome.

In Durban too the women – at first two hundred, then a thousand – were protesting to the Native Administration Department; and in Cape Town they marched through the streets. African men might be taken aback to see their women suddenly so independent and militant, breaking out of the conservative family structure, but they were proud. Walter Sisulu had observed the Union Buildings protest and asked: 'How could they *dare*?' The fact was, as Mrs Ngoyi, mother of three, explained,

'Men are born into the system, and it is as if it has become a life tradition that they carry passes. We as women have seen the treatment our men have – when they leave home in the mornings you are not sure they will come back. We are taking it very seriously. If the husband is to be arrested *and* the mother, what about the child?'

Early in 1956 when the Government began to force passes on women it was a time of drought and famine in the reserves. In Winburg in the Free State, many women were tricked into accepting passes – or reference books as the Government had retitled them. Mrs Ngoyi rushed there to explain the implications. When the Native Commissioner next came, hundreds of women marched silently to the magistrate's court and burned the books. Though it was not yet illegal to refuse them, it was illegal to destroy them; the women were arrested. All over the country women collected money for their defence and went on with their protests – 1,200 women demonstrated in Germiston, 2,000 in Johannesburg, 4,000 in Pretoria, 350 in Bethlehem, and so it went on. In Evaton, near Vereeniging – where for more than six months people had been boycotting buses against increased fares – 2,000 women walked seven miles to leave 10,000 protest forms with the Native Commissioner.

All this happened despite the usual obstacles. In Kimberley women organizing protests were dismissed from their jobs; permits for meetings were often refused. Mrs Annie Silinga, a big, cheerful asthmatic Xhosa living in Cape Town, who had joined the A.N.C. to defy in 1952, had been addressing meetings in distant villages despite being arrested and imprisoned several times, and even being banished for a while. One organizer turned out to be a police informer.

And there was always the problem of poverty. The Cape Town women asked if Mrs Ngoyi could visit them. The Secretary of the Women's League replied, 'I wish to point out to you the difficulty confronting the President. She is a person with a big family to support and has nobody helping her. We feel that a three weeks' visit means to her three weeks of having no money to support her family.' Due to the lack of funds much of the organizing had to be done by correspondence, with stenographers and typewriters non-existent.

Meanwhile the women prepared for their greatest protest. In August 1956 all over South Africa they packed their suitcases and hat boxes with the care and enjoyment they always put into such big events, and set off for Pretoria. In Port Elizabeth they raised eight hundred pounds for the fares and filled two coaches in the train, while from Durban twenty-three of them set off in cars owned by Indian friends, driving through the night and singing as they went. The African township of Lady Selborne near Pretoria threw open its doors and provided a grand concert.

The authorities announced that the women were forbidden to go in procession through Pretoria.

Early on the morning of 9 August there was therefore no procession. Instead there was something far more moving. Everywhere there were women, not more than three in a group, dressed in their Congress blouses or their saris or their best wear, some with baskets of food on their heads, some with babies on their backs, striding purposefully through Pretoria towards the Union Buildings, eager to tell the Prime Minister what they felt about the pass laws. In October 1955, 2,000 women – now, a year later, ten times as many. Twenty thousand women converged on the grassy slopes below the Union Buildings. Then, thumbs up, they moved up the hill between the pine trees. At their head were Lilian Ngoyi in Congress blouse, Helen Joseph in a dark suit, and Rahima Moosa in a glamorous sari. Behind them came the throng in gay colours. It took two and a half hours to file up and assemble in the great amphitheatre.

The Special Branch, some of whom had travelled on the same trains from other centres to watch the women, were there as usual. Civil servants came out to stare and the Press to record.

Lilian Ngoyi knocked on Mr Strijdom's door. Her left arm was weighed down by a vast bundle of protests. Others were similarly laden. The Secretary came out, said the Prime Minister was not there, and took the forms from them. Their leaders then rejoined the women in the amphitheatre and told them what had happened. The women rose to their feet. They stood with hands raised in the Congress salute for thirty minutes, to make their silent protest. Not a single child cried. There was complete silence. Then they burst into song, the warrior's song of the women of Natal with new words – 'Strijdom, you have struck a rock once you have touched a woman.' They sang the exalted 'Nkosi Sikelel' i-Afrika' and then dispersed.

'That was a marvellous thing in Pretoria. Oh, it was really a nice time!' one of the Port Elizabeth women said in recalling the occasion.

Many of them went on to attend the second national conference of the Women's Federation in Johannesburg. Several of its founders had been banned and could not be present. They discussed their progress. Fifty thousand had joined in widespread demonstrations during the past year. But they agreed this was small in a population of twelve and a half million. Mrs Ngoyi urged the need for work in the reserves, on the farms, the need for education in the laws and their effects. She concluded her address: 'Strijdom! Your Government now preach and practise cruel discrimination, it can pass the most cruel and barbaric laws, it can deport leaders and break homes and families, but it will never stop the women of Africa in their forward march to Freedom During Our Lifetime!'

The Prime Minister did not look at the petitions that twenty thousand women had gone to such lengths to deliver to him. They had been promptly removed from his office by one of the Special Branch.

Between 1957 and 1958 the women of Zeerust, a village in the Western Transvaal, were rising in profoundly felt resistance to the pass laws. Often such country people would claim to be members of the A.N.C. when they were not card carriers but simply were proud of it. In any event, though the A.N.C. played some part, the Government were always ready to blame it wholly for such resistance; blame that in African eyes amounted to praise. The Zeerust protests[1] spread into a revolt against Bantu Authorities – against the local tyranny given to stooge chiefs and their henchmen.

1. For an excellent account see *Brief Authority* by Charles Hooper.

Also in 1958 the Women's League, aided by Huddleston's successor, Father Martin Jarrett-Kerr, C.R., took part in protests against apartheid being extended to nursing: a profession in which African women were allowed one of their rare opportunities and had distinguished themselves.

Meanwhile, in the A.N.C. itself, though occasionally there were small local achievements to chalk up – such as a successful campaign against increased rentals in some townships – leaders were frankly analysing failures; but before such assessment could be fruitful a furious dispute began to rack the organization. It was obvious the Congress of the People made no impact on the daily problems facing the African people, and that Congress was not reaching peasants, factory workers or miners. However, when the Freedom Charter became the centre of dispute, it was on different grounds. It was angrily attacked by dissidents in the Transvaal A.N.C. who named themselves 'Africanists', and whose principal criticism was that the Charter's preamble spoke of South Africa belonging to all who live in it. They felt the land belonged to the African people and that only after the rule of an African majority had been accepted could others be naturalized and accepted as Africans or else foreigners. They claimed to be the guardians of the fundamental principles of the Youth League formulated in 1944. Yet its land policy at that time had envisaged the division of land among farmers and peasants *of all nationalities*. They argued that the A.N.C. was not carrying through the Programme of Action – for it still had not boycotted Advisory Boards. Professor Matthews argued that the Freedom Charter was a development of the Programme. The quarrel swept aside criticisms of the Charter which Lutuli and the Natal Executive had framed. These concurred with its general principle – a socialist basis to the State – but strongly urged full explanation to the rank and file of what nationalization and other factors meant.

During this time Strijdom at last had succeeded in destroying the constitutional safeguards entrenched in 1910. He next extended powers of banishment to 500 local authorities, and his Minister of Justice threatened the arrest of 200 people, with ominous hints of treason. Lutuli, from his exile in Groutville, powerless to make the personal intervention in the quarrel that might have been effectual, could only warn Congress not to dissipate energies by 'indulging in a fight on "isms" '. It was not simply an argument between 'right' and 'left', but between Africanism and interracial cooperation. A conference which was supposed to compose the dispute was chaotic. Lutuli was himself the object of public attacks from another source; Jordan Ngubane, a former pupil, one of the Youth League founders and a journalist, said Lutuli was being used by communists and Indians who had committed him 'to ridiculous policies so as to make him the laughing stock of the world'. Lutuli, who disliked personal controversies, remained silent. The State Information Department lost no time in quoting Ngubane to defame the A.N.C. Eventually Lutuli did reply. Ngubane's approach he described as one of narrow nationalism which undermined the A.N.C.'s broad alliance. Ngubane left the A.N.C. to become the most prominent African in the Liberal Party.

The Freedom Charter had by this time become a matter of principle and the genuine criticism people wanted to make on points of detail were lost. It thus became a victory for the left-wing who for the first time succeeded in bringing socialism into an A.N.C. programme. However the fears of some African leaders that the far left would try to replace the A.N.C. by a permanent Congress of the People were not realized. Nor were the hopes of those communists who had seen it as an opportunity of reaching thousands of new people and establishing the Peace Movement on a mass basis throughout the country.

In October 1956 the Government's *tour de force* in defence of apartheid, the long-promised Tomlinson Report which was to be its 'blueprint', appeared after six years' investigation. The Inter-Denominational African Ministers' Federation, led by the Rev. Zaccheus Mahabane, the former President-General of the A.N.C., the Rev. James Calata, and other well-known clergymen, summoned a conference of four hundred delegates from religious, social, cultural, economic, educational and political bodies (including Chief Lutuli and Duma Nokwe representing the A.N.C.) to discuss the Report. They unanimously rejected it. They demanded the repeal of discriminatory laws, sang '*Nkosi Sikelel i-Afrika*' and '*Mayibuye Afrika*', giving the A.N.C. thumbs up salute.

This was the time of the invasion of Suez and the invasion of Hungary. The attack on Suez by two imperialist powers touched deep emotions. The crushing of the Hungarian rising was viewed as the reflex to an invasion of African soil. An Anglican priest in the A.N.C., the Rev. W. S. Gawe, wrote to a Queenstown newspaper to say that Africans felt the fate of the people of Hungary was dwarfed by the sufferings of the people of Kenya, 'ruled by strangers'; at least in Hungary people shared on equal terms in the administration with the 'so-called oppressors'. This emotion strengthened left-wing influence in the A.N.C. Executive report. Whereas Lutuli and others condemned the 'ruthless intervention of Soviet Russia', the final report read: 'We believe that every nation is entitled to settle its own affairs, including the people of Hungary. The A.N.C. feels a sense of disappointment and regret at the bloodshed in Hungary, and sincerely hopes that peace will be restored without delay in this country.'

The space that Hungary, the rearming of Western Germany, and other cold-war issues took in Congress reports justified the Africanists' accusation that the Executive was being wastefully diverted into foreign ideological conflicts. It was also grist for the Government, and not long after, at a small private meeting of the A.N.C. in Johannesburg, Robert Resha spoke. 'When you are disciplined and told by the organization not to be violent, you must not be violent,' he cautioned. But, 'if you are a true volunteer and you are called upon to be violent, you must be absolutely violent, you must murder, murder, murder – that is all!' His flamboyant harangue met with tremendous applause. Secreted in the room was a Special Branch microphone.

Thirteen days later, at sunrise on 5 December 1956, throughout South Africa, in cities and in villages and locations, there was a knocking on doors. This was the beginning of the notorious Treason Trial.

14   1956–7: Could this be Treason? Could it be Communism?

The Chief and the 'Prof' in the Fort! As the news leaked out – dawn arrests, secret flights in military aircraft transporting Africans, and Indians, Coloureds and whites, from Cape Town, Port Elizabeth, Bloemfontein and Durban, to be imprisoned in Johannesburg jail, the Fort – for the first time since the Defiance Campaign, the A.N.C. and its allies were again in the world news. Afrikaner Nationalists approved their Government's vigilance 'in face of a dangerous plot'; English-speaking businessmen felt sceptical as they mounted the golf tee; Africans even in the Reserves felt proud of leaders they had often thought ineffectual. As the arrests swelled to 156 a Stand By Our Leaders movement grew, under the chairmanship of Father Jarrett-Kerr. Sisulu, Tambo, Nokwe and Resha were among the Transvaal accused and so was Moses Kotane. The Rev. James Calata was there and Father Gawe, along with militant Eastern Cape leaders, women too, including Lilian Ngoyi.

Though the intellectuals of Congress were represented, the backbone of the movement – drivers, clerks and labourers – made up the largest number. One or two Africanists were included. Friends kept apart by one ban or another could see each other again – Mandela and Meer, Lutuli and Dr Naicker, Gert Sibande and Ruth (First) Slovo.

The Government accused these people of being members of a conspiracy inspired by international communism to overthrow the South African state by violence. The Government's object clearly was to intimidate and to render the accused impotent. Its action had the opposite effect. The accused – the majority of the leaders of the true opposition in South Africa – who had

189

hitherto been separated by lack of funds or by bans, were now enabled to confer, as Lutuli put it, *sine die*. More important, the mass arrests gave a tremendous lift to the A.N.C. and its associates, who had previously been in a somewhat demoralized state. The arrests, moreover, proved as never before that the resistance movement in South Africa was above race; that black, white and brown were united against white domination. As never before liberals, Christians and socialists came together in organizing the Treason Trials Defence Fund: Alan Paton, the Bishop of Johannesburg, and the Labour Party M.P., Alex Hepple, joined with a leading member of the Institute of Race Relations, Dr Ellen Hellman, and Judge Frank Lucas. In London, Canon John Collins inaugurated a Fund that soon proved the substantial sympathy of the British people.

On 19 December 1956, the Preparatory Examination of the Treason Trial opened in the Johannesburg Drill Hall. From 5 a.m. vast crowds gathered in the surrounding streets, led by men and women carrying sandwich boards – WE STAND BY OUR LEADERS. A choir sang Congress songs and leaflets were distributed calling on people to remain non-violent. Through the crowd the vans of prisoners were driven – with the inmates singing as hard as they could, unable to see the crowds but aware of them from the noise. That day refugees arrived in South Africa from Hungary; one of the Johannesburg newspapers carried a headline about them: WE ARE IN A FREE COUNTRY NOW – THE REFUGEES CRIED. Inside the Drill Hall, the boss of the Special Branch turned up in a palm-beach suit. The prisoners, all races together, looked like delegates at a conference; after all, they had the sub-conscious certainty that ultimately their concept of justice would prevail. Immediately behind them on identical rows of chairs sat the public. During breaks in proceedings, prisoners, friends, the Press and the lawyers all mixed freely together – smoking, talking and sucking peaches. The whole day was marked by confusion and in-efficiency. The police gave up attempting to impose order after one of them – in trying to separate the sheep from the goats – had angrily ordered one of the prisoners off the premises. On the arrival of the magistrates it was discovered that not a word could be heard – the Drill Hall was designed for sergeants' harangues – so the court adjourned until the next day. Laughing and singing the accused piled back into the prison vans and were driven away. The Fort where they were imprisoned had originally been built by the British to keep the Boers out of Johannesburg.

The next day the crowd was greater than before. Only a minute proportion could be accommodated in the public gallery. Inside the Drill Hall the Prosecutor was droning on in a voice that, over the inadequate loudspeakers, sounded as if he were dictating in a room next-door; outside the people were in high spirits – African women dancing jigs under their big umbrellas; African youths striking clownish poses to tease the policemen.

The accused were trying to accustom themselves to the voice of the Prosecutor when suddenly there was a roar, a sharp burst of gunfire, and screams. An African woman among the prisoners jumped to her feet – she seemed to grow immensely tall – and with her eyes wide shouted: 'Oh, NO!' One of the men wept quietly. The accused began to surge forward, to be held back by the police. The Magistrate hurried from the court. The Bishop of Johannesburg rushed from the Hall and into the street.

The police had baton-charged the crowd and, after a gasping lull, people had thrown oranges and half bricks; the police, panicking, had fired. The Colonel in charge furiously ordered them to stop. Suddenly the Bishop and Alex Hepple – both small, mild men – could be seen right among the straining crowd of black people, calming them. As the people began to disperse, the Bishop crossed the road towards the Press who were watching, recognized the B.B.C. correspondent and thanked him for his Christmas card. Meanwhile the Colonel was angrily reprimanding the police. Although the young men looked not at all crestfallen, reporters could not remember a time when they had been thus publicly rebuked by one of their officers for firing on Africans. The journalists watched a white policeman, whose finger had been bitten, carried away by his comrades as if his back was broken. Twenty-two people, most of them Africans, were taken to hospital.

The authorities had learnt nothing, wanted to learn nothing. It was 1919 all over again.

Released on bail, the accused had a temporary respite when the court adjourned until the New Year. The head of the C.I.D. had remarked that the maximum penalty for high treason was death, but the leaders of the A.N.C. could understandably return home in sceptical gaiety for, looking back on the Congress record for thirty-five years, could this be treason?

The Prosecutor had forecast that the preparatory examination would last between six weeks and two months. It was to last for nine months. What the London *Times* described as the 'darkness and confusion' that prevailed, has often vividly been described. It could perhaps be summed up by Lewis Carroll's 'Barrister's Dream' from *The Hunting of the Snark*:

> And the judge kept explaining the state of the law
> In a soft undercurrent of sound.
> The indictment had never been clearly expressed,
> And it seemed that the Snark had begun,
> And had spoken three hours, before anyone guessed
> What the pig was supposed to have done.

The focus of the Prosecution's case was the policy of the A.N.C. between 1952 and 1956, with the Freedom Charter the key document. In all the muddle of the tens of thousands of documents seized at innumerable meetings (including SOUP WITH MEAT and SOUP WITHOUT MEAT!) and during innumerable police raids – there had been a thousand raids alone in the few months following the Congress of the People – and in the farcically incoherent evidence of many of the police witnesses, every wart on the face of the A.N.C. was to be studied through a strong microscope.

The Prosecutor said he would prove that the accused were all members of the National Liberation Movement whose speakers had propagated the Marxist–Leninist account of society and the state, and that the Freedom Charter envisaged steps in the direction of a communist state and, if necessary, was to be a prelude to revolution.

The Defence not only repudiated that the Charter was

treasonable, criminal, or a step towards a communistic state; it said it would positively declare the aim of the Congresses as expressed in the Charter and would contend that the trial was a political plot. It was not 156 individuals who were on trial 'but the ideas that they and thousands of others in our land have openly espoused and expressed'.

Against the background of the Trial the people of Alexandra, the township outside Johannesburg, were provoked to walk again, for in January 1957 the township was once more faced with a rise in bus fares. The A.N.C. had been holding meetings at which people discussed their problems and grievances, and the minimum wage claim of one pound a day which the A.N.C. and its ally S.A.C.T.U. originated began to catch on. But one pound a day was pie in the sky and it was the extra pence a day which aroused people to action. A mass meeting in Alexandra decided to boycott the buses. During the four months that the people walked, some of their local leaders went to the Drill Hall at lunch time for consultation with the A.N.C. leaders on trial. Solidarity boycotts were started by the A.N.C. in Port Elizabeth and other centres. The obdurate Minister of Transport said this was a political act. The Port Elizabeth A.N.C. agreed and asked: so what? In Johannesburg, the Bishop – who had earned African confidence by his blunt practicality and refusal to separate the social and religious from the political – was in the thick of the negotiations between boycotters and the Chamber of Commerce. But it was the people's own elected leaders in Alexandra who brought the boycott to a successful conclusion in April.

Meanwhile a Congress boycott of Afrikaner Nationalist firms went ahead. So nervous was one tobacco company that it obtained an interim interdict restraining the Congress Alliance from distributing leaflets calling for the boycott. In the Eastern Cape an A.N.C. boycott of oranges – because local farmers paid bad wages – was maintained until wages were raised slightly.

In mid 1957, from the Drill Hall, Lutuli called for a stay-at-home on 26 June in protest against apartheid and in support of the call for a pound a day basic wage. It was a daring act when A.N.C. and S.A.C.T.U. leaders were tied up in the Treason

Trial and unable to take a direct part in organizing. It paid off, the stay-at-home was 80 per cent successful on the Rand, with wide response in the dock area of Port Elizabeth, and token demonstrations in certain other towns. And protests against the extension of pass laws to women went on.

In the Drill Hall the Preparatory Investigation continued. For most of the time the boredom was acute. After seven months the Prosecutor announced: 'I am now going to call evidence of actual violence during the Defiance Campaign of 1952. I will show that bloodshed and incendiarism were engineered by the A.N.C. . . .'

Everyone sat up. Into the witness box walked a confident, bespectacled, middle-aged man, Solomon Mgubase. With aplomb the Crown led evidence from this witness who they said was a lawyer. He told the Court: 'Mr Sisulu and Mr Bopape' would 'arrange for ammunition and a certain gas powder' as part of 'Mau Mau' in South Africa, when Europeans in the Transkei would be murdered. He added that he had heard Mr Resha say that the gas powder would 'be used by secret soldiers to be trained in the Transkei'. So he went on, to the blatant diversion of the accused, when they were not enragedly reflecting that for this they were separated from their families, had sacrificed their jobs, and were on trial for their lives.

Had the highest law officers of the Government believed this rigmarole? If so it was staggering. Their witness had his antecedents briefly and precisely elicited by the Defence: Mgubase was no lawyer; he had served four terms of imprisonment for forgery or fraud; he had once been a police interpreter. Perhaps it was the usual contempt with which the Government treated the people of South Africa that led to such imbecile fantasies being put forward in a court of law. Having failed there, the Crown tried to pin a charge of organizing a 'cheesa-cheesa army' – 'burn-burn' – on Dr Arthur Letele – so ludicrous in face of the doctor's quiet integrity that the Defence could angrily declare it 'as foul a conspiracy as ever disgraced our courts' without rebuttal from the Prosecution.

The months dragged on; the strain on the men and women in

the Drill Hall stretched tight. One day Joe Slovo, one of the lawyers on trial, conducting his own defence, protested to the Magistrate on a legal point. There was a sharp exchange to which his fellow accused listened intently. The magistrate charged him with contempt of court. A dull growl escaped from the accused. They rose from their seats; it seemed as if they must surge forward towards the magistrate. In a moment Chief Lutuli was in control, calm, commanding: 'Sit down, sit down!' An ugly moment had been averted. The magistrate told those who wanted to register their protest to come forward. Subsequently not only were none of them prosecuted, but Slovo won his appeal against the charge.

Lutuli's authority was unquestioned – he united them through the most intolerable moments; as chairman of their Liaison Committee, he played an important part in consultations with the Defence team and the Defence Fund's organizers.

On 11 September 1957 the Preparatory Investigation closed. The Magistrate found 'sufficient reason for putting the accused on trial on the main charge of High Treason'. Meanwhile the accused could return to their homes to await trial.

Their excitement to be going home was tempered by a disaster – riots broke out in Johannesburg townships – more than forty Africans were killed or died of wounds, and scores were badly injured. The Government having once again refused to appoint a Commission of Inquiry, the City Council did so. The former Chief Justice, the Hon. A. van der Sandt Centlivres, led the inquiry which found among the root causes of the unrest the policy of ethnic grouping imposed by the Government; the effects of the migrant labour system; the breakdown of parental authority; rampant lawlessness and inadequate police protection; the utmost discomfort in trains in which Africans travelled to and from work; poverty; and lack of educational and vocational training and facilities for recreation and opportunities for employment for youths.[1] The Minister of Justice rejected the findings as of no practical value.

1. *A Survey of Race Relations in South Africa, 1957–1958* by Muriel Horrell.

For years the A.N.C. had struggled to organize in the townships amongst this lawlessness and violence, had tried to unite people of different tribes, had even given potential *tsotsis*[1] a sense of dedication in fighting for something beyond personal ends. But through eight years of increasingly harsh and widespread bannings, culminating in the virtual immobilization of established leaders in the Treason Trial, gaps in its organization were being filled by men without political experience. Some abused their new position of responsibility; some, harried by the constant attention of the Special Branch, got out of their depth.

Transvaal leaders anyway had a reputation for making bold calls to action without proper preparation – a circular would go out demanding 'The Pass Must Be Resisted', but without saying when or how. This gave the Africanists an access of strength in their vehement demands for reforms and militant action, though their attack on the 'communistic' Freedom Charter raised only five in 305 votes. Soon the quarrel burst into ugly brawls, not only in the Transvaal but in the Cape.

Lutuli and other national leaders were deeply shocked by such outrageous disputes. There were troubles enough without quarrelling amongst themselves. In Zeerust and in Sekukhuniland there were tragic upheavals as people opposed Bantu Authorities and the pass laws, while in the Transkei and in Zululand people began to stir. The Government's reaction – instead of seeking to discover what caused peaceable people to sacrifice everything in protests – was to let loose armed police in the areas and to blame A.N.C. 'agitators' for the disturbance. In fact it remained a weakness of the A.N.C. that it seldom rushed representatives to these rural areas at the first sign of discontent. The people had suffered to the point where they could bear no more. But they had no organization. The A.N.C.'s involvement consisted in the contact of a few members who came from the areas and in Mandela, Tambo and Nokwe being prominent in ensuing legal actions. Yet in March 1958, the Government banned Congress from these rural areas, penalties for infringement

1. Toughs; often juvenile delinquents.

being a fine of up to £300 and/or imprisonment of up to three years.

What was in fact a victory became obscured by all these happenings and currents: the Attorney-General withdrew the charge of high treason against Lutuli and Tambo – the A.N.C.'s senior leaders – and fifty-nine others. It was a vindication that Lutuli received with mixed feelings for, he said, 'the truth is I would be happier to see the whole thing through with my comrades'. He should therefore have been free to give the leadership Africans desperately needed at this time. But he was absorbed in a serious act of misjudgement. The left-wing in the Congress Alliance, particularly the Congress of Trades Unions, was intent on calling for a stay-at-home protest to coincide with the coming Parliamentary elections. S.A.C.T.U., though energetic and self-sacrificing, was not influential. The A.N.C. was badly disrupted and in any event the issue, the all-white elections, was ill-chosen. The Congress Alliance insisted. Lutuli made the call. The result: ignominious failure. The Africanists could justifiably attack such an abrogation of leadership on the A.N.C.'s part; but they had gone further, they had publicly and actively worked against it. (In the election the Nationalist Party gained a further seven seats.)

This further evidence that the Congress Alliance was out of touch with the mood of the people led to a further loss of prestige for the A.N.C. Lutuli was now ready to try to resolve the organization's dissensions. But the Government had just put a ban on all meetings. The trouble went on fermenting.

It seemed as if the men involved in the two factions had forgotten the Government and its oppressive policies as they attacked each other through their respective bulletins. The A.N.C. had revised its constitution: its stand for the 'creation of a united democratic South Africa on the principles outlined in the Freedom Charter' was hotly attacked by Africanists who declared the Charter emanated from 'vodka cocktail parties of Parktown and Lower Houghton'.[1] Africanists claimed that

1. Upper-class white suburbs in Johannesburg where in fact communists did *not* live.

Professor Matthews had 'unequivocally disowned' the Charter. For his part he could not think what all the fuss was about – the Charter 'did not seem to go much beyond African claims formulated in Xuma's time'.

'Africanism' had an obvious powerful emotional appeal especially to younger men, not only in negative retaliation to Afrikaner nationalism but in a positive assertion and in identification with what was happening in other African countries. The A.N.C. on the other hand, as Mandela put it, took account of the concrete situation in South Africa. They realized the different racial groups had come to stay, but insisted that inter-racial peace and progress depended on total abandonment of white domination, their goal being national freedom for the African people and a society where racial oppression and persecution would be outlawed. The most extreme of the Africanists, Josias Madzunya, a bearded rebel from Alexandra township, taunted Congress leaders for being 'puppets and tools, agents and touts and lackeys and flunkeys of their white and Indian masters'. Sisulu's attitude was: 'You judge a man by what he believes in and by what he does.'

There were white liberals attracted by the Africanists' anti-communist line who saw in them a force that could break the Congress Alliance. It was a curious dilemma for them that the generosity of the A.N.C. towards whites had derived largely from the consistent readiness of white leftists to be identified with the Africans' struggle ever since Bunting's day. The debate grew more heated as it went on.

The whole state of the Union strengthened the left. According to the Marxist prognosis as described by John Strachey, South Africa provides a classic situation for communist activity. All one needs is to insert 'African' in certain key phrases: unemployment endemic; misery of wage-earners and peasants ever-increasing; the violence, hysteria and general irrationality of the governing class mounting; fascism being established in a capitalist country.[1] South Africa also combines factors analogous to the industrial revolution of Great Britain, and to the Nazis'

1. *The Strangled Cry.*

rise in Germany. Another analogy, broadly speaking, lies between tribalism and the *concept* of communism in common ownership of land and 'democratic centralism'.

Marxists could genuinely share the African aim of a people's democracy – an intermediate step to their eventual target of a soviet system. Had the Labour Party of South Africa been socialist from the start, the country's history might have been different.

In the A.N.C., communists were judged by their actions over twenty or more years. Dr Xuma, for all his quarrels with communists in the forties, had found that J. B. Marks was 'neutral and did not push communist views'. Father Calata had found communists in the A.N.C. '100 per cent loyal' and Lutuli regarded Kotane as a man of admirable judgment and maturity. Mandela's view was that 'in spite of the criticism of communism as a creed, the record of those men from the point of view of sacrifice in the interests of African freedom was very praiseworthy indeed'. Professor Matthews summed up: 'The panic over communism existed for a long time and from time to time Congress branches discussed its influence and whether people would have dual loyalty. It was resolved on the basis that anyone who subscribed to the constitution was free to become a member.' When people complained about the left-wing he would ask, 'Have they gone against any resolution?' 'No,' the complainants would say, and add, 'but these fellows are very active, they get into office, when there is work to be done they are always first to do it.' To which Matthews would reply: 'Meet them on their own terms. Be tough and determined. The only way you can deal with them is by you yourself knowing where you are going.'

Attempts by the white left-wing to push their dogma met with the Africans' fundamental nationalism. As one former communist among the Africans remarked, 'Give a fellow Marx and he won't come to communism.' Three cyclostyled lectures prepared by a white communist, and sent to a few A.N.C. branches, remained untranslated and virtually unread – later adding to the Special Branch's already bulging files of confiscated documents.

Ultimately the left-wing was always faced with a force – the essential conservatism of African national life, based on a binding system from nation to tribe to clan to family; with, beyond, the African's belief in God, displayed in his higher life and deeper customs, a more significant influence, even if weakened by the erosion of tribal and family life, than the Christian teaching underlying the education of most middle-class Africans.

Communists could be grateful to the Government for attributing to 'communism' all militant opposition and for the frequent attacks by both the authorities and the capitalist Press which gave the ordinary African a strong impression that there must be good in communism. Besides, the left-wing's own Press consistently reported local African affairs and ceaselessly and courageously attacked the Government for its treatment of non-whites in a way that the white Press did not.

Through their identification with the non-whites, white leftists found an audience for their approach to foreign affairs, giving the African people a sense of identity with the peoples of Russia and China. At the conference founding the Women's Federation, Hilda Watts, the former Johannesburg City Councillor, spoke mainly about the hydrogen bomb and the destruction of Hiroshima; of all the suffering that both cold or hot wars led to. In an age when such a subject has been debased into a series of slogans, it is difficult to understand the freshness and depth of feeling with which many African women responded as they thought of all that the vast sums wasted in armaments could mean in providing education, better housing and medicine, but particularly food for their children in a country where malnutrition was rife. Fraternal greetings coming from communist countries or left-wing organizations – but also from African States, from Huddleston, Scott, Collins, and certain members of the British Labour Party – gave African conference delegates the warm glow of knowing all these friends existed in the world outside.

The significant influence in world affairs had two sources. One, the depth of African identification with the struggle of Africans elsewhere in the continent; this surfaced when Italy attacked Ethiopia, when Britain and France attacked Suez, when the Algerian war broke out; so that people asked: '*Who* is oppressing the Africans in Africa? *Who* has colonies here in Africa? Who is extending passes to our women? Is it communists?' The other source, which had become for African intellectuals the yardstick for judging the outside world, was the way countries voted at the United Nations. When apartheid was discussed they observed that year after year many of the western nations supported the South African Government; the communist countries never. One Christian in the A.N.C. commented: 'Even men who are anti-communists find it difficult to see much to criticize in Russia's policy towards Africa and are bound to find a lot to criticize in western policy.'

When it came to the day-to-day struggle against the Government, whether someone was a communist or not was irrelevant to most Africans: identification – always that concept – and friendship were what mattered. From the start, as in French Africa, communists had won the trust of Africans 'by behaving in ways the Africans had never seen Europeans behave; they were personal friends and comrades, rather than superiors'.[1] Lutuli explained: 'Now we don't know communism; all we know is that those men and women came to us to help us. I don't deny that some might have ulterior motives; all I am concerned about is that they came to assist me fight racial oppression, and they have no trace of racialism or of being patronizing – just no trace of it at all.' The latter was something not often appreciated by liberals; African politicians were quick to sense any sentimentality of approach. Also they liked the optimism of the left, however much it was regularly proved to be ill-founded! Optimism was a quality Marxists had in common with Christians – the logic of their respective faiths gave them both a belief in ultimate victory, whether here or hereafter.

Of the impression some liberals had that the A.N.C. was dominated by white leftists, Professor Matthews said there were so many South Africans accustomed to pushing the African from pillar to post so that they could not credit his being able to

1. *The Development of Political Parties in French West Africa* by Ruth Schachter.

do anything on his own initiative. The A.N.C. was the senior partner in the Congress Alliance.

In the Liberal Party there were an increasing number of individuals who showed themselves ready for sacrifice, and with whom some A.N.C. leaders were happy to work. But the suspicion that Liberals wanted to lead Congress instead of joining in the struggle as allies was slow to die; besides in seeking African members the Party competed with the A.N.C. Then to Liberals, joining with the A.N.C. meant working alongside the C.O.D., some of whom jealously guarded their entrenched position. Always the first to volunteer, offering abundant energy and a readiness to suffer, the C.O.D. played a leading part in committees despite their small numbers. Though not all were Marxists, on occasion their forcing forward of extraneous issues was sharply divisive – for instance the Korean war was pushed during discussions planning the Congress of the People – making cooperation difficult. But in the final analysis it was the courage and comradeship of the left that counted.

Representative of the A.N.C.'s attitude to white Christians was Lutuli's message of deep regret to Father Huddleston upon his recall to England. The Chief told him, 'You have challenged Christians most uncomfortably to live up to the tenets of their Christian faith.' Christian discipleship as both Huddleston and Lutuli saw it involved setting at liberty those who are oppressed, uncompromisingly resisting the injustice at the heart of the State.

Christopher Gell was an unorthodox Christian who played a significant role in the Eastern Cape. Gell, while Under-Secretary to the Government of the Punjab, had been stricken with polio from the shoulders down. Given only a few months to live in 1946 he had settled in South Africa with his wife, a physiotherapist, who came from there. Conservative by nature, he was precipitated into action by reading about farmers' ill-treatment of their workers. Through articles and letters to the Press, he began vigorously to campaign from his iron lung, hitting hard with powerful accuracy and acute analysis. It was as if his will to live was strengthened by the imperative need to resist evil.

In Port Elizabeth, during the few hours a day when he was freed of the encumbrance of the iron lung, A.N.C. leaders were regular visitors and would sit beside his bed while the Gell cat – a perpetually pregnant tabby – would doze on the foot of it. Temba Mqota, one of several whom Gell's pen rescued from banishment, was impressed by the concrete facts that Gell could quote and back up by telling him – 'look in *that* file for *that* paper' or giving him the page number of a relevant book. But what Mqota liked was to discuss the Bhagavad Ghita, or the music of Bach. Joe Matthews, while serving his law articles in Port Elizabeth, was another of Gell's friends; and when Govan Mbeki arrived in Port Elizabeth as local editor of *New Age*, the leftist newspaper, Matthews urged him to get to know Gell. Mbeki – an exceptionally able man, a dedicated communist – was suspicious, thinking Gell a Liberal: but when they did meet he found him 'very fine', and they saw each other often. The reason Mbeki felt Gell to be different from other whites was 'you could read as it were that the man was genuine, there was nothing up his sleeve. One got satisfied with discussions with him, with his writings.'

These men not only valued the clarity of Gell's thinking in which he trained himself while confined in the iron lung, but his ability to see through wishful thinking and to pierce dogma. He could expose rigid inflexibility in the left-wing and equally had no illusions about the A.N.C., its failures, personality conflicts, problems in face of tribalism, and the preoccupation of most Africans with getting adjusted to urban life. His empathy was such that he knew what it was to be African, to have one long problem, from birth to death, whereas the average white had everything laid on from the start.

Gell then, a sophisticated intellectual, believed South African communists were closer to nineteenth-century radicals, than to twentieth-century European ideological communists; that their driving force was not so much Marxism as detestation of the colour bar and the fact that there had been only the Communist Party to go to when opinions were being formed. He clashed with Patrick Duncan, a leading Liberal, who persistently attacked the A.N.C. for communist ascendancy. The Liberal Party Chairman, Peter Brown, made it clear Duncan did not represent the Party's view. Brown had no doubt there were communists in the A.N.C. but there were also nationalists and liberals and even conservatives in its ranks, all of whom had decided 'to sink their ideological differences and fight together their common enemy apartheid'. He appealed: 'Let us sink our ideological differences for the moment and get on with the job of disposing of the devil we know, and who daily rides roughshod over so many of our rights, rather than dissipate our energies in boxing a shadow which may never develop into anything more substantial.'[1]

The Government was about to investigate these very questions in the Treason Trial proper which opened on 1 August 1958 in Pretoria. The ninety-one accused were charged with high treason or with alternative charges under the Suppression of Communism Act. All pleaded not guilty. The Prosecutor was Advocate Oswald Pirow, Q.C., the Minister of Justice during the thirties. The Defence team was led by a man acknowledged to be the most brilliant advocate in South Africa, I. A. Maisels, Q.C., and among the others were Bram Fischer, Q.C., who had helped Dr Xuma frame the 1943 constitution, and Vernon Berrange. Sisulu, Mandela, Sibande, Mrs Ngoyi and several of the Eastern Cape people were among those still on trial; Helen Joseph was there too, Leon Levy the S.A.C.T.U. leader, and Indians long allied to the A.N.C.

Africans had a fresh link with the outside world – one of great significance – in the presence of distinguished observers sent by the International Commission of Jurists. One of them remarked that not since the Reichstag trial in Berlin – with the exception of the Nuremberg trials – had a trial attracted such international attention.[2] Also present was Professor Erwin N. Griswold, Dean of the Harvard Law School, who wrote in the London *Times* that the real opposition in South Africa was on trial. He met and was

1. *Contact*, 13 June 1959.
2. 'The South African Treason Trial: R. *v.* Adams and others'. L. J. Blom-Cooper in the *International and Comparative Law Quarterly*.

deeply impressed by Chief Lutuli who was attending the trial and remained clearly the leader even while sitting in the public gallery.

A week or two later Lutuli addressed the Pretoria Political Study Group – Europeans who had not before invited an African to speak to them. As the chairman was introducing him, about thirty whites burst in, shouting: 'We will not allow a kaffir to address this meeting!' They assaulted Lutuli and the chairman and women who tried to protect him. Foreign Embassy representatives were present as well as overseas Press correspondents; Lutuli's quiet dignity, his insistence on giving his address and the temperate manner in which he put the African case, enhanced his reputation at home and abroad.

Two days later Strijdom died. Dr Verwoerd became Prime Minister – the man who, more than any other, had caused bitter suffering for the non-whites of South Africa.

And Christopher Gell died, a death that, as Ruth First wrote, left 'an aching void . . . he was as much part of the Congress movement as any volunteer who went to prison during the Defiance Campaign, or branch official who participated in the hurly-burly of political activity in the townships. . . . There were some who thought he went too far – but they were generally those who themselves never dared go far enough.' But what Gell himself would have liked best was the conclusion: 'The tens of thousands who were spurred by his example will go on fighting his fight.'

In one of the innumerable running battles in the fight there was a small victory to chalk up: in the Treason Trial the alternative charge under the Suppression of Communism Act had been thrown out by the court – a notable event also in view of the debate on 'isms'. The charge of high treason remained – flowing from a 'conspiracy pure and simple'.

At the time the wives of several accused were taking part in anti-pass demonstrations. The overseas Press reported how nearly 500 women marched in a half-mile column, many with babies on their backs, singing and giving the A.N.C. thumbs up sign. As soon as they were arrested they climbed matter-of-factly into the police vans, some calling out: 'Tell our madams we won't be at work tomorrow!' Three thousand women went in disciplined protest to the City Hall. Sporadic demonstrations had gone on around the country during the past two years, but in face of intimidation and the wiliness of the authorities great numbers of women were persuaded to take passes. In Johannesburg 1,300 women were convicted and sentenced to between £3 and £50 fines and from one to three months' imprisonment, with suspension in some cases. Winnie Mandela, a social worker, Albertina Sisulu, and other leaders' wives served two weeks' imprisonment then paid a fine. But the A.N.C. had not planned efficiently; no one knew what its policy was supposed to be, whether women should remain in jail or be bailed out. Many women ready to serve sentence were angrily disappointed when they suddenly found themselves bailed out.

Altogether 1958 was a bad year for the A.N.C. Long delayed conferences to try to resolve the dispute with the Africanists were at last held in the latter half of the year when the ban on meetings had been raised. Lutuli presided at a Conference aimed at reuniting the Western Cape. He had small success. A leftist was elected President largely through trade union support; three branches broke away, to assert their Africanism.

The Transvaal's crucial conference took place in November. National leaders presided – Tambo in the chair, calm and conciliatory; Lutuli warning against 'dangerously narrow African nationalism' with its encouragement to people to return to a 'tribalism mentality'. To which Zeph Mathopeng, an Africanist, retorted that South Africa was divided into two groups – oppressed and oppressor and 'there can be no cooperation ... the whites must go back to Europe.'

Charge and counter-charge; recriminations and tempers rising. Josias Madzunya, expelled for furiously opposing the 1958 stay-at-home, forced his way to the platform to argue angrily with the credentials committee, and to insult Tambo and Lutuli. Two other leading Africanists recently expelled, Potlako Leballo and Peter Molotsi, brought supporters for a 'show-down'. Tambo decided the best strategy was to allow them time to have their say; particularly as they were accompanied by blanketed men carrying weapons. Through the night the argument went on. Lutuli, always anxious to understand the other man's point of view, leaned over backwards trying to retrieve the Africanists. The genuine grievances against the Transvaal Executive were lost in the uproar of abuse.

Next morning the atmosphere was tense but quiet. The A.N.C. had ensured that the blanketed men were outnumbered; both sides now had their strong-arm stewards. The credentials committee went on weeding out expelled men.

The Africanists left. They proceeded to hold their own meeting not far away from which they sent a message to the conference: 'We are launching out on our own as the custodian of A.N.C. policy as formulated in 1912 and pursued up to the time of Congress Alliance.'

The gulf had proved too wide to bridge. In the final clash it was as if the senior leaders were above a brawl that their followers engaged in. Lutuli and Tambo had had no part in the undemocratic actions of the Transvaal Congress that precipitated much of the trouble. Robert Sobukwe, the emerging leader of the Africanists, remained in the background.

Sobukwe, a tall forceful man, impressed favourably all who knew him. First active in the A.N.C. as a student at Fort Hare, his revolutionary language attracted young men. Potlako Kitchener Leballo, a former member of the A.N.C.'s Orlando East branch and a volunteer in the Defiance Campaign, was regarded as the brains behind the Africanists' tactics. They claimed Anton Lembede as their prophet, a claim rejected by Tambo who had known him well and declared he was a national not a sectional leader.

Fragmentation was a familiar story in mass movements but nowhere could it be more disastrous than in South Africa, where the only forces to gain by it were those maintaining white domination.

15 1959: Lutuli and Sobukwe Lead

1959 opened with the A.N.C. showing an astonishing upsurge of confidence. Not only had the hiving off of the Africanists jolted Congress leaders into a determined unity, but the Executive's recent disruptive tendency to waste time on 'cold war' issues was replaced by concentration on Africa. Congress sponsored the Pan-African Conference in Accra in December 1958, where its call for the boycott of South African goods found a hot response. And its annual conference, led by Lutuli and Tambo, decided to prepare for a 'long and bitter' struggle against the pass laws – 'the main pillar of our oppression and exploitation'.

Lutuli, after the years of being shackled by bans, was at last free to lead again. On 15 April 1959, he addressed an overflowing meeting in Durban to launch Africa Week, which culminated in 17,000 people gathering outside Johannesburg, most of them in tribal dress. It was like a carnival with gay processions, A.N.C. flags and banners, and pictures of Nkrumah, Azikwe, Nasser, Nyerere, Kenyatta, Mboya, Banda and Lutuli. Nokwe proclaimed: 'In South Africa we say "*Inkululeko*". In Tanganyika they say "*Uhuru*". But it means the same thing – freedom!'

A few days later, added cause for celebration, the indictment against sixty-one of the accused in the Treason Trial was quashed; of the original 156 arrested, only thirty remained on trial.

Lutuli set off to address meetings around the country. In Cape Town they greeted him with ovations. People of all races packed meetings to hear him. His theme was 'European fears and non-white aspirations':

We are not callous to the situation of the white man in this country, who entertains certain fears – fears that culturally, politically and economically he may be swamped and may lose his racial identity because of our numerical superiority. But must the white man, because of those fears, be excused for refusing his fellow man rights ? . . . The question is not the preservation of one group or another, but to preserve values which have been developed over generations and to pass those values on to generations to come.

His lucid, uncompromising approach inspired enthusiasm. After one meeting a crocodile of men and women of all races followed him down the street, singing 'Somlandela Lutuli' – 'we will follow Lutuli'. Swinging and swaying in the traditional steps – one, two, three, kick – 'we will follow, we will follow Lutuli...' His visit to the Cape was described as a 'triumphal tour' by the Johannesburg *Star*. The Transvaal was to be next.

The Government clearly could not stand his soaring popularity. Just before he was due to address a mass rally in Sophiatown, he was handed a banning order. This time it was for five years.

Nor dared they allow the A.N.C. freedom of expression. On the weekend when the rally was due, the Johannesburg magistrate banned all public meetings. Only a private conference would be possible.

However, though the ban on Lutuli's attendance at gatherings was immediate, he had three days before his confinement to the Lower Tugela area began. He set off for Johannesburg. A huge crowd of cheering, singing supporters saw him off at Durban railway station. All along the line people waved and sang Congress songs, and when the train stopped, brought him gifts of food.

And at the station in the Transvaal the crowds massed, singing 'Somlandela Lutuli', and cheering wildly when Lutuli raised his hand in silent greeting. The Special Branch were everywhere. To the conference of 900 Africans packed into the small Gandhi Hall, Lutuli's brief message expressed anger and disgust at the Government's ban on the rally. He added: 'I can promise you there will always be an A.N.C. to speak for the African people, despite reports from Cape Town that my Congress is expected to be banned soon.'

When the conference was not being raided by the police, it prepared plans for opposing the pass laws, taking encouragement from the fact that the bare announcement of their economic boycott of Nationalist products had induced one large firm to reinstate African workers victimized after the previous year's stay-at-home. The delegates were horrified by reports on the continued ill-treatment of farm labourers, particularly on potato and maize farms in the Transvaal. Twelve years after Sibande and Scott had made their disclosures, conditions were as bad as ever. Indeed worse because recently the Departments of Native Affairs and Justice together with the South African Police had devised a scheme whereby unemployed Africans or petty offenders were induced to accept labour on farms. As a rule they were sent to farms where the owner was so notoriously bad an employer that he could not get labour in any other way. The atrocious abuses under this system had been disclosed by a Johannesburg attorney, assisted by the Black Sash. There were still cases of farmers or their 'boss-boys' beating labourers until they died or were severely injured. Men had been virtually abducted to farms, locked up at night to prevent them 'escaping'; kept in over-crowded badly ventilated huts, where they had to sleep on filthy blankets or lousy sacks. Half drums were brought in at night for sanitary pails. There was little water for drinking, less for washing. Food was mainly mealie-meal.

The conference loudly applauded a decision to boycott potatoes and demanded a full investigation into the condition of farm workers in those areas. The boycott became a great success – a substantial achievement since potatoes were a staple food for Africans. In markets all over the country they were to pile up despite attempts by Government and farmers to break the boycott. (Subsequently the boycott, combined with protests from the Black Sash and other organizations, brought the Government to introduce reforms to the farm labour system – albeit limited ones.)

Lutuli's return to Natal, to virtual exile, was prefaced by

a great welcome at Durban airport. A convoy of cars filled
with people of all races escorted him along Natal's North Coast
road, as far as a rough dirt road straggling off the main road
through fields: this was Groutville reserve. It was an offence to
enter the area without a permit. Chief Lutuli got out, gave the
Congress salute to his friends and walked, upright, into his
exile.

His previous bans had met with little protest outside the
Congress Alliance and Liberal Party. Now the white Press of
South Africa came out with banner headlines and editorial
criticisms. Eminent citizens protested against the 'palpable
injustice'. There were protest meetings of all races in Johannesburg and Durban. The Africanists, too, condemned the ban.

To the Government Lutuli was a peculiarly dangerous man:
he, more than any other African leader in the country's history,
had profoundly affected the whites. The Government dreaded
that whites should come to know and understand Africans as
individuals, and therefore lose their fear of them.

Next Tambo and Nokwe were banned from gatherings for five
years. Nokwe had already suffered as an advocate in being
barred from having chambers in the city. Resha was banned
from gatherings and confined to the Johannesburg area for five
years. Gert Sibande, banned from meetings, was banished to a
distant dorp. It was not only the leaders – all the time the backbone of Congress was being attacked: banished, arrested.

Oddly, the Government took no such action against the
Africanists who toured the country holding meetings and recruit-
ing members. They had expelled the wild Madzunya and were
evolving a positive policy. In March 1959 they established the
Pan-Africanist Congress. Three hundred delegates unanimously
elected Robert Mangaliso ('Wonderful') Sobukwe, lecturer in
Zulu studies at the University of the Witwatersrand, as their
President.

Sobukwe, a man of intellectual vigour, capable of inspiring the
young and well-liked by those of his colleagues at the University
who knew him, had been born in Graaff-Reinet in the Cape
in 1924. Educated at Lovedale and Fort Hare College, he had

been a popular president of the Students' Representative Council before becoming a teacher in the Transvaal. Dismissed from teaching for taking part in the 1952 Defiance Campaign, he had gone on to lecture at 'Wits'. To the P.A.C.s inaugural conference he expressed the aim of government 'of the African, by the African for the African', everybody who owed his only loyalty to Africa and was 'prepared to accept the democratic rule of an African majority, being regarded as an African'. P.A.C. would guarantee no minority rights 'because we think in terms of individuals not groups'. Africanist foreign policy was, he said, an endorsement of the view of leaders such as Nkrumah and Mboya – positive neutralism – a rejection of totalitarianism. In economics they believed in 'the equitable distribution of wealth', aiming, as far as he was concerned, at 'equality of income'. The Africanists believed that there was only one race, the human race. In a subsequent statement on the Africanist attitude to Europeans, he said, 'We have admitted that there are Europeans who are intellectual converts to the African's cause, but, because they benefit materially from the present set-up, they cannot completely identify themselves with that cause.' Indian leadership, he wrote, was drawn from the merchant class 'tainted with the view of national arrogance and cultural supremacy'. He wished 'coolies' would reject this opportunist leadership and produce their own. 'In short,' he said in the words of Tambo to Xuma, before Tambo had had the experience of working alongside Indians and whites, 'we intend to go it alone.'[1]

The Pan-Africanist Congress's aim was to unite and rally Africans on the basis of nationalism and to fight for the overthrow of white domination, thus achieving an Africanist democratic society. The Conference heard messages from Nkrumah and Sekou Touré. They had hoped it could be opened by Dr Kamuzu Banda or Kenneth Kaunda but they were both detained at the time. Potlako Leballo was elected National Secretary. Born in 1922 on the border of Basutoland, educated at Lovedale, he had been a sergeant-major in the non-European army, serving in North Africa during the 1939–45 war. He had a

1. *Contact*, 30 May 1959.

reputation for flamboyant rebelliousness and for having led a small mutiny in his unit. He was one of the teachers dismissed for taking part in the Defiance Campaign. His Chairmanship of the A.N.C.'s strong Orlando Branch since 1954 put him in the centre of the Africanist revolt.

Peter Raboroko became a leading spokesman for P.A.C. In his words the reasons for its opposition to the A.N.C. or as he put it the Charterists, were that the A.N.C. had gravitated towards 'multi-racial liberalism', and had become a 'union of exploiters and the exploited' which repudiated a 'genuinely nationalist, socialist or democratic movement'. Thus it had resisted transfer of effective political power to the African people and betrayed their material interests. The only 'synthesis' of the categories of the 'dispossessed and their dispossessors, the victims and their robbers', he said, lay in Africanism.

The P.A.C. claimed not only that Africanists had given the Programme of Action to the A.N.C. in 1949, but that they had mainly planned, organized and executed the Defiance Campaign! In short that they were the legitimate successors of the A.N.C.'s ideology; 'sea-green incorruptibles.'[1]

The consolidation of Africanist feeling in this party was a significant political event, but all except a handful of whites pursued their ostrich course. For almost any white person South Africa remained a delightful place to live in. For Africans there were intensified discontent and serious upheavals. People had fled from the Zeerust area to Bechuanaland to escape the combined menace of police and Government-supporting chiefs; mass trials went on during the year. In Sekukhuniland it was the same story. In the Transkei, the enforcement of Bantu Authorities had set off what was virtually civil war. In Pretoria police baton-charged a peaceful meeting of African women. The A.N.C. was among the bodies – political and religious – which wrote to the Minister demanding a public commission of inquiry into the Pretoria assaults. The Minister refused. The Government bought eighty Saracen armoured cars from Britain.

There was the annual tightening up of repressive laws.

1. P. Raboroko – article in *Africa South*.

Apartheid was forced on universities despite six years of wide-spread protests from academic authorities at home and abroad. The Minister of Bantu Education took over Fort Hare University College. The great tradition and record of a college that in some forty years had produced some of Africa's most notable leaders, as well as South Africa's outstanding black intellectuals, was destroyed. Professor Matthews could stay on provided he resigned from the A.N.C. He resigned from Fort Hare. At the age of fifty-seven, he gave up salary and pension to begin a new life. For the first time he practised as a lawyer for which he had qualified twenty-eight years before.

The Treason Trial of thirty men and women continued. The State case had steadily narrowed down until it was limited to proving violent intentions on the part of the accused. On 12 May 1959, the Minister of Justice said, 'This trial will be proceeded with, no matter how many millions of pounds it costs . . . what does it matter how long it takes?'

All the while poverty gnawed at the lives of Africans. Up to 80 per cent in the urban areas lived below the breadline. Kwashiorkor – malignant malnutrition – continued to kill many African children, yet the Government continued to refuse them school feeding.[1] The African infant mortality rate for 1958 was 180·8 per thousand in seven towns, while the white rate was 29·4. The average African income was £27 a year against the white's £500 – the third highest in the world after the U.S.A. and Canada.

The Government chose this time to raise African taxes by 75 per cent. Already Africans were liable for tax from the age of eighteen whereas whites paid it from the age of twenty-one. Unlike whites they had no reduction in tax for married men with families. Unlike whites they had to pay tribal levies, in some areas hospital levies, municipal fees and hut tax. In country areas Africans were liable for ploughing, grazing and dipping fees. But for them failure to pay tax was a *criminal offence*: in 1957, 177,890 Africans had been arrested and tried, an increase

---

1. 1959–60 Numbers in Schools: whites 640,000, non-whites 2,020,000. Amount spent per head: whites £62 10s. od., non-whites £42, £7 per head being the share spent on Africans (1,608,000).

of more than 50,000 over the previous year. Meanwhile, Government and employers held each other responsible for deciding on wage increases, thus shelving responsibility. An interdepartmental committee disclosed that wages for Africans in commerce were: for 6,416 men between £51–£60 per annum, for 24,940 between £61–£70, for 47,744 between £101–110, with only 159 of the total of 79,259 men getting more than £180 a year. On farms cash earnings were estimated at between £29. 17s. od. and £49. 1s. od. per annum.[1]

In Durban, poverty was driving people to an extremity of despair. In the Cato Manor shack settlement women complained that their husbands' salaries were grossly inadequate and that the administration provided no lights and no sewerage. And they complained about nightly police raids, of a constant invasion of their privacy; a deep loathing for the police – both for their personal behaviour and as instruments of the oppressive laws – had taken root. A peaceful protest by women and children having proved virtually ineffectual, their grievances centred on the system of municipal beer halls. Throughout the country for thirty years resentment had simmered as the law preventing Africans from brewing traditional beer cut deep into their traditional forms of hospitality. Besides some men, instead of giving their wives the little money they earned, drank it away in the beer halls. The women argued that the halls should be closed and that they should be allowed to brew; also that this would supplement their husband's pay. The official reply was a refusal to close the beer halls and a reminder that police raids were the law of the land. The discontent exploded in June, when some 2,000 women had gathered to tell their grievances to a local official and, as in Pretoria, towards the end of the meeting the police broke up the crowd with a baton charge. As in Pretoria there were women with babies, some fell, some were seriously hurt; the predictable result – rioting. Through the night the rioters, including teenagers, burnt municipal buildings and vehicles. The beer hall, however, was preserved – the police shot

1. *A Survey of Race Relations in South Africa, 1957–1958* by Muriel Horrell.

and killed three Africans who tried to attack it. The disturbances spread.

The Director of Bantu Administration in Durban stated that the basic reason for the riots was poverty. He appealed for wage increases, pointing out that not one of the City Council's 7,700 unskilled African employees could afford the rent charged in the new townships. A senior official rejected his contention that the riots were caused by poverty and criticized the Municipality for inadequate control.[1]

In Natal the whole countryside was rising. The boycott of beer halls had caught on and women picketed them in a number of municipalities. The response of the authorities was to intensify police action against illegal brewing in Durban. As usual the Government refused a judicial inquiry into the disturbances at Cato Manor. In the rural areas the frustration and anger over the accumulating grievances focused on the dipping tanks for cattle which women were forced to maintain by unpaid labour. Throughout the tense province large numbers of the dipping tanks were destroyed. Sometimes the protests took the form of orderly deputations to the Bantu Commissioner, sometimes they were violent. Where police broke up the women's picketing of the beer halls by baton charges, the people burnt down the Bantu Education schools. The A.N.C.'s appeal for an end to violent demonstrations was ignored. A chain reaction had been precipitated. The upheavals went on. Hundreds of women were jailed – in one village a jail built for 115 prisoners held 482. Police trying to disperse a crowd of women found them kneeling down and praying in front of them. The police arrested the entire crowd – nearly 400 women – who were fined £35 or four months' imprisonment. None paid the fine; subsequently all were freed on appeal. Through the mass trials the spirit of the women of Natal remained uncrushed.

The A.N.C. quickly sent volunteers to the main trouble spots to win support for clear-cut demands and to mobilize people in a disciplined movement. A remarkable young leader had emerged – Margaret Mncadi, a doctor and a Roman Catholic who was

1. The Municipality announced small wage increases soon after.

prominent in the A.N.C. Women's League, and did much to attract new members. The potato boycott was at its height. Against the troubled background the 26 June 'Freedom Day' celebration at Currie's Fountain in Durban – the historic meeting ground of the great Indian gatherings in the 1946 passive resistance – was immense: estimates varied between 20,000 and 50,000 people. Despite the mass of bans and confinements earlier in the year the Congress was on a powerful upward surge.

In June the Minister of Justice resorted to one of his periodic scare announcements: the A.N.C., he alleged, were planning to assassinate Dr Verwoerd!

Two months after the first outbreak at Cato Manor, in mid August, Dr W. W. M. Eiselen, Secretary for Bantu Administration and Development, toured Natal consulting officials and magistrates. He declared that the senseless destruction could only be understood against the background of the 'sustained and exaggerated criticisms of everything the State does for the Bantu . . .'. He blamed the A.N.C. Simultaneously a senior police official said the A.N.C. were directly responsible for organizing the defiance, an allegation rebutted by Lutuli with a reminder that Congress was against violence. The A.N.C.'s volunteers organizing the discontent into a disciplined movement found people in remote areas spontaneously giving the thumbs up salute, singing Congress songs – particularly 'Somlandela Lutuli' – even wearing Congress uniforms. When the A.N.C. convened a special conference in September, people from the rural areas flocked to Durban. In Natal trade unions were also becoming more effective as S.A.C.T.U. worked closely with Moses Mabhida – the A.N.C. Vice-President. But this was the women's hour and at the conference a bright red banner proclaimed MAKABONGWE AMAKOSIKAZI – we thank the women.

In Pretoria, the Treason Trial continued. The cornerstone of the State case – the Freedom Charter – along with every conceivable document any member of the Congress Alliance had composed or read in the previous six years, had been minutely studied. A Pole, an expert on communism, had been imported from Switzerland. The unpublished opinion of Professor Joseph

217

Bochenski, D.D., Ph.D., on the Freedom Charter was that although communist phraseology was not used in it, it probably had been formulated by communists because of such proposals as land being shared amongst those working on it – a step advocated in the 'National-Democratic revolution' by Lenin towards 'a socialist revolution'. However the Professor added: 'There is nothing (in the Charter) to compel the reader to conclude that this is a communist statement.' It was 'a moderately socialist programme with stress on liberal theses'. For an expensively-imported expert witness this was not exactly what the State had hoped for; the Professor was not called to give evidence.

Somehow morale continued high among the accused. Philemon Mathole – mine striker in 1946, grocer in Moroka township near Johannesburg, defier in 1952, father of eight with a widowed mother and his late sister's three children dependent on him – though the three years of the Treason Trial had killed his small business, could nevertheless arrive in court grinning broadly. Asked how he did it he explained: 'Physical culture. I get up in the morning, do my exercises, have a wash, put on my clothes, put on my smile, come to court.'

1959 was drawing to a close. Police harassing continued ceaselessly. One of the latest victims was the Vice-President of the A.N.C. Women's League, and an indefatigable trade union organizer, Mrs Elizabeth Mafekeng, mother of eleven children, who because of her successful and brave fight on behalf of African trade unions was banished from the Cape to a remote area. She managed to escape to Basutoland where she settled.

Action was what the African people wanted. So for the third time in a few months they flocked to an A.N.C. gathering in Durban: the annual conference on 16 December 1959. A new factor was the crowd of peasant women who took part. Margaret Mncadi introduced them as her sisters. Zulu women who would normally be loyal supporters of their Paramount Chief announced, 'We recognize only one Chief, Lutuli.'

Despite the enervating heat the conference moved rapidly to a climax. When a message was read from Lutuli, advising careful consideration before action, it was swept aside by a delegate who rose to urge: 'Let us force our leaders into a tight corner! If they still think in terms of strategy we think in terms of action.' Thunderous applause followed. The theme was action. Nearly half a million Africans – almost one in twenty of the population – were convicted under the various pass laws every year. Anti-pass day was settled: 31 March 1960. Mass anti-pass demonstrations would follow in May and June.

A week after the A.N.C. conference had taken place the Pan-Africanist Congress held its first annual conference. They decided to launch a campaign against the pass laws. P.A.C. supporters should invite arrest, accept jail sentences – thus disorganizing the prisons and inconveniencing employers – and upon release should again seek arrest. The campaign should be non-violent. The slogan would be: NO BAIL, NO DEFENCE, NO FINE.

16 1960: Africa Year: Sharpeville and After

Africa Year. From South Africa when Africans looked to the North they saw new States burgeoning. And their cause was beginning to be taken up by the newly-independent States.

During January in Tunis the second All-African Peoples' Conference resolved to boycott South African goods. In Britain the call for boycott was taken up. In Cato Manor the poverty was unabated; the police liquor raids continued. A constable trod on a woman's foot; the avenging crowd killed five African policemen and four white policemen.

During February from Groutville Chief Lutuli warned South Africa that African resentment was high. In Cape Town, the British Prime Minister, Harold Macmillan, told the Government and the people of South Africa about the 'wind of change' that was sweeping across the continent. A typical A.N.C. comment was: 'We'll see whether he means it when Britain votes at the next U.N. Session.' Scepticism which proved justified.

As part of its anti-pass campaign, the A.N.C. joined a Committee of Fourteen Organizations (ranging from the Black Sash to the C.O.D.) in a deputation to the Johannesburg City Council, to demand abolition of the pass laws. A mass poster demonstration followed and pamphlets stating the case for abolition were widely distributed.

Meanwhile the P.A.C. were set for action and were making headway in areas where the A.N.C. was weakest: the Western Cape and parts of the Southern Transvaal. Robert Sobukwe and other leaders toured the country. The Western Cape, where the Government was wielding its latest weapon, was fertile ground. 'Endorsing out' was the euphemism for this weapon:

for driving Africans from urban areas to reserves under the notorious Section 10 of the Urban Areas Act. No African might be in an urban area for more than seventy-two hours unless he or she had resided there for fifteen years or worked with the same employer for ten years, or had a discretionary permit to reside and work there. Endorsed back to the reserve the victim of this law would be driven by poverty and lack of opportunity once again to an urban area – to be re-arrested. If the person endorsed out were married, it meant splitting up the family. The Western Cape had been declared a preserve of the white and Coloured people. Thousands of African women with their children had therefore been endorsed out of the Peninsula – sent away from husbands and homes. The husband, then labelled a 'bachelor', was forced to live in bachelor 'zones' in Langa – a township in the sand flats eight miles from Cape Town. Langa – supposed to house 5,000 people – in fact had a population of 25,000. Only 1,870 were women. Of the 20,000 men, 18,000 were housed under bachelor conditions. Into this hot-bed of frustration and discontent came a handful of young, able P.A.C. men. Nana Mahomo came from the Transvaal to study at the University of Cape Town in 1957 and began to organize for the P.A.C. He concentrated on building up leaders who moved into the 'zones', young men in their twenties. One of them was Philip Kgosana from Pretoria, who was studying medicine but soon abandoned his studies to take over from Mahomo. Their activist approach, their demands that Africans immediately throw off the pass laws 'to go it alone', found a ready response.

On 13 March, Stanley Uys, a noted political commentator, warned that a crisis point had been reached in South African politics; the tension in Parliament was so thick it could almost be cut with a knife.

On the 18th Sobukwe announced that within seventy-two hours the P.A.C. would launch a campaign for the abolition of the pass laws. They would call for a minimum wage of £35 a month. Thus, by ten days, they had cut in on the A.N.C.'s call. They also added £5 to the A.N.C.'s aim of £1 a day minimum wage. Sobukwe urged people to leave passes at home and to surrender themselves to the nearest police station. This, he promised, was the first step in achieving 'freedom and independence' by 1963. He instructed people to observe absolute non-violence. He invited the A.N.C. to cooperate. Nokwe replied that Congress would not support 'sensational actions that might not succeed . . .'

21 March, Monday morning, 7 a.m. Barefooted and determined, Sobukwe led a group of P.A.C. leaders to Orlando police H.Q. offering themselves for arrest for destroying their passes. They were immediately put into the cells. Thirty-five miles away, in Sharpeville, the African township of Vereeniging, and a few other areas of the Southern Transvaal, and in Langa, altogether some 50,000 people responded to the P.A.C. call. Natal and the Eastern Cape, strongholds of the A.N.C., produced a negligible response. In Evaton nearly 20,000 people inviting arrest were dispersed when Sabre Jets and Harvard planes dived menacingly low over them. Meanwhile the law-abiding people of the model township of Sharpeville were gathering in their thousands outside the police station. As the morning wore on, the crowd, which journalists found 'perfectly amiable', appeared to the police increasingly menacing. At 1.40 p.m. seventy-five members of the South African police force fired about 700 shots into the crowd, killing sixty-nine Africans and wounding 180. Most of them were shot in the back. At 4 p.m. a thundershower washed away the blood in the street outside the police station.

At 6 p.m. a thousand miles away, in Langa, some 10,000 people gathered outside the bachelor 'zones'. After a day of rumours and deflection of demonstrations, they believed the police were about to answer their demands that the pass laws be abolished. A fateful misunderstanding existed: many of the crowd were unaware that public meetings had suddenly been prohibited, on the other hand the police officer in charge of the force that came – a man said to be quiet and steady with a fine record – was unaware that the crowd was expecting him to make an important statement. He ordered them to disperse, gave a three minutes' warning which few could hear, and led his force of sixty armed policemen in a baton charge. Stone throwing, another baton charge, more stones, then the order to fire! Two Africans were killed, forty-nine injured. That night the crowd went berserk, burning Bantu education schools and public buildings in the township, killing a Coloured driver whom they encountered.

'SHARPEVILLE LANGA' flashed around the world.

Although in other countries – Algeria for instance – there had been far worse casualties, there had not been such an outburst of horror as shook the world on this occasion. The increasing abhorrence felt for South Africa's apartheid policies and the persistent non-violence which Africans and their allies had pursued for nearly fifty years, had deeply stirred the international conscience. In unprecedented actions, the Security Council of the United Nations, the United States Department of State, members of all parties in Parliament in Britain, and the Dutch Government, deplored the police action and the policy of apartheid from which it flowed. They sympathized with the African people. Dr Verwoerd praised the police and declared that riots were not unique. Mr de Wet Nel, Minister for Bantu Administration, remarked that race relations were better than ever.

In the first anguished shock Chief Lutuli and Professor Matthews called for a national day of mourning. The A.N.C.'s bitterness over what it regarded as the P.A.C.'s precipitate action was absorbed in the common sorrow. On 27 March Lutuli burnt his pass publicly in Pretoria, to be followed by many others. A few days later the pass laws were suddenly suspended; for a wonderful moment it seemed the campaign had brought victory.

A few days and . . . the pass laws were on again.

A nation's mourning found its outlet in the vast funerals for the victims of the shooting and in the countrywide response to Lutuli's call for a stay-at-home strike of mourning. Then the anger took over – rioting broke out in Johannesburg and in Worcester in the Cape.

It was at this time that the A.N.C., learning that the Government was determined to ban the Congresses, took an emergency decision to send Oliver Tambo, their Vice-President, abroad as roving 'ambassador'. He set out at once, without a passport, making for Bechuanaland, Tanganyika, London, and the United Nations.

On 30 March the Government blanketed the country with a state of emergency. As mass arrests began, with almost all leaders imprisoned, police in Cape Town were driving Africans back to work with swinging batons and sjamboks; four more Africans were shot in demonstrations in Durban.

At this time, when the country was in a state of emergency, when police were trigger-happy, when white South Africa was shaken as it had never been shaken before – when the African people were stronger than at any time in recent history, 30,000 Africans marched spontaneously to Parliament in Cape Town. They were led by a young student, dressed in shorts; this was Philip Kgosana. For a brief moment he captured the spirit of the whole movement. But, tricked by the Minister of Justice, he quietly dispersed the crowd and was arrested and imprisoned.

Then for a week, two weeks, the African labour force of Cape Town struck. This in the sleepy Cape, the safe haven, remote not only from the rest of the world but from the rest of Africa, its barriers of mountains protecting its Mediterranean rocks and vineyards. In Durban too there were mass marches, with A.N.C. and Liberals to the fore. What might have been achieved had Lutuli called for a *nation*-wide strike for a week or more?

Day after day as the police and army swooped, rounding up thousands of anonymous Africans to be imprisoned alongside their leaders, the enraged leaderless protests went on. Saracen tanks, armoured symbols of the hated Government, patrolled the townships arousing a vindictive anger which sprang from terror and bewilderment. By 9 April the death toll was eighty-three non-white civilians and three non-white police, while 365 non-white civilians and twenty-six non-white police were injured. No white policemen or civilians were killed; sixty were injured.

In the middle of it all the Minister of Justice called for calm. The Minister of Finance called for immigrants. The Minister of Native Affairs declared that apartheid was a model for the world.

The one Minister who showed momentary misgivings about Government policy – Paul Sauer – was quickly brought to heel. Mounting protests from South African industrialists and leaders of commerce were ignored by the Government. A white man tried to assassinate Dr Verwoerd.

The A.N.C. called again for a renewal of the struggle against the pass laws.

On 8 April the Government declared the African National Congress and the Pan-Africanist Congress 'unlawful organizations' – a 'serious threat to the safety of the public'. Parliament outlawed these organizations representing the mass of the people of South Africa by 128 votes to 16. The four Native Representatives and members of the newly-formed Progressive Party were alone in voting against the Bill. Under the Suppression of Communism Act, the penalty for furthering the aims of these unlawful organizations was imprisonment for up to ten years.

8 January 1912 – when the Native National Congress had been founded one of the delegates had said, 'We felt wonderfully optimistic. To us freedom was only round the corner.' Forty-eight years and two months later – after persistently countering the open force of successive Governments by civilized methods of struggle, and at a time when their fellows elsewhere in the continent were becoming Prime Ministers – the African National Congress, and its off-shoot the Pan-Africanist Congress, were driven underground.

The A.N.C.'s last legal action was to call for a National Convention to lay the foundations of a new Union of South Africa.

Not only A.N.C. and P.A.C., but almost all members of the militant opposition of all races were detained. The net dragged in many people who had not been involved in politics for ten years or more, even two missionaries. No radical opponent of the Government could feel safe. Some whom the police sought found refuge in the High Commission territories, others made their way to the north. According to the diary kept by Govan Mbeki in Rooi Hell, Port Elizabeth's jail, conditions for the Africans were abominable – over-crowded, often intolerably

225

filthy, with rusty tins for food that was bitter pap – and in most cases marked with the coarse brutality that the system breeds in its wardens. Yet the diary recorded other facets of their life as well. They sang freedom songs and had daily discussions on a remarkably catholic range of subjects: the pass system; music; marriage; Afrikaner Nationalism; sex education; should ancient customs and religions be restored after freedom? – a lively discussion revealing that apart from the few on the far left, the majority regarded the restoration of customs as essential. When they discussed leadership, the essential qualities, they agreed, were 'personality, dignity, alertness, knowledge, intelligence, sincerity, perseverance, determination, restraint and humility'.

Before long they were moved into better surroundings although the jail food met with curses all round. There were good moments: the knowledge that 'our own men abroad, such as Bishop Reeves and Oliver Tambo and others were sparing nothing of themselves to show up the brutality of this philosophy of racial supremacy'. Then, once again, came Africa Day, 15 April, 'magnified into a historical landmark' when a warder brought in a new broom which literally did sweep clean. Mbeki commented that Defence and Aid Committees under the presidency of the Archbishop of Cape Town – distributing food and warm clothing to the detained – 'sealed bonds of friendship between the Africans and that section of the white population which realizes that the narrow racial nationalism of the Nationalist Party cannot work in the world of today'. Exuberantly he recorded the Trinidad dockers' refusal to handle South African goods. There were the jail officials in whose moods the detainees took great interest: one, after demanding to be addressed as 'baas', called for mutual understanding as he told the detainees they might be there for two or even five years. 'Remember,' he added, 'thirty years ago we Afrikaners were in a similar position to yours.' The Africans were fascinated by the mental turmoil this revealed.

Bechuanaland's constitutional changes, the rise of the bank rate, the general unrest leading to a crisis in Pondoland, the Congo, all these were among the subjects that cropped up. And there was the warmth of comradeship so that when some detainees were released after three months, the parting 'aroused feelings of tenderness'.

31 May 1960 – half a century of Union. In Natal Mrs Lutuli, Alan Paton, Manilal Gandhi's widow and Ismail Meer's wife, Fatima, led the fasting and prayers to remind the country of all the thousands still in jail. Ohlange Institute, which Dr Dube had founded, took part.

The leadership of the A.N.C. and the P.A.C., according to the *Rand Daily Mail* on 25 August, had 'withered away'. But within the prisons leaders evolved new ways of working. The A.N.C. was to have a New Plan, reorganizing itself to function underground. Six days after the *Mail*'s remark, all the remaining detainees were released. Within two weeks, according to the Johannesburg *Star*, an A.N.C. caretaker committee had formed cells. Ten days later leaflets appeared attacking the pass laws. All over the country UHURU – the freedom slogan of East Africa – was written large: in Port Elizabeth, in Alice, on the Durban esplanade, on the floor of a post office and the front wall of a jail, and across Oxford Road in Johannesburg's upper class suburbs.

These signs displayed the contempt felt for the edict that to further the aims of the A.N.C. was a criminal offence. Besides, if anything was furthering its aim at this time, it was the Treason Trial instituted by the Government. In yet another example of South Africa's weird outlandishness, A.N.C. leaders and members – at the invitation of the State – were daily expounding the now-banned organization's policies and describing its activities. The trial was dragging through its fifth year.

The A.N.C.'s programme was the essence of the trial, yet its senior leaders, Albert Lutuli and Oliver Tambo, had been dismissed before the proper trial had begun. In the last resort the Crown's case depended on proving violence in A.N.C. policy. But attempts to discover violence in its campaigns against the Western Areas removals and against Bantu education had failed as had an attempt to link Congress with the riots in the Eastern Cape and Kimberley in 1952.

There remained the object – as the Chief Prosecutor, Oswald Pirow, Q.C., stated just before his death in October 1959 – of proving that 'the accused must have known that the course of action pursued by them would inevitably result in a violent collision with the State resulting in its subversion'. Involved in this was the question of the feasibility of non-violence in South Africa. The A.N.C.'s failure to avert the Western Areas removals was part of its failure to plan for the eventuality of the Government putting down non-violence by violence.

Robert Resha's 'murder, murder' speech had become a prize exhibit. The Prosecution's conclusion, from this and a handful of other speeches, that A.N.C. volunteers would be shock troops for a bloody revolution, was roundly rejected by Lutuli who pointed to the volume of evidence that volunteers in fact helped organize passive resistance.

Lutuli, ill and strained after arrest for burning his pass[1] and imprisonment in the Emergency, was questioned about the A.N.C.'s attitude to 'East' and 'West'. He said the tendency was to judge nations by their attitude to apartheid at U.N.O. The question of equality was very important and this probably was why the Soviet Union appeared to provide a pattern; but China, he said, played a more important part in their minds, because it was a non-European country that had suffered a form of oppression and achieved freedom. India also stood high in Congress circles, not only because it had gained freedom but because of its early lead at the U.N. on the question of apartheid. As for the A.N.C.'s leftist language – he himself had used this and had supported the Peace Movement because he understood it pursued a course that was very necessary.

Mandela gave evidence. Four years earlier, when the trial had begun, he had given observers an impression of being something of a playboy, handsome, well-dressed. But over the years, working behind the scenes, he had grown with the demands of leadership. During his evidence he was asked whether he had become a communist. He replied: 'Well, I don't know if I did

1. He was sentenced to a year's imprisonment or £100 fine. The fine was paid by friends.

become a communist. If by communist you mean a member of the Communist Party and a person who believes in the theory of Marx, Engels, Lenin and Stalin, and who adheres strictly to the discipline of the Party, I did not become a communist.' He had read Marx, he said, and was impressed by the absence of a colour bar in the Soviet Union, by the fact that it had no colonies in Africa, and by its strides in industry and science. He was 'very much attracted' to socialism but had not studied it deeply. Questioned about a one-party system he said it was not a question of form but of democracy: 'but if democracy would be best expressed by a one-party system, I would examine the proposition very carefully. . . . In this country, for example,' he pointed out to the Judges, 'we have a multi-party system at present, but in so far as the non-European people are concerned, this is the most vicious despotism you can think of, I can think of, at the present stage of world history.'

One of the points the Prosecutor frequently raised concerned Congress documents which referred to the struggle in other countries without condemning their use of violence. Mandela explained: 'Look, let us take the example of Kenya. We were concerned there with the fact that there was a colonial war. We condemned – we regarded Britain as an aggressor. We had never heard of the Kikuyu invading Great Britain, bombing their cities, bringing death and destruction to thousands of people by robbing their best land and breaking up their political organizations. These things Great Britain did in Kenya, and our concern was that Britain must leave Kenya. We were not concerned with the methods which the Kikuyu people used.'

The Crown asked: 'They were irrelevant?'

'They were absolutely irrelevant to us. Our own method here is non-violent, and they are the best judges of what method they should employ, it is not our concern.'

As for Sibande, he told his story of police victimization, of banning and banishment and imprisonment. Of his ten children seven were still dependent on him but since 1953 he had never been allowed to settle in any municipal area. He was asked by the Defence: 'I wonder if you would tell me, as a result of your twenty-odd years in the A.N.C., have you today a home?'

'I have no home.'

'Occupation?'

'No.'

'Have you anywhere you can live with your children?'

'No, My Lords.'

One defendant from the Eastern Cape, Simon P. Mkalipi, had only reached Standard Four in school. In the Defiance Campaign and since, he had frequently been imprisoned – for leading an unlawful procession, using a microphone without a permit, addressing a religious meeting declared unlawful, this last resulting in eight months in jail from which he had been extracted to be charged with treason. He was fast losing his sight, very slow-spoken with a deep voice. Asked what he knew of the liberatory struggles in other countries, he replied: 'Well – if – I remember reading in a book before the American Republic was established, I think the Americans revolted against the British. And they had fought for their liberation. But I don't agree with the way to which they fought, because there they took arms.'

He had left the Methodist church in 1953 when the minister had objected to A.N.C. volunteers wearing Congress armbands to church. Mkalipi said ministers of religion in the army had preached to people with uniforms on their bodies in 1940.

Ultimately the case had come to rest on the ability of the Crown to prove that the A.N.C. had advocated violent policies. Eleven rank and file members gave evidence. They included a fifty-seven-year-old tailor from Kimberley, a lay preacher from Cape Town, men and women from cities and villages and townships. They were pitted against the best legal brains the Government could produce, but they knew what they were talking about and the bogeys the Prosecution sought – violence and communism – were not to be found. Though there was a scattering of anti-white or anti-Afrikaner speeches on the record, they were leavened with African humour – when we get into power even the Dutchers will get education and they won't have to send their boys into the police any more!

Z. K. Matthews[1] was the concluding witness for the Defence. Asked whether he believed in the nationalization envisaged in the Freedom Charter as a solution to economic problems, the Professor replied: 'No, I am not myself particularly enamoured of nationalization. We have a certain degree of experience of it in this country in connexion with the railways. As a user of the railways myself I wouldn't say that nationalization has been particularly successful . . .' Anyway it was 'entirely wrong to suggest that these clauses in the Charter were due to communist influence – the same idea was once suggested by Schoeman, Minister of Transport, to nationalize mines, banks and key industries', he pointed out. It was 'simply a world trend'.

A Defence advocate put the Crown allegation that the bulk of the non-European population 'is likely to respond more quickly, more irresponsibly and more violently to illegal agitation than would be the case with a group whose general standard of civilization was higher'. The Professor replied: 'I'm a little sceptical about the use of this word civilization being higher; I don't know in what sense the word "higher" is used . . . but my own impression would be that even the so-called more highly civilized groups, subject to the same conditions to which the Bantu are subject in this country, would I think react more violently.'

With regard to the Crown allegation that on occasion the accused had 'deliberately created an explosive situation', Matthews retorted that an explosive situation had been created by the authorities and 'existed, I should say, since the State was created in 1910'.

When the Crown read an attack by A.N.C. members on 'Imperialist America' attempting 'to drag the world into a rule of violence . . .', he commented: 'No doubt many people of the A.N.C. have been concerned about the activities of America. The formation of power blocs in the world, with America on the one side and Russia on the other side, is likely to lead to a world war, and I don't think it is peculiar to the A.N.C. to think it a

1. He subsequently became a member of the World Council of Churches' staff.

crime against humanity to run the risk of creating such wars.' America had created the Nato alliance and the Seato alliance and had bases all over the world, whereas he did not know about Russian bases. But his remarks did not involve approval of the internal régime of Russia, he supplemented, for the A.N.C. had not had information about that. What they knew about was Russian delegates supporting the Afro-Asians in condemning colonialism. As for propaganda material from Rumania, Egypt, the United Kingdom, Bulgaria, there was 'no harm' in Congress receiving copies – 'As a matter of fact,' he mused, 'I think some of them might regard it as a nuisance receiving all this mail.'

In cross-examination he added: 'I am not personally anti-American. I have twice visited the U.S. and I found the American people very progressive and a likeable people.'

As for Britain's role, it was a great colonial power and its Government had passed the Act of Union. In the last five years, however, it had done more to grant self-government than in the fifty years before.

He agreed that the A.N.C.'s aim of universal franchise would mean the end of white supremacy, and said that it had been realized that the white supremacists would not really concede this, but even *they* would not be impervious to political and economic issues. The world wished for and was working for the extension of self-government to a wider group of people.

The A.N.C. had stressed the need for sacrifice, because working for political emancipation *always* involved sacrifice – money, time, hardship, loss of career, dismissal, even death. But Congress was optimistic: 'Our optimism was based upon the fact that this is not the only Government that has been relentless in the history of political struggle.' Others had been determined not to give in to attempts made by their oppressed subjects, 'and they have subsequently done so.'

On 29 March 1961, in an electric atmosphere the Court assembled. Mr Justice Rumpff, impassive as ever, prepared to give judgment. Nine years before Sisulu and Mandela had been in the dock before him on trial with other leaders for their part in organizing the Defiance Campaign. He had said: 'I accept the evidence that you have consistently advised your followers to follow a peaceful course of action and to avoid violence in any shape or form . . .' Now they stood before him again alongside their fellows. Now he stated that although there had been some violent speeches by A.N.C. members – 'a minute percentage of the total number of speeches made' – and although the A.N.C. under its 1949 Programme of Action decided by illegal methods to achieve 'a fundamentally different state from the present', the Prosecution had failed to prove that the A.N.C. 'as a matter of policy intended to achieve this new state by violent means'. And although the A.N.C. had had communist members before 1950, and 'a strong left-wing tendency manifested itself' from 1952 to 1956, there was no proof that it had become a communist organization nor that it had been infiltrated by communists.

Judge Rumpff asked the accused to stand: 'You are found not guilty and discharged,' he stated. 'You may go.'

Outlawed – but momentarily triumphant. Outside the court the crowd sang 'Nkosi Sikelel' i-Afrika', danced and cheered and wept.

Meanwhile in Pondoland, in the Transkei area, bitter hatred for Government-supporting chiefs had been inflamed by increased taxation and the ways in which land betterment schemes were enforced. In a virtual uprising eight of these chiefs and their councillors were murdered – as well as seventeen commoners – and huts were burned. In one of the police attacks on angry mobs eleven Africans were shot dead. The Government, by declaring a State of Emergency, by hanging a score or more and arresting or banishing hundreds, reduced the country to uneasy quiescence.

And meanwhile, Robert Sobukwe and other P.A.C. leaders were tried on charges of incitement or destruction of reference books. Sobukwe was sentenced to three years' imprisonment, Leballo to two, others to between six months and three years. Among the few who broke the P.A.C. 'no-bail' slogan, subsequently to estreat bail and leave the country, was Philip Kgosana, the young man who had had – and lost – his moment.

17 1961–2: Mandela Leads during a Historic Turning-point

It seemed that the movement for liberation must surely be numbed by the outlawing of the A.N.C. and P.A.C. and by the long imprisonments of the Emergency. At this moment Nelson Mandela was freed from successive bans for the first time in nine years. Though he had – like Sisulu – continued to work behind the scenes, the long imposed silence had been a drastic handicap. Now, his magnetic forcefulness came as a revelation when he addressed the All-In African Conference held in Pietermaritzburg in March 1961.

Forty African leaders – including former members of the A.N.C. and P.A.C., and Liberals and Progressives – had joined in calling the conference which was held despite police raids on the organizers and the arrest of thirteen of them. It took place against a background of a successful strike of African bus employees in Port Elizabeth, and continuing unrest in Pondoland and other rural areas, and its delegates included a remarkable number from Pondoland and Zululand. Mandela was elected leader of a National Action Council. He accepted, knowing the implications: the other members were to remain secret as protection against police persecution, he was to be the public figure to take the rap; his prosperous legal practice, above all his family life, would have to be sacrificed. He renewed the demand for a 'truly' National Convention to establish a new Union of *all* South Africans; if the Government did not comply, he said, there would be a three-day stay-at-home at the time when a Republic of white South Africans was due to be established.

Immediately the police started massive searches but many people, including Mandela, had gone underground. However,

Duma Nokwe and the twelve others already arrested – who included Ngubane of the Liberal Party – were charged with furthering the aims of the A.N.C. The State seemed unaware of the irony of thus charging members of the Liberal and Progressive Parties, and even the P.A.C., some of whom had anyway withdrawn from the Conference. On the very day of the Parliamentary election in 1961, when white voters were freely expressing their political views, these men were sentenced to a year's imprisonment for advocating one man one vote, abolition of the pass laws, no taxation without representation, and compulsory education for all. On appeal, however, they were acquitted, the judge saying there were probably many organizations in the country with aims similar to some of those of the A.N.C. and that it could not be said that the All-In Conference had promoted or tried to revive the A.N.C.

Between March and the end of May Mandela and Sisulu secretly toured the country, organizing the anticipated three-day stay-at-home. A warrant was issued for Mandela's arrest, the Government acquired power to imprison without trial for twelve days, and gatherings were prohibited.

Meanwhile the call for a National Convention was taken up by a multi-racial National Convention, widely representative of liberal, religious and academic opinions, while Coloured leaders were founding their own Convention to make a similar call.

The Government took no notice of the desire thus expressed on behalf of the vast majority of South Africans. But it did not ignore Mandela's call for the stay-at-home. It called out police, army, commandos, citizen forces and Saracen armoured cars. As white civilians were sworn in to be special constables and gun shops sold out their stocks of revolvers to whites, police arrested thousands of Africans throughout the country and pursued their leaders, imprisoning many under the twelve days' provision. Mandela still eluded them. From underground he renewed the call, still touring, organizing, seeing both supporters and opponents. He even wrote to the leader of the United Party, Sir de Villiers Graaff, pointing to what widespread support the Africans' call for a National Convention had achieved.

Where, he asked, did the United Party stand? Graaff did not reply.

As 29 May drew near, overseas Press representatives arrived, anticipating another Sharpeville. The local English language Press suddenly swung from objective reporting of the call to warnings against it. The *Rand Daily Mail* reported a secret plan for the non-whites to invade cities. Mandela's denial of this trumped-up plan was rejected.

But the greatest blow at this time, when African feeling was strong, when the Coloured people were promising to give support as never before, was the decision of the P.A.C. actively, bitterly, to oppose the stay-at-home.

On the eve of the stay-at-home, authorities warned that strikers would be sacked from their jobs or endorsed out of towns; police would move into the townships in force to drive residents to work. During the night helicopters flew low over townships flashing searchlights down on the matchbox houses and rough roads. Police and army were ready. A sudden undeclared state of emergency again took hold of the country.

Yet on Monday, 29 May 1961, hundreds of thousands of Africans risked jobs and homes to respond to the call. In Durban Indian workers and in Cape Town many Coloured workers also stayed away. (The South African Broadcasting Corporation, which had deteriorated over the years into a Government mouthpiece, repeatedly announced all was 'normal'. On 30 May it announced that all had 'returned to normal'.) And on 30 May in Port Elizabeth – after night-long organizing in the townships – there was a 75 per cent strike. In several areas a significant response came from African schools which struck in a chain reaction to the call. But there was no doubt, the response was disappointing, and on the second day Mandela called it off. In secret interviews with overseas journalists he conceded partial failure; but, he said, the massive mobilization of armed forces by the State had been a 'striking testimony of our own strength and a measure of the weakness of the Government'.

This was a climax in South Africa's history.

If naked force was to crush every peaceful demonstration, it was futile to rely on non-violent methods. Having come to this conclusion, Mandela and a handful of African leaders came together in June 1961 to decide what form their counter-violence should take. They joined with several whites and Indians – most of them communists – in establishing *Umkonto we Sizwe*, 'Spear of the Nation', to sabotage selected installations, with an express object of not harming people.

But in October 1961 the first outbreak of sabotage was committed by a group of white liberals and an ex-communist who had founded the National Committee of Liberation – later to become the African Resistance Movement, though its African membership was but a gesture.

Umkonto we Sizwe – M K – declared itself on Dingaan's Day, 16 December 1961, with sabotage of electric installations, and Bantu affairs and municipal offices, in Port Elizabeth and Johannesburg. One of the saboteurs was killed in the explosion he had set off.

Only a few days earlier, in Oslo on 10 December, Chief Lutuli, in the presence of King Olaf of Norway, had received the Nobel Peace Prize for 1960. He accepted the honour in the name of the 'true patriots of South Africa', giving credit for the Africans' policy of non-violence and non-racialism to the leaders of the A.N.C. who, over fifty years, had set the organization steadfastly against racial vaingloriousness.

Meanwhile, some former P.A.C. members, rejecting sabotage as useless, were forming Poqo – meaning 'pure', 'we go-it-alone' – in cells mainly active in the Western Cape. Their objective was to fulfil the P.A.C.'s promise of freedom in 1963. Their method was still to be disclosed. In August, near Paarl in the Cape, at what was ostensibly a dance, 750 P.A.C. members met to plan action.[1]

Overseas, there had been a brief rapprochement when representatives sent abroad by the A.N.C. and Indian Congress formed a United Front in exile with P.A.C. representatives to assist in the substantial lobby against the South African Republic being kept in the Commonwealth. (As a result of the lobbying,

1. *Drum*, February 1963.

Commonwealth Prime Ministers stipulated that apartheid be abandoned, and Dr Verwoerd left the Commonwealth.) But the rapprochement did not survive bitterness caused by P.A.C. activity in South Africa – in virtually supporting the Government's attempts to break the May stay-at-home.

Internationally the African cause edged forward. At the United Nations' annual debate on apartheid, for the first time Britain and Australia voted against South Africa. And symbolic of closer ties with African states was Nelson Mandela's secret tour of the continent, to address the Pan-African Freedom Movement Conference in Addis Ababa, early in 1962, and to confer with many heads of state. He was given military instruction during a visit to the Algerian army, before going to London where he met the leaders of the Opposition Parties – Hugh Gaitskell and Jo Grimond. For the first time in his life he was free of white dominance and arrogance.

By this time three or four hundred members of the A.N.C. and P.A.C. had left South Africa in a steady flow. President Nyerere had been a particularly generous host in accepting missions in exile, and Algeria, Egypt, Ghana and Britain were early host countries. Some who went were refugees, some potential scholars, others went for military training in one of several African countries, and some were police informers. At home sabotage continued sporadically, almost as if it was a period of dress rehearsal.

But not for the Government. A new Minister of Justice was in power, a suitable incumbent for Oswald Pirow's inheritance: Balthazar John Vorster, formerly a general in the Ossewabrandwag. His powers to ban and restrict were harshened and lavishly inflicted. It became a criminal offence for one banned person to communicate with another (husbands and wives were given dispensation); for some banned people to have visitors; for banned people to fail to report regularly (some even daily) to a police station; for some to prepare *anything* for publication; and for anyone to publish an utterance or writing of a banned person.

He routed the Left, outlawing the Congress of Democrats, banning *New Age* and, when that was replaced by *Spark*, driving that out of existence by prohibiting the key members of its staff from taking any part in publishing. Yet when he released a list of communists to the Press in November 1962, he could produce the names of only 129 whites and 308 non-whites – some of whom had been politically inactive for years. However, he had a new bogey to hand: Communism was not the biggest danger confronting South Africa. Liberalism was a far greater enemy. And the English Press, he warned, must not think his eyes were closed.

Lilian Ngoyi and other men and women were each confined for five years to the small area of the townships in which they lived. Nor was it only the active who received such attention: Canon Calata – though he had not been a member of the A.N.C. since 1956 – was charged with furthering the aims of the unlawful A.N.C. The grounds? Two twenty-year-old pictures of A.N.C. deputations hanging on his wall – as they had done since they were taken. He was sentenced to six months' imprisonment, suspended for two years.

Vorster's next weapon was house arrest, served first against Helen Joseph – the British-born social worker. Soon Sisulu and Kotane were among those placed under twenty-four-hour house arrest. Most victims among the whites were former communists and before long the torment of existing in this physical and psychological cage drove them into exile in London.

Mandela, meantime, having returned to South Africa, continued his underground work despite a nation-wide police net. But in August 1962 he was captured. He was sentenced to five years' imprisonment: for having incited the people to stay-at-home in May 1961, and for leaving the country illegally. He told the court: 'When my sentence has been completed, I will still be moved by my conscience to resist race discrimination.'

Even while his trial was taking place, members of the underground A.N.C. were conferring in Bechuanaland with representatives from A.N.C. missions in African states. Under its New Plan the A.N.C. continued secretly to organize and its policy remained non-violent – the intention being even at this late stage to educate people politically and to raise funds for the defence of those continually arrested; but to unsophisticated people used to public meetings and all the trappings of annual conferences, to function discreetly in cells came hard.

1962 ended in widespread violence. Umkonto's controlled sabotage was by this time in many instances proving to be carefully perpetrated as power pylons, telephone installations and railway signals were blown up. But in East London, a member of M K initiated unbridled petrol bombing of houses of pro-Government chiefs. In one of them an African child was killed and another injured.

And in Paarl, in the Western Cape's beautiful fruit-growing valleys, where wives and families of workers had been cruelly endorsed out, so that 2,000 'bachelors' lived in barracks, grievances mounted. It was a ready-made opportunity for the extremists of P.A.C. who had formed Poqo, offering 'freedom' at twenty-five cents a time and no questions. In the intimidating going on at least eight Africans and Coloured people had been murdered in the location, and the arrest of seven men for these crimes on 21 November set a mob marching to attack the police station and on till they swept into the white part of Paarl.

In the riots two whites were murdered, others injured, while five Africans were shot and some wounded. A one-Judge inquiry was held with substantial evidence given of the grievances that had fertilized Poqo and its terrorist outcome, yet this ferocious warning was ignored as was another – the murder of three African policemen in Langa, where enforced 'bachelors' – 12,000 of 18,000 in barracks being married men – still fomented frustration. In Paarl hundreds were arrested. Endorsing out of wives and children from the Western Cape continued unabated.

At the United Nations the annual debate on apartheid gathered steam. The Afro-Asian states once again advocated economic sanctions as the only potentially non-violent way of bringing an end to that policy, and this time they achieved the necessary two-thirds majority. Britain, the United States, Canada, Australia and most of Western Europe (excluding Scandinavia) made up the sixteen countries that opposed the resolution.

18 1963–4: The Violent Years

1963: *Freedom* year, the year in which Robert Sobukwe and other P.A.C. leaders had promised 'freedom and independence'. Sobukwe was to be freed on 3 May.

And the Acting President of the P.A.C., Potlako Leballo, had settled in Basutoland after serving his two-year sentence. The combination of forces at his disposal was dangerous. The question would be, dangerous for whom?

There was the mystical respect thousands of young Africans felt for Sobukwe. There was the monstrous frustration of these young men, born and bred and – most of them – barely educated in the faceless townships of the Transvaal and Western Cape; their highest prospect to make tea and carry messages for the white 'master' (the modernization of 'baas'), their more likely one to become labourers or cleaners or garden boys or, rejecting such 'opportunities' for living their only lifetime thus, to become *tsotsis* and at least have the excitement of fully-fledged crime ahead. There was *that* promise of freedom in 1963. And there was the force of Leballo's recklessness.

Violence was in the air. A P.A.C. document referred to a P.A.C. 'task force' which 'started killing innocent people, plundering, burning and terrorizing . . . exercising their instincts of self-impotence [*sic*] freely and unchecked', an 'instinct' which, with the coming of Poqo, was repressed a bit, 'because there was some organization and discipline in the fighting forces.'[1] Leballo was alternately reported as claiming P.A.C. and Poqo to be the same, and denying this. In the Transkei Poqo was suspected of

1. Memo on *Commands and Commanders*.

241

the murder of a tribal headman and of attacks on the Government-supporting Chief, Kaiser Matanzima, whose accession to power caused upheavals, which police, aided by his impis, subdued. Armed Poqo groups were arrested travelling from the Western Cape; in one clash with the police ten Africans and a white policeman were killed and others wounded. On 2 February, near the Bashee River, five whites in a road camp were slashed to death. Scores of Africans were arrested. Six men from Langa, when sentenced to death for the murder of a Transkeian chief, said Poqo had driven them to it.

On 13 February, Leballo, according to State evidence, sent an 'Urgent Warning' from Maseru in code: The situation was 'graver and graver'. The 'forces of darkness' (police) had wiped out certain P.A.C. branches. 'I am directing you, the FINAL WARNING . . . the date of a JIVE SESSION (attack) has now been chosen.' Sometimes the signature was 'Macdonald, Acting Director – Dance Association', sometimes, in a jumble of codes about going to the 'tournament or twist session without football kit', it was 'Blackburn, Acting Referee, S.A.A. Football League'. A batch of such circulars was captured by the South African police, who had embargoed mail from Basutoland; the recipients were arrested, some of them on 21 March.

From Maseru, on the same day, Leballo put out a newsletter declaring: 'African Nationalism is now poised to unleash invincible knock-out blow against white supremacist savagery of Verwoerdism in South Africa.' Two days later he gave a Press conference, and announced that the P.A.C. 'with shocking determination stands by its pledge to free the African people in 1963 by Positive Action, which is now imminent'.[1] Throughout South Africa police raided and arrested, capturing many more missives, including membership lists. On 2 April Basutoland police raided his office, detaining thirteen P.A.C. members and seizing cartons of documents, including a list of 10,000 names. Leballo escaped and went into hiding.

Meanwhile, Patrick Duncan renounced his belief in a policy of non-violence to become the P.A.C.'s first white member,

1. Documents handed in as evidence in P.A.C. trials.

leaving immediately to lobby for support for its policy in Britain and America.

8 April was said to be the day Leballo had chosen for the rising. By then thousands had been arrested.

And meanwhile the one-man inquiry into the Paarl riots, Judge Snyman, though he reckoned Poqo membership to be only several thousand, strongest in Langa and Nyanga, had urged swift action to deal with its activity and plans. The result went far beyond his recommendations, and on 24 April the Minister of Justice said the police had been operating with obsolete weapons, therefore the General Laws Amendment Bill of 1963 was needed. Detention without trial, in solitary confinement, for periods of up to 90 days which could be cumulative – till 'this side of eternity' the Minister mocked – during which detainees would be interrogated until they replied 'satisfactorily' to all questions put. This was the most heinous of all the new 'weapons'.

But there were others: much increased powers against those suspected of belonging to unlawful organizations and the use of provisions of the Suppression of Communism Act against any unlawful organization. (As a result, Press headlines frequently labelled trials of A.N.C. and P.A.C. 'Red'.) Between five years to death was imposed for anyone convicted if, at any place outside South Africa, since 26 June 1950, he had advocated bringing about change (including social or economic change) by 'violent or forcible' means, or any of the statutory objects of communism by the intervention, guidance or assistance of any foreign government or institution; or if he had undergone training or obtained information of use in furthering the aims of communism or of unlawful organizations.

One of the other clauses was directed against – for the time being – one man: Robert Sobukwe. It gave the Minister of Justice power to detain political prisoners after they had served their sentences. On 1 May the law was passed. On 3 May Sobukwe was *not* freed. He was transported to detention on Robben Island, the flat bleak island off Table Bay which, apart from occasional diversions such as housing a leper colony, had for centuries been a penal settlement.

By June, according to the Minister of Justice, 3,246 Africans had been arrested on Poqo charges, of whom 124 were convicted for murder.

In numerous trials evidence was led of a planned uprising against the whites. State witnesses included accomplices and spies planted as P.A.C. members. Some of the accused, who included sixteen-year-olds in school blazers, insisted they had only been to a couple of meetings, most denied all knowledge of the plans and any 'intent of violence'. Others admitted collecting bombs and hiding them. In a Pretoria trial, defence application for adequate adjournment to prepare the case, after a hurried and vague indictment had been successfully questioned, was refused and the accused were left to defend themselves. One of them, who had allegedly been assaulted in detention and received a broken ear-drum, seemed incapable of comprehending; the Court record, when it came to his defence, read: Accused No. 7 (*wishes to maintain silence*).

The trials concerned attacks planned in Pretoria, Benoni, Cape Town, Johannesburg, Kingwilliamstown, Lady Frere and Germiston, with resulting sentences ranging from five to twenty years. One eighteen-year-old was among the six sentenced to imprisonment for life.

All this while Leballo hid. As soon as the Basutoland Government's warrant for his arrest expired, in September, he surfaced. *Drum* magazine referred to the 'dismay and anger' he had caused 'among many Africans'.[1] With Sobukwe indefinitely incarcerated, he would continue to lead the P.A.C.

P.A.C. and A.N.C. were as mutually hostile as ever, a hostility vented abroad as well as at home where Leballo's March newsletter had attacked the A.N.C. as 'puppies and puppets of foreign powers' – and accused the Congress not only of planning to assassinate the entire leadership of the P.A.C. but of selling out Mandela. Indeed P.A.C. abroad went further and claimed Mandela had been sold out by communists because he was moving towards the P.A.C.! In May an A.N.C. circular read: 'The A.N.C. Spearheads Revolution. Leballo? No.' The way to

1. May 1963.

'smash' the 'instruments of white power' was 'well-planned strategic violence', it went on. 'The Leballo way is useless. . . . Umkonto has no need to boast. The people are with us. . . .'

If many of the youth followed Sobukwe, more mature men, ranging from labourers to university lecturers, were 'furthering the aims' of the A.N.C., or had joined Umkonto. MK sabotage had been stepped up since November 1962; the townships might be thrilled; white South Africa – to judge from the brief and almost casual Press reporting – went on its way. Only occasionally, as in January 1963, when a Nationalist newspaper office in Natal was blown up, did a sabotage story rate substantial headlines. By May damage in 29 cases was assessed at just over £22,000 – most of it due to sabotage to railway property, but in fact by then there had been some 200 cases. Among the captured saboteurs were young Indians who had tried to blow up a signal box and – evidently through an *agent provocateur* – been trapped by police. Three of them, while in detention, alleged torture by assaults and electric shock 'treatment'. They were sentenced to twelve years' imprisonment. But the great majority of saboteurs were Africans, as were those leaving South Africa for education or military training abroad.

Through the assistance not only of the Southern Rhodesian but the Federal police, in Northern Rhodesia and Nyasaland, several groups of men were arrested while travelling north or south and handed over to the South African police, to be sentenced to between two years for leaving South Africa without travel documents, and, in the case of men found guilty of being A.N.C. returning from three months' training in Ethiopia, to an additional twenty years' imprisonment. They were tried in camera. In one such case men were convicted on the evidence of accomplices. Their attempts to get legal defence had failed. (Later a lawyer took the cases to petition and the sentences were reduced to a total of twelve years.)

Probably the record for being persistently persecuted was held by Walter Sisulu. Of the six occasions when he had been arrested in 1962, only one had resulted in charges that stuck and in March 1963 he was sentenced to six years' imprisonment for furthering the aims of the A.N.C. and inciting people to stay-at-home in May 1961. He was granted bail of £3,000, pending an appeal, and the twelve-hour house arrest imposed on him in 1962 was promptly doubled to twenty-four hours. On 20 April he went underground. An A.N.C. Press statement declared: 'He remains, and at all times will be, at the disposal of our Congress and in the first ranks of our leadership.' On 26 June he broadcast on a secret Freedom radio in South Africa.

Meanwhile on 20 June his wife, Albertina, had been the first woman to be held under the 90-days law, when she and their seventeen-year-old son Max were both imprisoned for interrogation. The four younger children had to be left in the care of a fourteen-year-old cousin for several weeks.

90-days: in effect, on 1 May South Africa's white Parliament – which claimed membership of the Western civilized world – had enacted the most abominable law in the country's history, legalizing torture. The opposition United Party had supported the Bill at its third reading. Only Helen Suzman of the Progressive Party had voted against it at every stage.

A week later arrests had begun. Throughout South Africa the Security Police moved in with their new weapon. Non-whites had long been accustomed to harsh treatment, if not assault, in the police stations and jails. Now they and whites were subject to a new and subtle 'technique' – legalized – justified in the minds of its users, when 'communistic', 'liberalistic' enemies were attacking the very foundations of the State.

In no time at all, 90 days in solitary confinement had produced a busy crop of informers – some of whom decided to save their skins after only a few hours, some of whom held out until psychologically broken, some of whom were tricked into believing their comrades had broken before them, some of whom were physically tortured. None of whom had had any conception of what solitary confinement in itself could do to a human being. A macabre and startling facet was that some who went in for treachery in a big way went even beyond minimum facts. It was as if they hoped to win their interrogators' admiration by spewing forth information, involving unknown people, sending the police net ever wider, sometimes embroidering statements falsely.

All the while the Government was doing its best to whitewash South Africa's image, with the very considerable aid of the South African Foundation, led by Sir Francis de Guingaud and other prosperous industrialists and businessmen – even including Harry Oppenheimer of the Progressive Party. *Apartheid* was acknowledged to be a dirty word abroad. 'Separate development', 'parallel streams', 'self-government' of 'Bantu homelands' within a South Africa 'commonwealth' – all these were tried out, but the most felicitous came from Dr Verwoerd himself: South Africa's policy, he said, was 'four-streamed vertical separate development'. The outside world remained unedified.

'Self-government' with its 'separate freedom' was there to behold in its early stages in the first Bantustan, the Transkei. It would have a flag, an anthem – ironically *Nkosi Sikelel' i-Afrika* – and Xhosa as its official language. The white South African Parliament would retain power over defence, external affairs, police, post office, railways, immigration and other subjects including the Transkeian constitution, leaving the Transkei government a limited say in its budget, the maintenance of law and order, control of lower courts, of land settlement and agricultural and similar services, and a number of local matters. *All* laws passed by the Transkei Assembly required the State President's assent.

The Government having previously confirmed Kaiser Matanzima, pro-apartheid chief, to be Chairman of the Territorial Authority, and the majority in the Assembly being reserved for sixty chiefs (Government appointments), the elections for the other forty-five seats would be the proof of the people's desires. Thirty-eight of the forty-five seats were won by Chief Victor Poto whose Democratic party stands for multi-racialism. Matanzima, with the majority of chiefs behind him, became the first Prime Minister. His serious acceptance of the Government's professed policies from the start led to utterances provoking a quick slap-down. His early reference to the White man as having no claim to land between the Fish River in the Eastern Cape and

Zululand brought a reproof from Verwoerd: 'There can be no question whatsoever' of that whole territory becoming a 'Bantu homeland'. Significantly, throughout the elections and during Matanzima's initiation as Chief Minister, the emergency regulations, with detentions and banishments without trial, remained in force in the Transkei.[1]

As for the seven million Africans living and working in the so-called white 87 per cent of the country – described by apartheid theoreticians as 'guest workers' or 'loan labour' – in 1963 they became subject to yet further harsh controls. The Bantu Laws Amendment Act, despite impassioned and carefully argued protests at home and abroad, was passed. Helen Suzman described the new law as stripping the African 'of every pretension he has to being . . . a free human being in the country of his birth', reducing him 'to the level of a chattel'. As in 'political' offences, a new factor – contrary to any normal practice of justice – was that in any ensuing legal case the onus of proof would be on the accused and not on the prosecution.

By 23 August some 300 men and women were held under 90-days. On 5 September Looksmart Solwandle Ngudle, from Cape Town, a man regarded by his friends as tough and brave, was found hanged in his prison cell. He had only been detained since 19 August. After his death the Government imposed a ban on him, and any statements he made during his lifetime could thus not be quoted. The State declared Ngudle had committed suicide after giving information to the police which led to arrests. An advocate who had seen a fellow-prisoner was informed that Ngudle had died as a result of torture. Either way, the interrogators could claim their first life.

Meanwhile Dennis Brutus, who had been banned for his initiative in fighting racial discrimination in sport, was arrested and charged with breaking his ban. He fled to Swaziland, then on to Mozambique, hoping to make his way to the Olympic Games Committee meeting due in Germany, but the Portuguese police arrested him and, despite his Federal passport and birthright from Salisbury, handed him over to the South African

1. And are still in force at the time of writing.

police. Back in Johannesburg he made a desperate attempt to escape; the police shot him and before long he, too, was to join the growing ranks of non-white political prisoners on Robben Island, to serve eighteen months.

By November, a 90-day detainee, Elijah Loza, was re-arrested upon release after serving two terms totalling 180 days. The Minister of Justice declared that if a detainee refused to give information to the police, they had no option but to rearrest him. 'Torture by mind-breaking' was the all too apt description to be given to this activity on the part of the South African police.

A 'Summit Conference' of thirty leaders of African States meeting in Addis Ababa had adopted an All-African Charter and sent a delegation to inform the Security Council of the explosive situation in South Africa. They also set up a Liberation Committee in Dar-es-Salaam to administer a fund to aid liberation movements.

The U.N.'s Special Committee on the Policy of Apartheid, set up at the end of 1962, was busy producing impeccably annotated reports. The military build-up in the Republic was detailed and the call for an embargo on arms to South Africa was winning support from forty-four countries, including the United States. But Britain and France insisted on continuing their trade in arms. As resolutions condemning racialism and warning of the dangers unless radical change came soon drew wider support, an initiative from the Scandinavian countries was adopted: the Secretary-General was to appoint a group of experts to seek a constructive way out of South Africa's deadlock.

But the most remarkable vote on any South African issue in the U.N. came on 11 October 1963, when the General Assembly, by 106 votes to 1 (South Africa) called for the immediate and unconditional release of political prisoners, and an immediate end to all the political trials – including those under the 'Sabotage' Act. Even Britain voted for this resolution.

During 1963, 3,355 men and women (201 of them juveniles) were detained – 1,186 of them without trial, either under the 90-days law or under the Transkei's emergency regulations.[1]

1. Minister of Justice's statement to Assembly, January 1964.

The desperate anxiety of the families of these people, many of whom could get no news of their relatives, swelled the intense disquiet continually expressed by South Africa's shrinking body of public-spirited whites. In December the extreme mental suffering and possible lasting mental effects of solitary confinement had been exposed by sixty leading psychiatrists, psychologists and medical specialists in Cape Town when they appealed for abolition of the 90-day system. This infliction of such mental suffering was no less abhorrent than physical torture, they declared. On 24 January 1964 James Tyitya was found hanged in his cell in Port Elizabeth jail.

According to the Minister of Justice, 177 policemen and 177 members of the Prisons Department were convicted of irregular treatment of people in custody between 1960–3. He told the Assembly that only 49 complaints of assault had been lodged by 90-day detainees, and none was found to be of substance.

Mrs Suzman riposted that detainees were afraid to complain, being in the hands of the very people who assaulted them, or, if freed, running the risk of rearrest under the 90-day clause. She and others continually urged the need for judicial inquiry into alleged assaults.

The Minister refused. But in one case, in March 1964, like the peak of an iceberg, evidence of police violence was so blatant that even white public opinion was scandalized.

A Police station commander and four white policemen at Bultfontein – a village in the Free State – were charged with the murder, by whipping, by electric shock treatment and by suffocation, of an African suspected of stealing a small sum of money. One of the policemen remarked that he did not think there was a police station in the country that did not use such methods of interrogation. Two of the policemen were found guilty, not of murder but of culpable homicide with intent to do grievous bodily harm, the others of lesser offences. Their sentences ranged from three to nine years, some with strokes.

Meanwhile, the death penalty was imposed on three Africans from Port Elizabeth, found guilty on accomplice evidence of ordering the shooting of a State witness, and of sabotage. One of

them, Vuyisile Mini, trade unionist and A.N.C. member, had
been in the Treason Trial. Subsequently three other men – one
of whom was found guilty of the actual killing – were also condemned to death for this murder.

19 1964: Rivonia and After

Meanwhile in the African states, in London, Washington and at the United Nations, doubtless in Moscow too, attentive diplomats and civil servants followed the proceedings of what was to become South Africa's most spectacular trial.

The armed State forces surrounding the Palace of Justice in the centre of Afrikanerdom, Pretoria, magnified the drama of the opening of the proceedings against Nelson Mandela and Walter Sisulu and others captured on 11 July 1963, and emphasized the reality and the fantasy: the reality of the State's immense physical power and its fear of these few men, which only enhanced their dignity and calm confidence in the justice of their cause; the fantasy that the Court must be protected from potential armed attack.

Gone were the one-time relaxed courtroom scenes of the Treason Trial, the mixing of accused and public and lawyers. The significance of the Rivonia trial – as it was called – apart from the stature of some of the men in the dock, was the ultimate underlining of the change from non-violence to violence: the State, by outlawing non-violent African nationalist organizations, had forced them to give up, or to turn to secret violence.

The drama had begun on a mid winter afternoon, when policemen, hidden in a dry-cleaner's van, drove from Johannesburg to the spacious outlying suburb of Rivonia. There, at Liliesleaf Farm, they made their great coup. Walter Sisulu, Govan Mbeki (who had also gone underground), and others were there – most of them disguised. Also there were 250 documents, many relating to the manufacture of explosives, one of them – for some fantastic reason not destroyed – Mandela's

252

diary of his tour of Africa, and – amongst others open on a table in the house – a draft memorandum with the title *Operation Mayibuye.*

On 12 August two of the whites held, Arthur Goldreich and Harold Wolpe, by promising a bribe to a warder, made a spectacular escape from South Africa, while another, Bob Hepple, who had agreed to give evidence for the State, fled rather than do so.

Nelson Mandela was brought from Robben Island while Sisulu and the remaining eight were to be held in solitary for eighty-eight days while the State prepared its case. Sisulu later declared in evidence that he was asked to testify against his fellows, or give information confidentially, under threat of the death penalty.

In the Trial, which opened at the end of October, the State, after initially alleging 222 acts of sabotage against Umkonto, reduced the number to 199, only to have its indictment quashed at the request of the Defence – led by Abram Fischer, Q.C. Under the final indictment the accused were alleged to have recruited men for training with the object of causing a violent revolution and of assisting units of foreign countries should they invade the Republic. The acts of sabotage for which they were allegedly responsible were now reduced to 193, of which the Defence conceded 20. The State in the event failed to prove more than this.

The trial again focused the attention of the outside world. The amazing U.N. vote of 106 to 1 reflected growing anxiety for the welfare of Mandela, Sisulu and others, and indeed had been partly achieved through the lobbying of their friend, Oliver Tambo. Most white South Africans might see the Rivonia accused as sinister conspirators, the outside world saw them as men driven to an extremity – yet even then trying to act with restraint – in struggling for the birthright of the African people. That almost all the whites named as accused or co-conspirators of Umkonto were communists was on the whole regarded as an unfortunate but understandable factor emerging from South Africa's policies and history.

The State closed its case in February 1964. The accused were a microcosm of the country: six Africans, three whites (of whom one was quickly freed with charges withdrawn) and an Indian. When they were called to the witness box, they did not defend themselves so much as make a positive affirmation of what they represented.

. Mandela's address to the Court from the dock made a historic impact abroad and in South Africa where, as never before, whites were forced to recognize that it was not white agitators leading the blacks, but Africans of imposing authority.

He recalled the long history of the A.N.C.; the tyranny, exploitation and oppression; the ultimate decision to turn to violence only after a 'calm and sober assessment' of the political situation. Terrorism had been rejected. Always he and other A.N.C. leaders were moved by the belief that South Africa belonged to all who lived in it but by June 1961, he said, 'it could not be denied that our policy to achieve a non-racial state by non-violence, had achieved nothing . . .'.

In the life of any nation, he pointed out, 'the time comes . . . when there remain only two choices – submit or fight. That time has now come to South Africa. . . .' Umkonto, by its policy of controlled sabotage, hoped to bring the Government and its supporters to their senses before it was too late. It hoped also to affect foreign trade. As for the decision to send men out for military training, this had been necessary so that a nucleus of trained men would be available if guerilla warfare started. He had had some training while briefly in Algeria as he wanted to be side by side with his people. He spoke of the creed of the A.N.C. being one of African nationalism – a 'concept of freedom and fulfilment for the African people in their own land' but not of driving whites into the sea. 'Our fight is basically against poverty and lack of human dignity' and meticulously he enunciated the facts of life as lived by Africans.

The aspirations of his people, he expressed with profoundly moving directness: 'Africans want to be paid a living wage. Africans want to perform work which they are capable of doing, and not work which the Government declares them to be capable of. We want to be allowed to live where we obtain work and not to be endorsed out of an area because we were not born there. We want to be allowed to own land in places where we work. . . . We want to be part of the general population and not confined to living in our ghettos. African men want to have their wives and children to live with them where they work and not be forced into an unnatural existence in men's hostels. Our women want to be with their menfolk, and not to be left permanently widowed in the reserves. We want to be allowed out after 11 o'clock at night and not to be confined to our rooms like little children. We want to be allowed to travel in our own country and to seek work where we want to and not where the Labour Bureau tells us to. We want a just share in the whole of South Africa. We want security and a stake in society.

'Above all, we want equal political rights.'

Why must whites fear this? 'The A.N.C. has spent half a century fighting against racialism,' he pointed out and 'when it triumphs, as it certainly must, it will not change that policy. . . .

'Our struggle is a truly national one. It is a struggle of the African people, inspired by our own suffering and our own experience. It is a struggle for the right to live.'

At this point Mandela ceased reading from the long statement he had prepared. The Court was still. There was at this time a real fear that he and others might be sentenced to death. He looked up at the Judge, Quartus de Wet, and said quietly:

'During my lifetime I dedicated myself to this struggle of the African people. I have fought against white domination and I have fought against black domination. I have cherished the ideal of a democratic and free society in which all persons live together in harmony, and with equal opportunities. It is an ideal which I hope to live for and to achieve. But, if needs be, it is an ideal for which I am prepared to die.'

He sat down. From the galleries came a sort of deep sigh; then absolute silence.

Bram Fischer rose: 'I call Accused No. 2.'

Mandela's concluding words, so quietly spoken from the dock, were to ring out in unexpected places, inspiring black and

255

white in far-away continents: even in the streets of New York outside the United Nations, where Ossie Davis, Negro actor and writer – a man with something of Mandela's nobility of aspect – was to read them to a crowd protesting against the Rivonia trial and all political trials in South Africa.

Accused Number 2, Walter Sisulu, was the main Defence witness and came under prolonged attack from the Prosecutor, Dr Percy Yutar.

Once he had taken the measure of the Prosecution it was as if Sisulu forgot he was in the witness box. It must have been eleven years since he had last appeared on a public platform and now again he dominated the situation.

To him and Mbeki fell the main task of defining the distinction between the A.N.C. and Umkonto. He had remained with the A.N.C. and been the main link at the topmost level with Mbeki, who, early in 1963, joined Mandela and others of all races on the High Command of Umkonto. The A.N.C., after going underground with its new plan for functioning secretly, had retained its all-African membership and non-violent policy for, Mbeki explained, it would have been 'political dishonesty' to transform it into a violent organization which would have exposed its members, including old men in their seventies, to charges of sabotage. Umkonto was essentially small, with specially trained men of all races. In 1963 the A.N.C. had planned an anti-pass campaign and boycott of the Transkei elections, but the 90-day detentions had blocked its organizing. However, one thing could not be explained away – the fact that A.N.C. missions abroad were used equally by A.N.C. and Umkonto at home.

One of the most important pieces of evidence at the Trial was *Operation Mayibuye*. It had been drafted by Arthur Goldreich, architect and stage-designer, a flamboyant man who, astonishingly, had been recommended by Mandela as a member of Umkonto, and who had lived in Lilliesleaf Farm – a property bought by the Communist Party, where Mandela and Sisulu were able to stay from time to time while underground.

Number 9 accused, Elias Matsoaledi, was a quiet-spoken man

who had the painful experience of seeing his wife, Caroline, suddenly taken off from the Court by police into 90-day detention, with their seven small children left to the eventual care of a grandparent. From the dock this man made a statement. A clerk, aged thirty-nine, he had grown up as one of ten children in Sekukhuniland. He had got a job in a boot factory at 24s. a week but upon asking for a rise had been sacked. So he had joined a trade union and the A.N.C.; it was 1948 when the Nationalists had come to power. He said: 'I know this is not the place to describe in detail all the heavy burdens which an African has to carry, but I am telling the Court of some of these matters which make our hearts sore and our minds heavy. When I was asked to join Umkonto we Sizwe it was at a time when it was clear to me that all our years of peaceful struggle had been of no use. The Government would not let us fight peacefully any more, and had blocked all our legal acts by making them illegal. I thought a great deal about the matter. I could see no other way open to me. What I did brought me no personal gain, what I did I did for my people and because I thought it was the only way left for me to help my people. That is all I have to say.'

His wife was to be re-arrested, at the end of 90 days, for a further time of detention. No charge was ever laid against her. He too had been held under 90 days and alleged he had been given electric shock torture, yet he had refused to make any statements to the police or betray his friends. Indeed, a memorable feature of the trial itself was the absolute refusal of all the accused to answer any question that might implicate others.

Among the broad issues that emerged was one concerning the Indian people. Kathrada who, as a schoolboy had been a passive resister in 1946 and a member of the Young Communist League, had come early to the conclusion that taking small concessions from the whites was no solution for his people; that they could only achieve true freedom if they threw in their lot with the Africans. And Lionel 'Rusty' Bernstein – who had been at Liliesleaf Farm to discuss what could be done about 90-day detentions, and who was to be acquitted – gave evidence about a pamphlet he had written after Sharpeville, warning of the

257

dangers of another Algeria, and urging whites to negotiate to meet the demands of non-whites and thus avoid an ultimate period 'of great civil bitterness'.

On 11 June Judge de Wet gave his verdict: Mandela was the prime mover in founding Umkonto to perform sabotage. The defence contention was accepted that the leaders gave instructions 'that care should be exercised that no person was injured or killed' but they should have contemplated that the saboteurs 'would probably get out of hand'. The defence had conceded that more than 300 men had left for military training outside the country. Sisulu's denial of membership of Umkonto was unimpressive; MK and A.N.C. executives were virtually the same thing. As for a remark of Mandela's that in parts of Africa 'there are great reservations about our policy and there is a widespread feeling that the A.N.C. is a communist-dominated organization', despite Mandela's denial that he was a communist or had communist sympathy, Judge de Wet shared that 'feeling' after hearing the evidence. However, he found that the plans for guerilla warfare had not been accepted by the leaders.

Alan Paton, speaking in mitigation of the sentence, expressed the Liberal Party's 'highest regard' for Mandela and recognized the 'great courage' of Sisulu and Mbeki, their determination, resolution and great ability. 'None of these three is known as a person who is obsessed with any desire for vengeance, any kind of racial vengeance,' he said, and he spoke of their 'deep devotion to the cause of their people'.

On 12 June 1964, the Judge pronounced sentence. The crime of which he found all but Bernstein guilty was, he said, essentially high treason, but as the State had not seen fit so to charge them, he would not impose the death sentence. He sentenced them to life imprisonment.

So on 13 June Mandela, Sisulu and the other non-whites were sent to Robben Island maximum security prison. They did not appeal – those who were leaders because they accepted full responsibility for their acts, the others because they felt even if they succeeded, they would be immediately detained.

Like virtually all political prisoners, they were graded Category D – one half-hour visit every six months, one letter every six months, food for Africans that was grossly ill-nourishing and yet on which they had to do hard labour. Most would have periods for limited studies.

At this time Sobukwe, the only one living under detention among the Island's thousand or more prisoners, applied for an exit permit to leave South Africa, and was refused. His detention was renewed for another year.

All these events found an echo in the Security Council which passed two resolutions in June. One – from which Britain, the United States and France abstained because the Rivonia Trial was still in progress at the time – called for an end to the trial, and an amnesty for all political prisoners – including Mini and others under sentence of death. The second – nine days later – after the Rivonia judgment, repeated the appeal for an amnesty, and for the abolition of imprisonment without charge or trial. But it also – with the qualified support of Britain and America – agreed to set up a committee to study the implications of measures under the Charter which could induce South Africa to change her policies. The Soviet Union was among abstainers because the resolution was not strong enough.

And the British Government drew the attention of the South African Government to widespread criticism in Britain of the length of sentences in the Rivonia Trial, and the desirability of reducing them. For Britain it was an unprecedented action, among the many similar messages sent by Governments, organizations and individuals, to the State President and Dr Verwoerd.

During the Rivonia Trial Umkonto laid off sabotage, and few cases were reported. But immediately after the verdict explosions damaged post offices and pylons in various places, and an attack was made on the walls of Johannesburg jail – the Fort. Hundreds of arrests followed and massive searches took place even of the homes of white academics, of journalists and, for the first time, of a member of the Progressive Party. In Port Elizabeth's townships what was now becoming typical was a raid in the small hours of the morning, when forty-one men and women were dragged from their beds and, humiliatingly, were not

259

allowed to dress properly despite the mid-winter cold, before being hustled off to 90-day detention.

But it was after the rounding up of numbers of whites that the already powerful protests against 90-day detention became vehement, for, during the four months these men and women were detained while the State obtained its evidence, reports accumulated of a new form of torture: the statue torture learnt from Algeria where the French had used it with horrible effect, but described long before in Koestler's *Darkness at Noon*. Tough, confident young men could be reduced by this combination of solitary confinement and interrogation while standing in one spot for forty-two hours or more to tearful, tremulous disintegration.

A startling new factor was that the detainees included not only men and women banned under the Suppression of Communism Act, but university lecturers, students and journalists, most of them known members of the Liberal Party. Then on 9 July Abram Fischer, Q.C., was detained, to be released a few days later but ultimately re-arrested and charged with others for leadership and membership of the Communist Party.

Early in the year a group of Coloured teachers in the Cape had been tried with others for membership of the Yu Chi Chan Club. Their leader, a brilliant graduate of a German university, Dr Neville Alexander, explained that they had studied ways of overthrowing the Government by revolution but had made no plans, nor taken any action. He and four others were sentenced to ten years' imprisonment.

Soon it transpired from evidence given by accomplices that the young white liberals held – most of them from Cape Town and Johannesburg – were members of the African Resistance Movement, a new title for the National Liberation Committee, which had performed the first sabotage in October 1961. The originators had left the country to settle in Britain and several leaders of the A.R.M. escaped from South Africa while their fellows were being arrested. The non-white membership of A.R.M. proved to be a token, though its one Coloured member, Edward Daniels, found guilty of sabotage, was to get the heaviest sentence – fifteen years. The white members were sentenced to between two to ten years for their various parts in A.R.M.'s sabotage or organization.

These young men and women, several of whom expressed a profound sense of futility about their activity when they came to be sentenced, represented the atrocious frustration felt by young white intellectuals at being unable to halt South Africa's progress towards racial conflict. Though they opted for sabotage, and the young whites who were later to plead guilty to being communists had gone slogan painting and had circulated memoranda (including one about 90-day detentions) for which they were sentenced to between one and three years' imprisonment, common to all of them was desperation at their growing isolation from Africans. Whether it was the young liberals trying to find a suitable African or two to join their *African* Resistance Movement, or the young communists painting A.N.C. or Umkonto slogans, they were symbolic of the same tragedy: the gulf between white and black that Verwoerd and Vorster had so successfully blasted. And to the cost of both groups, a former close, respected colleague would be the chief witness for the State, inexplicably brought to such treachery within a few hours of detention, and without torture. (The other witness against the young communists was to be a spy whom the police succeeded in planting after ten years of communist underground activity.)

But if these had been violent years, if even Umkonto leaders had been ingenuous, and been disobeyed by some followers whose planting of petrol bombs in the houses of police or informers had resulted in two or three deaths, not even Poqo's anarchistic murders rocked the country as did the first act of terrorism: an outrageous protest against an outrageous regime which, far from achieving its purpose of bringing home to white South Africa the disaster of its policies, dealt a shocking blow to the struggle for justice. On 24 July 1964, when a time bomb exploded in Johannesburg Station's 'Europeans only' concourse, a number of people were seriously injured. As a result an elderly woman died and one small girl was monstrously harmed.

As was the case in 1960 in the attempted assassination of Dr

Verwoerd, the perpetrator was a white man with a record of mental disturbance. But the station bomb explosion was a fully political act, John Harris being an active Liberal and organizer of the campaign against racial discrimination in sport, who had joined the A.R.M. And while horror at the act was doubtless uppermost in most people's feelings, there were those who regarded Harris as a hero, and who said: 'It's time whites suffered a bit, as we have suffered so long.'

Throughout 1964 the political trials continued in every area, the major ones for sabotage but scores for furthering the aims of the A.N.C. or, less often, the P.A.C. Between the times when he himself was arrested, Bram Fischer led the defence of the 'little Rivonia' trial, when Andrew Mashaba, Peter Mongano and six others – waiters, trade unionists and domestic servants in Pretoria – were found guilty of sabotage as members of Umkonto. Fischer, arguing in mitigation of sentence, said that while Mashaba and Mongano were the leaders of Umkonto in Pretoria and as such bore a greater responsibility for the offences (which included an attempt to blow up the Treason Trial court – the old Synagogue), it should be remembered that it was they who had kept the organization under control, and prevented loss of life. 'Symbolic sabotage' such as this was unique in history. These two leaders were sentenced to fifteen years, others to between five and twelve years. It was in this trial that a State witness, when brought into court, shouted his refusal to give evidence against his leaders. It was a brave and splendid gesture and all too rare.

The High Command of Umkonto had been renewed after the Rivonia arrests. Wilton Mkwayi – a Port Elizabeth leader who had been in the Treason Trial of 1956 – with two others – a white and an Indian – was found guilty of carrying this on. Mkwayi told the court his story. His striking demeanour and the simplicity of his words moved some who heard him even more than had Mandela in his more sophisticated declaration. Mkwayi's father had been an A.N.C. member, and had made Wilton one in 1940 at the age of seventeen. Poverty precluded education; labourer, office boy, factory worker, Mkwayi naturally became a trade unionist and, because of this and his A.N.C. interest, 'what whites like to call an agitator'. Since 1947 he had taken a leading part in the Port Elizabeth bus boycotts, the stay-at-homes, the Defiance Campaign, the Congress of the People, and in campaigns for higher wages and lower rents. He compared the long non-violent struggle with such acts of Government violence as the crushing of the 1946 mine strike and the 1950 May day strike, the armed threat against the Sophiatown community, Sharpeville. Driven to counter-violence, he had helped to found Umkonto but, he explained, 'Sabotage is not the beginning of a war, but a letter of invitation to the Government and the white minority' to come to a National Convention. Since going underground in 1960, he had toured Europe and Africa on trade union missions before undergoing military training in small arms in China, 'so that I too could fight for my country if necessary'. 'After all,' he pointed out, 'in South Africa white women, and boys and girls of sixteen, are taught to handle small arms.' He had been at Rivonia on the day of the arrests, but had managed to escape and continue working underground until captured. Because a State witness had opined that he was a communist, he dealt with the question, though he regarded it as of no great importance: 'I am not a communist' but, he added, 'We are oppressed not by communists but by a white minority Government' and in his experience communists had 'worked and fought side by side with the oppressed people . . .'.

He and his brothers – two already serving long sentences on Robben Island, a third sought by the police – were all fighting for liberation of their people from the tyranny of racial discrimination. He concluded by repeating Mandela's last remarks. He, too, was sentenced to life imprisonment, his companions to lesser terms.

By this time some 900 men and women had been held under 90 days, 134 of them for a second period and 13 for a third. Nearly 500 of them were being tried, mainly on the evidence given to the State by two or three hundred of the others. A law passed earlier in the year enabled the State to imprison recalcitrant witnesses for successive periods of a year unless they had a just excuse. Affidavits alleging assault, from standing torture to severe physical attacks, had been made by a number of men and women of all races, including men imprisoned on Robben Island, and had received substantial publicity at home and abroad. As a result conditions on Robben Island were said to have been somewhat improved, but the 90-day law remained an incentive to sadism, physical and psychological – sadism laced with zealotry.

Just a year after the death of Looksmart Ngudle, in September 1964, came the third violent death of a detainee: Suliman Salojee, a solicitor's clerk, jumped to his death from the seventh floor of security police headquarters in Johannesburg. At the time he was under interrogation.

On 5 November, the Minister of Justice spoke at a dinner about the 2,000 letters and cables of protest he had received from all over the world – which included an appeal from U Thant – concerning the death sentence on Vuyisile Mini and the other trade unionists found guilty of the murder of a State witness and of sabotage. He quoted an Afrikaner poet who had said one swallow did not make a summer, but that one bluefly could spoil a herd of cattle. 'Blue-flies can be dealt with in only two ways,' Vorster told the dinner guests. 'One can either kill them with a swat or you can open the window and let them out. This is exactly what we are doing in South Africa. Those who try to instigate political thuggery do not succeed; many of them are no longer with us.'[1]

At dawn the next morning Mini, Khayinga and Mkaba were hanged.

Overseas, the call for economic sanctions against South Africa had been invigorated by an international conference in London – initiated by Ronald Segal and other exiles and the Anti-Apartheid Movement. The resulting studies were of use both to a conference of forty-seven non-aligned nations, in Cairo in October, which supported the call for sanctions, and to members of the United Nations.

The Committee of Experts set up by the Security Council, headed by Mrs Myrdal and Sir Hugh Foot, had meanwhile made

1. *Contact*, 27 November 1964.

its report, combining a grave warning of the dangers of race conflict ahead if South Africa pursued its white supremacist policy,
with a genuine search for constructive, firm measures. The Committee concluded the only way out of the impasse was for a
National Convention of representatives of all races in South
Africa, with an amnesty of political prisoners an essential prelude. But – recognizing that the Government and white electorate were unlikely to make so beneficent and brave a move,
the Committee felt forced to recommend economic sanctions as
the only way of achieving a rapid transformation with the minimum of suffering and dislocation.

In all these activities the A.N.C. missions abroad, led by
Oliver Tambo, and exiles of other races, played a part – sub-
mitting memoranda, testifying to the Organization for African
Unity and to United Nations Committees. By this time missions
existed in Dar-es-Salaam, London, Cairo, Accra, Algiers, Lusaka
and Cuba. From South Africa Moses Kotane, Duma Nokwe,
and J. B. Marks had been sent abroad, after being under house
arrest in Johannesburg.

The P.A.C. remained active in Africa, but ambivalent both
towards the United Nations and the policy of sanctions. Its
'counter-method' was not disclosed. However, when Sobukwe
was refused an exit permit to leave South Africa, Leballo cabled
African leaders: DEMAND SANCTIONS EXPULSION MILITARY
ACTION AGAINST PRETORIA GOVERNMENT.

But the P.A.C.'s missions abroad were rent with regrettable
dissension, not surprising among men whom events – rather
than natural authority or political experience – had thrown into
positions of leadership, or whom exile, as so often in history,
could corrupt. One faction suspended Kgosana soon after his
arrival overseas and Peter Molotsi while in East Africa while, in
mid 1964, after a successful tour of the United States where he
was welcomed by the American Federation of Labor, Nana
Mahomo found himself suspended on return to London. So
serious were the splits that Leballo left Maseru in August 1964
not only to lobby abroad but to visit the missions in a 'desperate
attempt to close ranks' and 'eradicate these cancerous practices'.

Meanwhile those who carried out the suspension were intent on persuading African leaders that the P.A.C. was in the vanguard of the struggle in South Africa. One of the P.A.C. representatives in exile insisted: 'We are faced with the tasks of having to manœuvre carefully and brilliantly everywhere in order to destroy the false image of the A.N.C. and S.A.C.T.U.' It would therefore pay to 'stifle' the reports of expulsions and splits, especially any suspensions for misappropriation of funds which would discourage the P.A.C. being given financial support. And, he told the Maseru office, evidence of P.A.C. activity in South Africa was urgently needed.

The P.A.C.'s policy had changed considerably since its formation. During 1964 it was establishing 'close ties of solidarity' with China. It was a curious position for Patrick Duncan, for so long an acrimonious anti-communist, to be in. Meanwhile young P.A.C. men who had left South Africa for military training abroad deplored the 'dog eats dog policy', and appealed for reorganization.[1]

The P.A.C.'s need for Sobukwe's authority and power to lead and unite was greater than ever, but the South African Government was to renew his detention yet again, in 1965 and in 1966.

As for Chief Lutuli – an elder statesman – he was further restricted, being confined to the small area of Groutville Reserve, forbidden even to attend church services.

Mandela, Sobukwe and Lutuli were joined in the tribute paid by Martin Luther King to the African peoples and their allies throughout the long struggle in South Africa, when he spoke in London on his way to receive the Nobel Peace Prize. In a powerful speech he advocated withdrawal of American investments in South Africa and economic sanctions as the one hope of achieving change non-violently. In December 1961 Lutuli had been in Oslo. Now in 1964 King was there, both men symbolizing recognition of noble qualities of leadership in what was widely seen to be the gravest issue facing our era.

In the 1890s Dube had been inspired by Booker T. Washington; in the 1920s peasants in the Ciskei had awaited Garvey's

1. Documents laid in evidence in trials.

coming; many links of fact and of philosophy existed between the struggle for a birthright in South Africa and in America. In September 1964, at a Conference in Washington, Negro leaders faced up to the potential of the Negro vote in influencing American policy towards South Africa. From the United Nations, African Ambassadors emphasized that potential.

But meanwhile American and British investment mounted; 1964 was one of the best in South Africa's economic history – the main stimulus coming from a sharp increase in investment – 18 per cent higher than in 1963. And Defence expenditure was increased by 45 per cent over the previous year.

20 1965–6: Boere en Bandiete

South Africa 1965: a stable surface, a model of law and order; sunny, rich, inviting investors to enjoy phenomenally high, quick profits, and tourists to enjoy beaches, country clubs, flora and fauna with the titillating recollection that this is the country said to endanger world peace.

The only time the Nationalist Government was remotely near to breaking was after Sharpeville, and then it was rescued by British and American investors: the cracks were papered over. The chance that Mandela's call for a stay-at-home in 1961 would open the cracks was thwarted by all the power the State could galvanize, power that since has been fortified. The Congo, overseas condemnation of apartheid, sabotage, Poqo, above all the station bomb, rallied and hardened white support for the *status quo*.

The *status quo*? Rule by 'die Volk', led by Dr Hendrik Verwoerd and Balthazar Vorster – both supporters of Hitler in the 1940s; its ethos to be an inspiration for the 'sick' western world and, according to a broadcast by the Broederbond Chairman, Dr Piet Meyer, to 'make a decisive contribution to the consolidation of the entire West as a White world united in its struggle against the joint forces of the Yellow and Black races of the Earth'. 'Die Volk' – embattled forever in its spiritual *laager* against the forces of 'communism', of 'liberalism', of 'sickly humanism'.

Surely somewhere, in this apocalyptic delineation, there must be some aberration, some rebels who yet maintain the generosity, independence and bravery of the best of their forebears? But this tiny handful – Christians, academics, artists, lawyers –

268

cast out by 'die Volk', railed against as 'communist' and 'liberalist', are without physical or numerical power. One of them, Bram Fischer – while on trial, accused of leadership of the South African Communist Party – went underground early in 1965 to continue to oppose the 'monstrous policy' of the Government rather than face wasteful years of detention, only to be captured, to be brought to trial in March 1966.

And so 'die Volk', less than 2 million whites empowered by massive armaments and prosperity, orders the lives of $14\frac{1}{2}$ million non-whites. Yet in all the world, the only avowed supporters of apartheid are Portugal, the Rhodesian rebels, and a handful of societies such as the Ku Klux Klan, the John Birch Society, and the League of Empire Loyalists. Such is the power of gold.

And so 'die Volk's' ultimate argument can be put by one of its most persuasive spokesmen: if Africans were to be admitted to Parliament, Afrikaners would revolt, and 'our underground will be the best armed, the most sophisticated, the world has ever known; we shall be far more devilish than any Bantu could ever be'. (The moral seems to be: if you think we are dreadful in power, you can be sure we'll be even worse in opposition.)

But if this small tribe is intent on narcissistic self-preservation to the point of self-annihilation, what of the one and a half million English-speaking whites? For most, preoccupying motives remain profit and pleasure and a quiet life under the hot sun with, concomitant, political apathy. Though Anglo-Boer hostility simmers, to be brought to the boil regularly by Ministerial speeches on commemoration days, on one thing there is unity – the shoring up of white supremacy. The life-denying canker at the heart of this 'dogma' inevitably breeds cruelty, and cruelty is masked by mythology.

It is masked by the myth of ultimate 'separate freedoms' and in the delusion that, more and more, Africans are becoming satisfied with the Bantustan policy.[1]

1. After eighteen years of Nationalist rule, there is still only one Bantustan, the Transkei, which is still under a state of Emergency. Nine years after the Government's blue-print for economic development of the reserves

This mask was robustly cast off when Transkeians of both parties threw out Bantu education, and every one of the Transkei's primary schools in 1965 rejected the vernacular or Afrikaans as the medium of instruction, to choose English.

Cruelty is masked by comparisons with other parts of Africa, comparisons which are wholly irrelevant for South Africa, a wealthy, highly industrialized country in which the only valid comparisons are within its own borders, between its own citizens of whatever race.[1]

Cruelty breeds a sick society; a society where robbery with violence has become endemic, where the prison population is more than twice that of Britain (which has three times South Africa's population),[2] having doubled in ten years *but* where, significantly, something like three quarters of the prisoners are serving sentences of under four months for 'offences' such as under the pass laws, throwing ordinary people amongst criminals and breeding wholesale contempt of the law. A society which hanged 135 human beings in 1963, and 85 in 1964; which provides 25 farm jails so that farmers can have cheap labour; and which stunts education for African children so that they emerge apathetic, devoid of ambition or anarchistic.

Occasionally whites are forced to face the cruelty unmasked, as when the case was reported, in September 1965, of a ninety-

- the Tomlinson Report – said 50,000 jobs should be created annually, less than 4,000 have been, in reserves *and* border areas, the latter at 'iniquitously' low wages, to quote the President of T.U.C. (figures from *Race Relations News*, mid 1965).

1. Estimated *per capita* income 1962–3: whites £624, non-whites under £37. Average starting cash wages per month for African men in Johannesburg, £16. 2s. 6d. In Provincial service, it is £8. 2s. od. Minimum required for family of five to live on: £24 per month. On the mines, average wage for 1963: whites £1,281 p.a., Coloured and Asians £229, Africans £76 (in addition, compound accommodation and Native food). Prime Minister Kaiser Matanzima blamed British and American Mining Companies for the Transkei's poverty. In Education, annual expenditure on white child, £60–£68, on African child, £6. 10s. od. (Statistics from *A Survey of Race Relations*, 1964, and subsequent Education Report in 1965).

2. 1963 daily average in Britain, 30,896; in South Africa, 66,575.

year-old African who, on his way to collect his pension in Johannesburg, was arrested by police who refused to listen to anything he had to say and imprisoned him. Six days later his frantic relatives, who had tried hospitals, even mortuaries, in search of him, with the help of his former employers traced him to jail and he was released. At much the same time a seventeen-year-old orphan girl was imprisoned for six months for leaving her reference book at home, and for overstaying the seventy-two hours to which Africans are limited when visiting urban areas. For three and a half months her relatives had searched for her. The police would not let her send any message to them. By chance, her case also came before the public's attention, and an anonymous white paid a fine for her release.

But these are only two among the some 350,000 pass-law convictions of African men and women above the age of sixteen that take place in any one year and will go un-reported because they have been allowed to become a fact of daily life.[1] Just as only a rare case is reported among the 170,000 African men and women endorsed out of urban areas, to denuded reserves, to quote only one fifteen-months period, up to March 1965. 170,000 individual tragedies meaning, in very many cases, entire families broken.

But apart from Black Sash activity, and comment in the *Rand Daily Mail* – which under its editor, Laurence Gandar, has earned a superb editorial reputation – in the Port Elizabeth *Evening Post* and sometimes one or two other English-language newspapers, nothing is done and the mask is quickly readjusted.

The physical and spiritual deserts and abysmal poverty in which the thirty-one men and women still banished from their homes live – never charged or tried – reached one South African Sunday newspaper only after a columnist read their tragic stories in the *New York Times*. Subsequently severalmore were banished.

And a recurring scandal in so rich a country is the famine in African reserves repeatedly struck by drought. Sometimes, tardily and inadequately, the Government has provided relief,

1. In 1962 384,497 were convicted.

but it has also rejected aid from charitable relief organizations despite continuing hunger and malnutrition.

Credit must be given where deserved, however, and in its eighteen years of rule the Government has much improved (though regimented) *some* African housing, and introduced one reform: the extension to Africans of the right to buy liquor – this, despite Dutch Reformed Church objections and in response to Afrikaner wine distillers/voters who wished to increase their sales.

The myth is at its most lunatic when Chinese, as well as Indian and Coloured South Africans, are harshly discriminated against and are steadily shoved out into their respective group areas, distant from the towns in which they have struggled to build up a living, whereas Japanese are honorary whites – because Japan buys pig iron.

Of course, all the while economics make nonsense of apartheid and, immigrants being insufficient, labour shortages are the constant cry of the building trade, of factories, railways and the post office. A tug of war goes on between the Government, insisting that the law be adhered to, and employers illegally using Africans for semi-skilled or even skilled work. But for the time being the number of Africans benefiting from this turning of a blind eye is minimal, and usually at a cheap rate.

In the eighteen years of apartheid, and in spite of all the endorsements out, the number of Africans flowing inexorably into so-called white urban areas has almost doubled. By 1978 however, so the Government promises, the tide *will* be turned!

If 'die Volk' could live isolated, servantless, labourless, on a deserted island, their anachronistic beliefs would seem merely pathetic or amusing. But it is the manner in which they wield power over a majority of voteless, voiceless people, that arouses the anger of the world. Nor is the anger ill-informed: in all history there cannot have been any situation so lavishly documented as this one. The dread of racial conflict brings a sense of alarmed urgency to all the warnings, all the resolutions seeking a solution for South Africa.

Afro-Asian States, as yet physically powerless to force change, use every peaceful form of pressure available. At the request of African leaders and other Government opponents in South Africa, they have banned South African planes from over-flights, and ships from ports; and from international labour, health, social welfare, technical and sporting organizations they have achieved, or press for, exclusion of the South African Government. Some African and communist countries continue to trade with South Africa, but such trade is minute compared with British and American involvement. However, with the Labour Government coming into office in 1964, Britain joined the United States and virtually all countries except France and West Germany in the boycott of arms. The pressure grows for an oil embargo, as a prelude to wider economic sanctions. The International Court's judgment on whether South Africa has abused the Mandate of South West Africa will bring a fresh opportunity for united action – whatever the outcome. And meanwhile the power of the Negro vote has been given a fillip by President Johnson's introduction of the Voting Rights Act.

Closer to home is the unpredictable effect of the impending independence of Basutoland and Bechuanaland which, in 1965, voted for African Prime Ministers and legislatures and which – with Swaziland – have already been up to their necks in acceptance of South African political refugees.

In a physical *laager*, the South African Government is allied with Portugal and Rhodesia, to defend white supremacy in all of Southern Africa. It is a peculiarly powerful grouping in a cynical world busy with existing wars and not prone to taking constructive preventive action. Yet, powerful as it is, there is no doubt that South Africa fears economic sanctions, as evidenced when Rhodesia brought the threat much nearer by declaring UDI. The ultimate threat lies in a warning President Julius Nyerere of Tanzania gave in June 1965. He asked: 'Does anyone really believe that little decadent Portugal and minority governments in Southern Rhodesia and South Africa could stand out against determined pressure from the other powers of the Western bloc?' African nations might be forced to get arms from communist countries, he said, and might find themselves fighting the West, unless Southern Africa is quickly freed from white rule.

The Minister of Justice had told his Party in August 1964 that communism in South Africa would be broken for ever within the next six months. Yet, incessantly he continues to ban and restrict people under the Suppression of Communism Act. Before that he had said Umkonto was broken, and before that, Poqo was beaten on a 'knock-out'. 'It is our duty to defend this Republic, if necessary, against the whole world. Ultimately,' he said, 'the struggle in South Africa will be between those who want one man one vote, and those who are uncompromisingly opposed to that.'

A year later, again addressing his party, Vorster said the next phase of action against the State would be the infiltration of professional saboteurs. But, he added, thanks to the measures taken in the past, South Africa was quiet and peaceful.

'Quiet and peaceful'; a model of law and order? Yet political trials continue, so much a part of life that often they go unreported. In 1965 trials of men found guilty of training in guerilla warfare and sabotage in China, in East Africa, and sentenced to between five and twelve years, and also occasional sabotage trials of both A.N.C. and P.A.C. In P.A.C. cases a distressing, even sinister, development was collaboration between the South African and Basutoland police. For instance, during a trial in Maseru, where all the six men accused of conspiring to overthrow the South African Government by violence were acquitted on appeal, evidence was given by a State witness that the South African police – after holding him in 90-day detention and threatening he would never be released unless he made a statement – took him and another witness to the border, there to hand them over to the Basutoland police. After they had given evidence, the Basuto police returned them to the South Africans. P.A.C. men from the Paarl area were sentenced to between three to five years. In Molteno, in the Cape, thirty-three men, of ages ranging from seventeen to seventy-two, were alleged to have planned a violent Poqo uprising for early 1965, with intent to take over this village. For all the allegations, they were simply found guilty of membership of the Poqo/P.A.C. and were sentenced to between one and six years. In a confusion of evidence several of those accused alleged police torture. A Press story which, even if read in the Gobi Desert would be recognizably South African, reported that one man, Lorry Thembani, said a Bantu detective nicknamed 'Big Brain' tramped on his head with a booted foot. The 'booted foot' recurred in a Cape Town trial where both Defence and State witnesses alleged police trampled on their necks, or kicked them, with 'booted feet', and spoke of electric shock torture and the placing of a paraffin tin over the head, the tin then being beaten on or filled with smoke. In the Molteno case the Court rejected the allegations of assault as deliberate lies.

Meanwhile the authorities attempt to destroy by attrition such parties or organizations as they have not tried to destroy by outlawing.

By regular banning, silencing and restricting of officials or members, the Government is trying to break the Liberal Party, the Indian Congress, S.A.C.T.U. and the Defence and Aid Fund which, since the 1960 emergency arrests, has helped to provide legal defence for political accused, and to aid their families. Perhaps the case which best symbolizes the magnitude of this Fund's achievements was the 'Goodwood' case in which forty-five men and women were arrested between May and November 1963, to be held under 90-days detention until the first charges were laid. Twenty-two of them complained of assault. One man whose grave illness was wrongly diagnosed and whose treatment in hospital was delayed because of a 'shortage of |police vans', died of cancer. When the trial began in May 1964, three men were discharged – having each spent at least six months in jail. The rest were tried for membership of a new organization, the African Youth League, on the grounds that it was an A.N.C. cover. Another eight were discharged and ten found not guilty before, on 24 August, the magistrate sentenced twenty-three men and women to between three and five years. On appeal, in February 1965 seventeen were acquitted, the sentences of three were reduced and only in the case of three were the sentences confirmed. Had it not been for Defence and Aid providing lawyers throughout, who knows how many of the forty-five would now be on Robben Island? As it is, only six were ultimately convicted. *Ultimately* – the cost in pain and misery to the families and to the accused in the intervening time, of some eighteen months, can be all too inadequately indicated. One man who had spent twenty-one months in jail before the final acquittal was promptly put under 24-hour house arrest upon release, two others under 12-hour house arrest, and five others under restrictive bans. All are in poverty and in debt, for funds for aid are always minimal in face of the gargantuan task of coping with so many thousands of victims.

South Africa is a society in which justice was long ago subverted by a spate of unjust laws and now is subverted by the whole process of administration of those laws.

Nowhere is this more evident than in the Eastern Cape, an area of prosperous American and British-owned factories. There the State, through its political police, is intent on purging Port Elizabeth's townships, New Brighton and Kwazakele – so long the centre of militant A.N.C. activity – of the last drop of political consciousness. Between October 1963 and October 1965 about 1,000 men and women were arrested and in a plethora of trials were charged with belonging to the A.N.C. or, in a handful of cases, the P.A.C.; many cases relate to 1961.

The accused have been imprisoned awaiting trial for anything from five to nineteen months. Virtually all the trials have been held *in camera*, in villages remote from Port Elizabeth, on the grounds that State witnesses fear intimidation or reprisals, with resulting difficulty in finding defence counsel and in the Press being able to cover them, so that a dreadful pall of anonymity settles on the Trials.

But where injustice is most apparent, though blessed by the law, is in the framing of the charges, for these have been broken down under multiple counts: membership of an unlawful organization, furthering its aims, collecting funds for it, attending meetings, allowing premises to be used for its meetings, distributing leaflets; the maximum sentence on each count being three years; with in some cases each meeting, each leaflet, treated as a separate count! The severity of sentences thus became a striking feature: whereas admitted rank-and-file members of the Communist Party – who collected subscriptions, distributed leaflets, painted slogans and attended more than twenty cell meetings – were sentenced to two years, A.N.C. members have been sentenced to up to ten years for a lesser series of activities.

A prime factor in the pattern the trials took related to violence. *Acts* of violence, such as sabotage, automatically went before the Supreme Court, and though violence came up in speeches quoted in some trials, fictional violence became 'deliberately introduced' by State witnesses, to quote one defence lawyer, through 'heinous' allegations, with the effect of aggravating a possible sentence. The fiction related to the past – a State witness alleging that in the A.N.C.'s stay-at-homes there was violence, or a policeman alleging that the A.N.C. was responsible for violence in the 1952 riots. And it related to the A.N.C.'s New Plan, for instance State witnesses who had given detailed evidence in early trials about discussing the New Plan at a meeting in February 1961, suddenly – when referring to the same meeting, alleged that the Plan involved violence – and the meeting had happened six months before even Mandela had considered the change in policy that led to Umkonto!

But the pattern was particularly alarming when State witnesses were studied. One had already given evidence against sixty people, one learnt his evidence off by heart, one, as Defence Counsel remarked, had the history of a man who is in the pay of the police. The material witnesses virtually all claimed to be former colleagues, accomplices, of the accused, most of whom had been arrested and held in 90 days. As with State witnesses elsewhere, they would vehemently deny torture or pressure of any kind. They had come to court to tell 'the truth' and – in a startlingly repetitive manner – they would volunteer: 'I was not *forced* to make a statement.'

Increasingly, corroboration of small details of what happened in 1961 or 1962 by witness after witness stretched the credulity of anyone studying the trials. It was like hearing parrots come to court. And in several instances, the Defence elicited the fact that State witnesses during a trial had slept – sometimes two or three together at a time – in a room with the Bantu (*sic*) security sergeant, Gaza, a gat-toothed man with a Hitler moustache, widely feared; but they insisted nothing concerning the case was ever discussed.

Tommy Charlieman, a S.A.C.T.U. man aged about sixty, after being imprisoned in four different jails for a total of nineteen months, was released in December 1964 without any charge being laid. In January 1965 he wrote to the Minister of Justice claiming damages for loss of health and wages. He was then re-arrested, and charged with A.N.C. membership, and other counts emerging from a meeting in November 1962. He was found guilty and sentenced to eight years. An appeal was noted.

Nursing Sister Zebia Mpendu, aged forty-seven, had been trying to get a passport to study paediatrics in Britain when she was arrested in March 1964. She was held, in prison – apart from a brief couple of weeks when bail was allowed – for sixteen months, awaiting trial. When Defence counsel questioned the Security Police sergeant in charge of her case about this period, he replied it was 'perhaps not too long'. He added: 'There were others who were more important, who had waited longer.' Yet bail had been withdrawn from her fifteen months before and the State Prosecutor had given as a reason that she was the 'most dangerous' of the sixty-one prisoners awaiting trial before the court at the time. Fifteen months in prison, a 'most dangerous' woman, and when it came to her trial, she was charged with a different set of facts from those for which she was arrested. The Prosecutor – in Addo Court, in July 1965 – declared her case centred on the 'disposal of a motor van'. It was alleged that her man had been given the van by the A.N.C., and after his arrest, she had taken over its sale. She denied the charges. State witnesses said she told them the sale was to raise money for the A.N.C., and would be used – according to one or another of them – for ammunition; explosives; firearms; petrol bombs;

machine-guns; rifles; revolvers. The magistrate found her guilty on four counts: A.N.C. membership, raising funds, meeting in her house, and stamping a receipt with an A.N.C. sign. Allowing for the eighteen months she had by this time been in custody – he sentenced her to a further two and a half years, in all then, four years. On emergence she still hopes to study paediatrics.

Then there have been the bus strike cases, involving the employees of the Port Elizabeth bus company, who had successfully struck for better conditions in 1961. At that time they had been charged with participating in an illegal strike and the company had helped them pay admission of guilt fines. Four years later, in batches of ten or twelve, some of these men found themselves arrested and charged on the grounds that the strike had been an unlawful activity and that arson was committed. The first group, acquitted on the A.N.C. charge, were found guilty of arson and sentenced to four years, the second were found guilty of A.N.C. activity.

What of the few found not guilty and acquitted? By July 1965 most of the thirty or so acquitted were promptly re-arrested, and there were three recorded cases of men re-arrested a fourth time after being thrice freed either by the courts or by having the charges withdrawn. Clearly the Government, preferring to function within ostensible legality, chooses not to invoke the 'Sobukwe clause'. Therefore those whose spirit remains unbroken by imprisonment are likely to be recharged on release, or, like Dennis Brutus on release in July 1965, placed under house arrest and the severest of restrictive bans.

And all the time – in the background – are the anguished families; in the Eastern Cape alone for the 1,000 men and women arrested in the area by October 1965 (of whom about 150 became State witnesses) there are about 3,000 women and children and other dependents for whom local welfare committees could provide only a tenth of the poverty datum sum.

Many of South Africa's political prisoners believe they will never be released from Robben Island or other prisons until the day of Freedom comes. Men who will one day be among rulers of South Africa are today *bandiete* – bandits, prisoners; their warders are *Boere* – Boers; embraced for the moment in cops and robbers slang – for the moment.

But for who knows how long? The Security Police, in the Eastern Cape particularly, relentlessly producing many hundreds of arrests and providing the evidence for conviction, are here to stay – until that day.

Excruciatingly, the picture of these townships has become one of dispirited people, terrified of the Security Police, deadening the atmosphere in courts with their hopelessness in face of the law, South Africa's law. Why have so few risen in court, to make a positive assertion of their beliefs, an avowal that what they did was honourable and history will prove it to be so? Almost all have pleaded 'not guilty' to the point of denying almost all knowledge of the A.N.C. or P.A.C. For anyone to make such an assertion – as did Mandela and Mkwayi and a few others – calls for the considerable strength of a mature politician. Besides – the courts, South Africa's justice – have come to mean nothing to them.

Nor is the only end result that hundreds of decent ordinary wage-earners are being turned into bitter rebels. Vile corruption of the life of whole communities results from the activities of former colleagues turned informer, sometimes brother against brother. Elsewhere in the world this and the police terrorism that goes with it have driven desperate people to counter-terrorism. So far, apart from Poqo, in Paarl in 1963, there has been astonishingly little revenge in the townships; a few attempts at petrol bombing of guilty men's houses, two or three murders. But what will the future be?

The hundred and fifty or so Xhosa informers in the Eastern Cape, and the two or three hundred elsewhere in the country, who have helped the Afrikaner Government imprison their fellows are a far cry from Makana's followers in 1819, who refused to betray him even when they were threatened with extermination.

Perhaps any one of us, faced with interrogation, or other pressures, under solitary confinement, would do the same. Or perhaps the rot is inevitable in a sick society where it pays to lie and cheat and to fawn 'Ja, baas' to a man for whom only deadly contempt is felt. Today's informers are partly a reflection of all that has been done to a subject people in a century and a half. African leaders have not only had to counter the activities of small-time informers and *agents provocateurs*, but also the escapism of many of their people who turn to exotic religions, to the self-centred pursuits of middle-class society in the townships, to dagga (marijuana), drink or crime.

Certainly, now, informers have become big-time. Yet ordinary people do not see them so much as *themselves*, as what white power and white brainwashing has turned them into. As one woman in New Brighton put it: 'We are going to end up, not seeing the faces of individuals – just seeing WHITE.'

The quantity of whites who fight on for justice has shrunk enormously – though some who have gone abroad, communists and liberals – work in the exile groups seeking to help end apartheid. But the quality is enhanced. Exhausted they may become – these few lawyers, intellectuals, journalists, Christians, communists, liberals, Black Sash women, and the one Progressive Member of Parliament[1] – and isolated they may be from local white society, and – far more tragic – from the nonwhites with whose struggle they have identified themselves at one level or another, but they will, they can, only fight on, for a part of their being needs to live by principle. Probably each one is aware that by the time 'liberty' is achieved, the gulf deliberately driven by Verwoerd and his Government between black and white will be unbreachable – and blacks *will* only see WHITE. The truth has long been that not even through imprisonment, or torture, can a white find equality with a non-white – always he has a superior material condition; except – as was brought home when John Harris was executed before dawn on 1 April 1965 – except on the gallows. There, black and white are equal.

A stable surface: with, to quote the Minister of Justice, giving facts for only the limited period of February 1963 to December 1964, 2,436 people charged with sabotage and other

1. Two Provincial Counsellors won the Coloured representative seats in 1965. In the March 1966 election Mrs Helen Suzman will defend her seat.

subversive activities (of whom about 1,000 were discharged or found not guilty); with, to quote a reported statement by the Chief Commissioner of Prisons while in Sweden in 1965, some 8,000 political prisoners;[1] with 1,095 men and women, of whom only 272 were convicted, held under the 90-day law until its suspension in January 1965, while 241 had as a result given evidence for the State. (Even a year after release some of the 854 who refused to give evidence against their fellows feel the subtle, alarming after-effects of the psychological torture.) And with in 1965, the 90-day detention law suspended only to be replaced by an even more terrible law – 180-day detention, without charge or trial, ostensibly for the holding of anyone likely to give material evidence for the State in criminal or political trials!

On 1 September 1965, Isaac Heymann was imprisoned under the 180-day law. He tried to cut his throat and wrists, but he survived. Before long some twenty-three more, men and women, were detained under this law. Those subsequently refusing to give evidence were sentenced to up to a year's imprisonment.

Looking back over half a century, though the African struggle for a birthright fluctuated, the A.N.C. was always at its heart; for long too trusting, too cautious and middle-class, but with inspired moments. In the early decades the I.C.U., under Kadalie's exciting leadership, was the first organization to respond to the needs of workers and to frighten the authorities – until power corrupted and Kadalie shrank from fulfilling his promises of mass resistance.

In all the fifty years the only financial scandals were those of the I.C.U. in the late twenties and, latterly and muted, of the P.A.C. in exile.

The A.N.C.'s main weakness lay in concentrating on nation-wide protests and strikes – however successful in some places – rather than in action affecting the daily lives of the people. The bus strikes proved people would *act* when it was a question of pence.

Perhaps the failure of any African leader to plunge his followers into the unknown and to precipitate continued militant mass

1. It has become impossible to discover the precise number of political prisoners.

resistance remains the key question. The answer is a composite: the vast obstacles placed persistently in the way of African political organizations and action over generations; the psychological effects of oppression; and the immeasurable impact of life in a complex industrial society. Certainly there has been no lack of individual courage and readiness to face suffering in recent years. The A.N.C.-led Defiance Campaign was the great time of the 1950s and, with Sobukwe and Kgosana's startling capturing of the mood of the people in 1960, there was, in the Cape especially – after the Sharpeville tragedy – a time of spontaneous action such as the country had not experienced, though whites had always dreaded such a moment. But P.A.C. leaders quickly showed their inexperience, their inability to control Poqo extremism, and their failure to realize the seriousness and complexity of the prolonged struggle. Internecine disruption seemed inevitable.

Umkonto's campaign of sabotage, with its intention that human beings should not be harmed, was in a real sense a development from the A.N.C.'s non-violence, so consistently maintained despite every provocation. The campaign's objective of bringing South Africa to the conference table failed utterly, but in the outside world, and especially in the United Nations, it brought home African desperation, determination – and discipline.

But the great failure – true of all the African nationalist and trade union organizations, and indeed of their allies and others of all races opposed to the Nationalist Government – was the failure to face the fact of the ruthlessness – not only of successive Nationalist Governments but, terribly exemplified in the 1946 mine strike, of the power structure, rooted in Goli,[1] in the City of London and in Wall Street.

The A.N.C. has, over fifty years, a record of generosity, of almost foolhardy decency. Seme's founding of the Congress was an act of unification rare in South Africa's history. And in the 1950s, the A.N.C. and its allies became something rare in the world; symbolizing all its conflicting forces: black, white, brown, Christian, Jew, Hindu, Moslem, pagan, communist,

1. African name for Johannesburg, City of Gold.

283

conservative, liberal. Although it was the negative force of apartheid that brought them together, nevertheless they came together, and as such made a creative contribution to humanity. In face of this the Nationalist Government appeared dangerous and stupid in turn, at once pathetic and terrifying in its self-chosen isolation from international society and civilized standards.

That anyone should be criticized for decency is a measure of the decadence of our world, implying – a grim implication – that until the men and women struggling for their birthright become as ruthless as those who withhold it, they will never succeed.

Yet, if the Portuguese Minister of Justice could declare an amnesty of political prisoners, in August 1965, may there yet be hope that his counterpart in South Africa could be persuaded? . . . So far 'die Volk' has not responded to generosity. In the 1914 rebellion of extremist Afrikaners against the Government, resulting in hundreds of deaths, only one leader was executed, Jopie Fourie, and he because he was in the Defence Force at the time and responsible for a high proportion of the deaths. All the other 281 ringleaders were released within two years. And that very violent revolt was in wartime. But the mercy shown to their people does not appear to stir any similar feeling in the Government now for African rebels guilty of comparatively trivial offences.

In a conflict symbolized by Boere and Bandiete, how can victims not become executioners? It is the question of all times.

If the surface seems calm, what cauldron of frenzied rage does it conceal? When, in October 1965, one of the ceaselessly overcrowded trains of African workers crashed, killing ninety-one passengers, survivors battered to death a white man who came to their aid.

Yet so far, white fears of black 'swamping', of black revenge, should be countered by history; which shows that the black man has far more cause to fear the white, has suffered far more at the hands of the white man, than the contrary. And countered by facts of present-day South Africa: in the one area where Africans have a partial vote, the Transkei, a majority of voters chose a multi-racial society despite every inducement and reason to opt for black domination. While, in Zululand, an important section of the Zulu people are resisting the mockery and racialism of a Bantustan, led as they are by Chief Gatsha Buthelezi, whose strength, brave integrity and intelligence represent in a new, sophisticated form traditional pride and valour. And Mandela, even today on Robben Island, represents the stand against racialism.

Robben Island, a small world of Boere and Bandiete: Laski once wrote – 'The political criminals under a tyrant are the heroes of all free men.' Makana in 1819, Mandela, Sisulu, Sobukwe, a thousand more today; and in addition the unknown numbers of 'politicals' in other South African prisons. In his last statement, Mandela, before being imprisoned for life, described how, in his youth in the Transkei, he listened to tribal elders talking of heroes who had defended their fathers' land: Bambata, Hintsa, Moshoeshoe, Sekukhuni, Dingane, Makana. . . . From that time he hoped life would offer an opportunity for him to serve his people: to 'make my own humble contribution to their freedom struggle, this is what has motivated me in all I have done. . . .'

If South Africa today presents a picture of white complacency and black apathy, of an 'underworld' of power rampant over the crumbled resistance of men and women whose leaders are imprisoned or training abroad, from Robben Island came proof of a new spirit. An ordinary man – a labourer and A.N.C. member – Terrance Makwabe came to give evidence for the defence in one of the Eastern Cape trials. The Prosecutor reminded him that the effect of his evidence might well be to lay him open to renewed prosecution and a longer sentence. Makwabe, a slight, bespectacled, modest-voiced man in his early forties, agreed.

'Why, then,' asked the Prosecutor, 'are you giving the evidence?'

'*Andi soyiki*', replied Makwabe, which, being interpreted, means: I am no longer afraid.

Main Leaders of African Nationalist Organizations and Unions

African National Congress (A.N.C.)

1910S

Dr Pixley Ka Izaka Seme
Rev. John L. Dube
Sol T. Plaatje
R. V. Selope Thema

1920S

Rev. Z. R. Mahabane
Mrs Charlotte Maxeke
J. T. Gumede

1930S

Dr Seme
Rev. James A. Calata
Moses Kotane (and Communist Party)

1940S

Dr A. B. Xuma
Rev. J. A. Calata
Anton M. Lembede ⎫
Oliver Tambo   ⎪
Walter Sisulu   ⎬ *Youth League*
Nelson R. Mandela ⎭
J. B. Marks (also African Mine Workers' Union and Communist Party)

1950s

Dr J. S. Moroka
W. Sisulu
Albert J. Lutuli
O. Tambo
N. Mandela
M. Kotane
Mrs Lilian Ngoyi
Duma Nokwe
Professor Z. K. Matthews ⎫
Dr James Njongwe ⎪
Robert Matji ⎬ *Eastern Cape*
Govan Mbeki ⎭
M. B. Yengwa ⎫
Dr Margaret Mncadi ⎬ *Natal*

National Action Council
1961

Nelson Mandela

Industrial and Commercial Workers' Union (I.C.U.)

1920s to 1930s

Clements Kadalie
George Champion
T. Mbeki

All-African Convention (A.A.C.)

Mid 1930s

Dr D. D. T. Jabavu

1940s

I. A. Tabata

African Democratic Party (A.D.P.)

Mid 1940s

Paul Mosaka

Pan-Africanist Congress (P.A.C.)

Late 1950s

Robert M. Sobukwe
Potlako K. Leballo
Philip Kgosana
Nana Mahomo
Patrick Duncan
P. Raboroko

Sources

The following books and documents were particularly referred to when writing this book.

Prologue: *Narrative of a Residence in South Africa* and *Afar in the Desert*, Thomas Pringle; *Time Longer than Rope*, Edward Roux; *The Unification of South Africa 1902–1910*, L. M. Thompson; *Closer Union*, Olive Schreiner.

Chapter 1: *Native Life in South Africa*, Sol T. Plaatje.

Chapters 1–3: *The African Yearly Register*, T. D. Mweli Skota.

Chapters 2–4: *Time Longer than Rope*, and certain issues of the *Star*, *Rand Daily Mail*, *Pretoria News* and *Abantu-Batho*.

Chapters 3–4: A. W. G. Champion papers.

Chapter 5: *Cape Times* and other Press reports.

Chapters 6–7: *The Treason Cage*, Anthony Sampson; Press reports.

Chapter 8: *Passive Resister*, Native Representative Council Reports, *Rand Daily Mail*, The *Star*, Court Records and unpublished material by Lionel Bernstein.

Chapters 8–12: *The Struggle for Equality* and *Unrest in South Africa*, P. S. Joshi.

Chapters 9–18: United Nations reports.

Chapters 10–14: *The Treason Cage*.

Chapter 13: Women's Federation pamphlet.

Chapters 11–16: Treason Trial record and documents put in in evidence and Press reports.

Chapter 14: *African Political Parties*, Thomas Hodgkin.

Chapters 16–19: *Action, Reaction and Counter-action*, Muriel Horrell Court records, documents handed in in evidence, Press reports.

Chapter 20: Court records, documents and press cuttings.

General Background: A History of Southern Africa, Eric Walker;
The Politics of Inequality, Gwendolen Carter; *A Handbook of
Race Relations*, and Annual Surveys of the Institute of Race
Relations by Muriel Horrell.

Invaluable historical material came from the writings of H.
Selby Msimang in *Contact*, 1960; and of Professor Z. K.
Matthews in *Imvo*, 1961-2. Cyril Dunn provided vivid notes
used in Chapters 1, 2 and 14.

But the book depends mainly on personal interviews throughout South Africa, on attendance at trials, and general research,
during the period from 1957 to 1965.

Other relevant works: *No Easy Walk to Freedom*, Nelson Man-
dela; *Let My People Go*, A. J. Lutuli; *Passive Resistance in
South Africa*, Leo Kuper; *If This Be Treason*, Helen Joseph;
Brief Authority, Charles Hooper; *I Will Still Be Moved*, ed.
Marion Friedmann; *The Rise of Congress in South Africa*,
Julius Lewin; A.N.C., A.A.C. and P.A.C. publications; other
books in the Penguin South African Series.

Acknowledgements

During the historical and personal research which I did in South Africa from 1961 to 1962 and since January 1965 I received generous and valuable information and advice from a variety of South Africans of all races. From some I was able to get reminiscences going back fifty years – before it was too late. Among those I saw during that earlier period, were leaders and followers who are now imprisoned or in exile, some of whom, I am proud to say, are my friends. For obvious reasons – the laws of South Africa being what they are – I am not thanking anyone individually and for this reason also I hope possibly frustrated scholars will forgive the reticence of my list of sources. Police raids over generations of course removed many of the written records that existed.

Anthony Sampson encouraged me to write *The African Patriots*, on which this book is based, and I am also grateful to Ronald Segal for ensuring that this more popular yet more comprehensive and up-to-date story should be published by Penguins.

Index